JACK THE RIPPER: ANATOMY OF A MYTH

by

William Beadle

ISBN 0952 448 904

Typeset by: In-House Typesetting
PO Box 227
Brighton
Sussex BN2 3GL

Printed and Bound by:
Redwood Books, Trowbridge, Wiltshire.

Published by:
WAT TYLER BOOKS
P.O. Box 17
Dagenham
Essex RM10 8XF

IN MEMORIUM:

JAMES JOSEPH CLEMENTS
1930 — 1992

Who always listened to me
and encouraged me to make
this odyssey.

By The Same Author:
The Killing of Leon Beron

Acknowledgements and thanks to the following Publishers and Authors for permission to quote from their works:

Eric Dobby Publishing, 'Jack The Ripper': The Final Solution' by Stephen Knight.

Churchill Livingstone 'Taylor's Principles And Practice of Medical Jurisprudence', Edited Professor Kieth Simpson.

Random House and Joel Norris: 'Serial Killers: The Growing Menace'.

Daniel Farson, 'Jack The Ripper'.

Robson Books: Murder and Madness: The Secret Life Of jack The Ripper' by Dr David Abrahamsen.

Weidenfeld And Nicholson And Martin Fido: 'The Crimes, Detection And Death Of jack The Ripper'.

Brian Marriner: 'A Century of Sex Killers'.

Gerald Duckworth And Co Ltd, 'East End 1888' by William Fishman, and 'The Ripper And The Royals' by Melvyn Fairclough.

Cassell and Terence Sharkey: 'Jack The Ripper: One Hundred Years Of Investigation'.

Arthur Barker and Elwyn Jones and John Lloyd: 'The Ripper File'.

Donald McCormick and Jarolds: 'The Identity Of Jack The Ripper'.

Virgin Publishing and Michael Harrison: 'Clarence: The Life Of H.R.H. The Duke Of Clarence And Avondale 1864—1892'.

Virgin Publishing and Donald Rumbelow: 'The Complete Jack The Ripper'.

Virgin Publishing and Norman Lucas: 'The Sex Killers'.

Harper Collins Publishers Ltd and Richard Davenport-Hines: 'Sex, Death And Punishment'.

Hodder And Stoughton and Thomas Boyle: 'Black Swine In The Sewers Of Hampstead'.

Robinson Publishing and Jonathan Goodman: 'Masterpieces Of Murder'.

Paul Begg, Martin Fido and Kieth Skinner: 'The Jack The Ripper A to Z', Headline Books.

The Authors of the last named Book have asked me to make it clear that the quotes used come from the first edition of their 'A to Z', and that some of them may not appear in subsequent editions. A new edition has in fact recently been published.

Other Authors and Publishers could not be contacted.

My thanks to the Scottish Public records Office in Edinburgh for their courtesy and efficiency during the research for this Book.

Finally, my thanks to Chris who did an excellent and enthusiastic job of typing my manuscript.

CONTENTS

INTRODUCTION

'Some Monster in human form whose desperate wickedness goes free and undetected by force of its own terrible audacity— (a) woman killer who renders the midnight streets dreadful with the footfalls of death'

Thus spoke the 'Daily Telegraph' on October 1st, 1888, the day after Jack the ripper had butchered two women within an hour of each other in the streets of London. A myth was in the process of being created, of the sexual deviant as Superman, a myth which would spawn countless books, Films and theories and fashion a legend from an enervating creature who deserved only repugnance.

Students of the Ripper have awarded him an 'ology' and his own house magazine, "Ripperology". Ripper "Clubs" have been mooted. One book proclaims his crimes to be Britain's Watergate; another uses him to rewrite our history books. The latest links him to a second great Victorian murder mystery. There seems to be an endless conveyor belt of "solutions" each one more ridiculous than the last as if the Ripper were some gruesome soap opera filling lives that are tedious and stale.

The truth is more simple and more sad. Jack the ripper and his victims were products of the society in which they lived. Colin Wilson, doyen of Ripperologists, terms him as an alienated outsider and forerunner of today's multicides. Wilson is correct, but the Ripper also represented an alienated Society, the residues of which are still with us today. Victorian Society divorced humanity to marry gold. During this process it became sexually abnormal. The Ripper reflected this. His victims were already victims, used and outcast, doomed to wander in blind alleys until they died. Victorian England was an evil place.

Jack the ripper's identity will come as a disappointment to all those with their heads full of nonsense about Royal Princes and machiavellic plots. 'Jack' was a very ordinary individual. This truth has been apparent for some time. Wilson in his book 'The Criminal History of Mankind' says: 'The truth is probably that the ripper was some anonymous unknown'. Echoing him, Donald Rumbelow in 'The Complete Jack the Ripper' writes that when his identity is at last revealed: 'we shall turn and look with blank astonishment... and say "who?"'. These assessments are correct.

Researching this book took me to the Scottish Public Records Office in Edinburgh. I am also indebted to Paul Begg, Martin Fido and Keith Skinner for their superb compendium of factual data on the case, 'The Jack the Ripper A to Z'. Their work, published as an aide to writers and researchers, saved me much time and trouble. Whilst I am scathing towards Ripperology and its 'philes', my criticisms do not extend to them.

Part One

Thanatos, The Nights of The Ripper

PROLOGUE

Take heed of yonder dog!
Look when he fawns, he bites;
And when he bites,
His venom tooth will rankle
To the Death:
Have not to do with him,
Beware of Him;
Sin, Death, and Hell, have set their
Marks on him,
And all their ministers attend
On him.

(Richard III Act 1 Scene 3)

Chapter One: Victorian Values

In 1982, when Margaret Thatcher waxed lyrical over Victorian Values in the House of Commons, a Labour M.P. asked what had impressed her most, the appalling levels of poverty and unemployment, the dreadful crime rate or the never ending series of Colonial Wars!

The Nineteenth Century was a time of plenty for the few and few for the plenty. The enclosures of the Agricultural revolution had changed the face of Britain forever. The vast bulk of the population, hitherto rurally based, was quite literally uprooted and herded into the rapidly expanding cities and townships, there to provide canon fodder for the Industrial Revolution. The new population densities fueled the birth rate and the resulting over crowding, coupled with slave labour and trade recessions, in turn spawned slums, poverty, unemployment and crime. A social miasma had been created: An iron tyranny of profit gripped fast those whose lives held no profit.

Yet Britain, their country and their flag, ruled the greatest empire in history. The contradiction was staggering. Whilst a significant proportion of the populace existed just above, on or below the poverty line their Rulers either owned or dominated around 40% of the World. Visiting the Great Exhibition at Crystal Palace in 1851, the Novelist Charlotte Bronte could only stand and marvel at:

> *'The carefully guarded caskets full of real diamonds and pearls worth hundreds of thousands of ponds.'*

Just five years earlier many thousands of men, women and children had been allowed to starve to death during the Potato famine: just a few miles away from this vast orgy of wealth many thousands of people lived in unimaginable squalor, clawing desperately at the crumbs brushed from the banqueting table of super profits.

Bronte went on:

> *'It seems as if only magic could have gathered this mass of wealth from all the ends of the earth.'*

The "magic" grew out of the barrel of a gun. The vast concentration of riches on display had been looted from all round the globe.

According to its own propaganda Britain was 'the Workshop of the World'. This was the image. The reality was a cruel sweatshop, the incarnation of the factory scene from Fritz Lang's "Metropolis". The story can be told in reams of statistics or harrowing descriptions of toil and drudgery, but it is best depicted by the stories of ordinary people themselves. What toil actually meant can be gleaned from the evidence of Elizabeth Bentley, a Yorkshire Millhand, to a Parliamentary Inquiry into working conditions in 1815. Bentley had been put to work at the tender age of six. Depending on how busy the mill was her hours were either 5 a.m. to 9 p.m. or 6 a.m. to 7 p.m., with one forty minute meal break. If she flagged through weariness she was chained up and beaten with a strap. By the age of thirteen her job left her permanently deformed, bent over like an old woman and in constant pain. Ten years further on and now unable to work properly she was eeking out her existence in a Workhouse. Asked whether her dreadful conditions of employment had ruined her life, Bentley broke down and was unable to answer.

Over twenty years later when Victoria ascended the throne little or nothing had been done to ameliorate the conditions which had crippled little Elizabeth Bentley. The Factory Acts only commenced in the 1840's and owed very little to philanthropy or humanitarianism. Shorter hours and improved working conditions meant more production and profit.

Two years after Bentley gave evidence to the Parliamentary Commissioners another Inquiry heard about the fate of Thomas Pitt, a Chimney Sweep's Climbing Boy. Pitt was ordered to climb down into a chimney only moments after the fire had been extinguished. A little while later the sweep, becoming anxious, ordered him to climb back up again. The piteous response was 'I cannot come up Master, I must die here.' He did. In a chimney, literally roasted alive, his flesh burnt off right through to his bones. Thomas Pitt was just eight years old.

The Inquiry advocated that the use of Climbing Boys be abolished. This recommendation was ignored.

'The great social mill crushes and grinds, beneath its steel gearing, the lowest human stratum', wrote Hippolyte Taine, a French Visitor in 1861. Forty years later the social mill was still crushing and grinding. In London alone 1.8 million people lived on or below the poverty line with a further 1 million just above it, a week's wages separating them from pauperism. Elizabeth Bentley was doubtless long dead but her apparition visited 500,000 toilers every year, suffering death or disablement from disease or injury incurred through their work. Almost 1.3 million Londoners existed on an income of £1.05 per week, per family (about £65.00 in today's values) and in London's poorest district, the East End, 55% of all children died before the age of five.

Contrast this with the opulence of the so-called 'great and good', Britain's ruling elite. 500 hereditary (a euphemism for self perpetuating), peers owned 20% of England and they and their functionaries lavished on themselves £370 million annually; — 32% of the wealth created by the nation's workforce. That this wealth dripped with the blood and ruin of half a million Elizabeth Bentley's and the exhaustion of many millions more, was a matter of supreme indifference to those who owned Britain. Beneral William Booth, founder of the Salvation Army, delivered this searing indictment of Victorian values:

> *'Those ... who grind the faces of the poor, and who rob the Widow and Orphan and who for a pretence make great professions of public spirit*

and philanphropy, these men nowadays are sent to Parliament to make laws for the people. The old prophets sent them to hell - but we have changed all that. They send their victims to hell, and are rewarded by all that wealth can do to make their lives comfortable.'

The worst of all the hells was London's East End. Once a prosperous area and a centre of the silk weaving trade, East London was by the Nineteenth Century the poorest of the poor, home to a throng in rags, the epitome of starving and suffering Britain. Let us enter it through the eyes of Jack London, the American writer:

'Nowhere in the streets of London may one escape the sight of abject poverty, while five minutes walk from about any point will bring one to a slum; but the region my hansom was now penetrating was one unending slum'.[1]

Slum indeed. The overcrowding was barbaric. The average number of people per acre for London as a whole was 50; in Whitechapel 176. But Whitechapel paled into insignificance beside neighbouring Spitalfields. There, Bell Lane was 'home' to a grotesque 600 persons per acre, nearby Pearl Street 500. Both streets were officially condemned as unfit for human habitation in 1877. By the time of the ripper murders eleven years later nothing had been done about them. Living conditions resembled the black hole of Calcutta. The inquest on a four month old child revealed that the family, nine all told, lived — if that is the right word — in a room only 12 foot square and that the baby had suffocated through overlying. 17% of East End children died under the age of one.

The Metropolitan Board of works was unmoved by such statistics. They could find no money for Spitalfields, plenty to effect whatever improvements were needed in the West End. William Fishman in his study of conditions in the East End sums it up accordingly:

'We may well ask where is the "Home Sweet Home" of Victorian song and legend. Certainly not here.'[2]

"Home Sweet Home" was just another fiction, a product of Victorian hypocrisy.

General Booth estimated that 35% of the population of the East End lived either on the poverty line or below it in the direst form of economic hardship. There was no safety net of social security, no sick pay, no injury compensation or disability pension. The poor either worked or starved. Jack London movingly

1   The People of the Abyss p12/13
2   East End 1888 p22

depicted the fate of a latter day Elizabeth Bentley, a man who had permanently injured himself lifting a heavy load:

'He put his back under too great a load of fish, and his chance of happiness in life was crossed off the books.' [1]

Unemployment was rife. When work did present itself men literally fought each other for it. Ben Tillett, the Docker's Leader, has left this description of casual labourers waiting outside the Dock gates, 600 of them to fill the 20 jobs that would be needed that day:

'Coats, flesh and even ears were torn off. The strong literally threw themselves over the heads of their fellows and battled through the kicking, punching cursing crowds to the rails of the "cage" which held them like rats - mad human rats who saw food in the ticket.'

The imagery here, of mad human rats fighting one another for a pittance, is a horrifying one, but is eclipsed by Beatrice Webb the Socialist and Labour Leader's initial impression of the Dock casuals:

'they are like the circle of the suicides in Dante's Inferno: they go round and round within a certain area.'

This image can be taken quite literally: suicide was a common way of escaping a dreadful existence. London recounts the story of one, Alfred Freeman, an unemployed twenty year old who had attempted to drown himself in Britannia Lock. He was "rescued" by the Lock-Keeper's Wife but as fast as she could pull him out Freeman crawled back and attempted it again. He was arrested and appeared at Magistrates Court the following morning where the Magistrate complimented the Lock-Keeper's wife on her physical prowess. London wrote:

'the Court Room laughed; but all I could see was a boy on the threshold of life, passionately crawling to muddy death, and there was no laughter in it.' [2]

Compare the dark tragedy of this young man's existence with the lifestyle of Britain's rulers, a day out in the country, spent slaughtering the nation's wild life, with Queen Victoria and her consort, Prince Albert. Victoria wrote:

'Albert had already killed the stag; ... he was a magnificent animal, the beauty that we had admired yesterday... we heard that another stag had been seen... we saw one below the road looking so handsome. Albert fired - the animal fell.'

1   The People of the Abyss p43
2   The People of the Abyss p106

4

The stags, 'magnificent', 'beautiful' and 'handsome' are killed for idle amusement. We may wonder if there is not an analogy here with the treatment of Victoria's subjects.

*****

Hand in glove with economic enslavement went subjugation of a more personal nature. The enforced exodus into the new slum cities meant an accelerating drift away from the Church. By the end of Victoria's reign 80% of the population had ceased formal religious observance although the overwhelming majority still held to a basic belief in God. Hitherto the organised Church had been a very useful instrument in keeping the masses in their place. (It is not an accident that the British Aristocracy has traditionally awarded itself the title of 'Lord'.) Now, as the Church's grip weakened, so Britain's rulers became increasingly worried about losing control. Richard Davenport Hines in his book 'Sex, Death and Punishment' crystallises the issue:

> 'This rejection of obedience to God... coupled with the filth and degra-dation of slum life seemed to portend the decay of towns and cities into lawless badlands where the old etiquette and deference were lost. "Men's instincts are utterly corrupt and... everywhere, except under the influence of religion and tradition, they resort to practices ruinous to their race and lower than any that are practised by the beast", warned the Duke of Argyll in 1896.'[1]

What the Noble Lord actually meant by "utterly corrupt instincts" and "practices ruinous and lower than that practised by the beast" was sex! As disenchantment with the Church grew the ruling classes attempted to step into the breach and impose a set of moral standards designed to protect their authority. Victoria's ascent to the throne in 1837 provided them with the excuse. Colin Wilson:

> 'With an eighteen year old virgin on the throne... England felt the need to mend its morals - or at any rate its public attitudes.'

Overnight sex became a taboo, an unmentionable vice.
Wilson:

> 'Women became embarrassed if they had to refer to a chest of draws... table legs were swathed in frills because a naked leg... might invoke impure thoughts ... (later) the frills... were replaced by long table cloths.

1   Sex, Death and Punishment p157

Prudely induced a kind of galloping inflation in euphemisms.' [1]

What was actually taking place was a gross abnormality. Normal, healthy human desires, and with them love, affection and tenderness, were being perverted to create a sanitised society wholly alien to human nature. That control of people's behaviour - and through it the maintenance of the social order - was the ultimate aim of this unhealthy puritanism is made clear by Davenport Hines:

> *'Some Christians in authority were content if their dependents buckled under to show the resemblance rather than genuine faith. It was conformity to authority - obedience - that was prized.'* [2]

Cosy illusions were planted, like artificial flowers on a waste ground. Wilson again:

> *'Their ideal seemed to be a world rather like that of Tolkein's hobbits drowsing in their warm hobbit holes, or John Betjeman's small boy tucked up in bed, "safe inside his slumberwear".'* [3]

Behind the illusion lurked the reality. Suppressing natural feelings led to a cramped, inward looking and neurotic society, impeccably summarised by Thomas Boyle in his book 'Black Swine in the Sewers of Hampstead':

> *'Society, in these accounts, often appears to be teetering on the brink of madness, whilst presenting to the outside world an image of buttoned up respectability.'* [4]

What Boyle is portraying here is a facade, a Society living a lie and bleeding from its own hypocrisy. And hypocrisy it was. The Victorian upper classes never paid more than lip service to the ideals which they sought to impose. Whilst the Clergy's ever diminishing voice exalted the poorer classes to emulate their 'betters' and practise restraint, the young Aristocrats of Victorian Britain nightly prowled the streets debauching the daughters of the poor. The Bishop of London estimated that there were 80,000 prostitutes in the capital alone. Others felt this figure was too conservative!

Anaemic debates over figures are strictly secondary to the reasons which forced these women out onto the streets and into a life of misery and deprivation. Conditions of employment for women - when they could find work in the first place — were harrowing. Typical was Bryant and May, the Matchmakers. 'Match Girls', as they were known, found plenty in common with Elizabeth Bentley and

---

1   A Criminal History of Mankind p496
2   Sex, Death Aand Punishment p157
3   A Criminal History of Mankind p483
4   Black Swine In the Sewers of Hampstead p34

her generation many decades earlier. Forced to toil long hours for minimal wages and sacked if they became sick, the nature of the work inflicted a particularly unpleasant disease called 'Phossy Jaw' on the Match Girls. 'Phossy Jaw' inflamed the teeth and jaw causing intense pain and terrible disfigurement; 'their jaws eaten out of their heads in order that matches should be sold cheaper and shareholders get a higher percentage for their investment' as the socialist leader H M Hyndman put it. In order to cut labour costs and keep their employees in line, Bryant and May also employed a significant number of outworkers making Matchboxes. Each matchbox involved fourteen different operations and the girls were paid 2 ¾d[*] per gross (around 80 pence today), which meant that even to earn a shilling a day — starvation wages — they had to produce 600 matchboxes. The work caused numbness and pain in the fingers and after a while permanently damaged the eyes. Small wonder then, given conditions such as these, that many young women turned in despair to prostitution.

Others had been prostituted from a very young age. Child prostitution was rife, a delicacy for the depraved. Donald McCormick writes of 'Children.... with rouged faces, kicked out of their homes... and told to stay out until some monster of a man would give them a couple of shillings'.[1]

What prostitution actually created was a pool of impoverished young women on whom the wealthy could slake their carnal thirsts; 'ruining the daughters of the working class to gratify their passions' railed the Socialist journal 'Justice'. Far from practising restraint and observing their own code of morality the upper classes simply used the poor as substitutes for the women of their own class whom they eventually married. By reducing women to penury they had created their own reservoir of amusement; pleasures born from the flesh of poverty.

Around this grew up a microscopism of Victorian Capitalism, a system based on a system and fueled by its mores and hypocrisies: - the white slave trade. By the middle of the nineteenth Century there was a flourishing Cross Channel trade in young women bound for the brothels of France, Belgium and Germany. Most were victims of poverty and unemployment; some coerced by threats and beatings, others simply abducted and drugged. Once abroad they were committed to a treadmill life of loveless sex in a brothel. Sometimes they were even auctioned to procurers for brothels in South America. One observer at such an auction in Belgium recalled a young Englishwoman weeping piteously as she was sold — naked and prodded and poked like a prize heifer - to a brothel in Buenos Aires.

Unscrupulous employers, particularly the owners of sweat shops, also took

1   The Identity Of Jack The Ripper 2nd (revised) Edition p19

*   Pre-decimal Currency

sexual advantage of poverty as General Booth makes clear. Such employers:

> *'Hunted from pillar to post... a young penniless girl, confronted always by the alternatives - starve or sin. And when the poor girl has consented to buy the right to earn her living by the sacrifice of her virtue, then she is treated as a slave and an outcast by the very men who have ruined her.'*

William Fishman takes up the story:

> *'On being seduced the girl was often so appalled by the shame and horror of her deed, that she had no alternative but to acquiesce in her future role as "unfortunate".* [1]

Here we see the way in which evil begets evil, predators using the values of a deformed Society to their own advantage. The girl is seduced and then regards herself as ruined and unclean, her only future now a life of prostitution. There are also stories of young women being deliberately raped by procurers to achieve the same result. Poverty and perversion hand in hand to consign their victims to hell.

Hell is hardly too strong a word. Prostitution offered no escape for its victims. For most there was no let up from economic hardship. Instead their lot was degradation, disease and ill health, their only relationships with the brutal and degenerate men who 'minded' them and fed off them. The conditions in which some prostitutes existed — it cannot be put any higher than that — sometimes defy belief. The girls who worked the Army barracks at Aldershot slept in holes in sand caves, half naked, diseased, verminous and perpetually drunk. Their counterparts at the Curragh Barracks lived under hedges. Booth again, describes sick London prostitutes as 'lying in many a dark hole... positively rotting away' and cared for only by their fellow prostitutes.

The economic law which had driven them onto the streets was compounded by the judicial law. Under the Contagious Diseases Act (1864) — passed by the Commons at dinner time with only 50 M.P.'s present — any woman out alone within a three mile radius of an Army or Naval Barracks could be arrested by a Policeman and on a Magistrates' Order compulsorily hospitalized and examined for Venereal disease. The Act was refined in 1866 (this time at 2 a.m. in the morning) and existed until 1883 when it was scrapped only to be replaced by new laws against soliciting on the grounds that prostitution was "degrading to Women", a catch all phrase also used against women who had extra-marital affairs. That prostitution was, and is, degrading no one can doubt, but when set in the balance against starvation or debility it was a choice which many found unavoidable. The Act only succeeded in degrading pros-

1   East End 1888 p123

8

titutes even further by criminalising them and forcing them deeper into the clutches of pimps and ponces. It paid no heed to the economic conditions which induced prostitution and added a new dimension to the hardship; — the necessity to pay the fine which could only be met by further prostitution. Small wonder that Oscar Wilde characterised moralists as 'heartless, cruel, vindictive, log-stupid and lacking in humanity.'

The story of the Jack the ripper murders is the story of some of the victims of Victorian values. The women who died, randomly slaughtered by a vicious homicide, were not exceptional cases. Their killer had a vast army of working class victims to choose from. The ripper himself reflected the warped values around him. Thomas Boyle writes of a 'World which - beneath the pretence of sanitised respectability - is randomly violent'; where 'Acts combining brutality and sex... are not exceptional' and a 'dismal swamp honeycombed with quicksand and teeming with predators'.[1] To pick one case out: In 1850, Jane Wilbred, a servant girl, summonsed her Master, one George Sloane for cruelty. Wilbred was forced to do her duties naked from the waist up. She was beaten regularly. When she cried she was beaten again. If she used the chamber pot at night Sloane's wife made her eat her own faeces in the morning. Beside this, being forced to eat raw turnips stuffed with dirt seems almost decent! Admitted to Hospital, Wilbred was found to weigh only four and a half stone. The Sloanes were sent to prison.

Decency lies in the person and not the outward trappings of society. Ostensibly, Sloane was a pillar of respectability, a Director of the Church of England's Assurance Institution. Compare his behaviour with that of ripper victim Mary Kelly who on the last night of her life attempted to dissuade a young friend from becoming a prostitute. There was in fact no actual difference between the Sloanes and Jack the ripper in terms of cruelty and degeneracy. Where the similarity ends is that the ripper's abnormality overcame him completely. But both he and the Sloanes reflected the values of an amoral and inhuman society, blushing with its own obscenity.

Jack the ripper summed up a dirty, dismal and best forgotten century.

---

1   Black Swine In The Sewers Of Hampstead p21

Chapter Two : The Birth Of A Myth

'Jack the Ripper' did not lurk in the shadows; he did not spring out of the fog, carry a little black bag or write mocking letters to the police. These are all canards created by tabloid journalism and saloon bar gossip. So much nonsense has been written about these murders that it is sometimes difficult to believe that the ripper was a real person and not a mythical or semi mythical character like Sweeney Todd or 'Spring heeled Jack'. Unfortunately he did exist. The one thing about him that was not mythical was the trail of torn and broken bodies which he left on his bloody rampage.

To begin with he was not so much the Whitechapel Murderer as the East End Murderer: of the twelve victims who have been linked with the ripper only four, Emma Smith, Martha Tabram, Mary Ann Nichols and Alice McKenzie, were slain in Whitechapel itself. Three, Elizabeth Stride, an unidentified torso found in Pinchin Street and Frances Coles, died in the Parish of St Georges In the East. Annie Chapman and Mary Kelly were murdered in Spitalfields, Catharine Eddowes in Aldgate, Rose Mylett in Poplar; and Ada Wilson was attacked in Mile End. In short these crimes, some of which can be attributed to the same man and some of which cannot, spread like a cancer throughout the whole of London's East End.

Equally, Jack the ripper may not have been the only serial killer at large in London at this time. On October 3rd, 1888 workmen discovered the remains of a dismembered female corpse which had been dumped on their building site in Whitehall. Ironically the building under construction was New Scotland Yard! In May and June of 1889 parts of the body of a West London prostitute named Elizabeth Jackson were recovered from the Thames, and on September 10th the aforementioned Pinchin Street torso was discovered. Like the Whitehall victim she could not be identified although she may have been a prostitute known as Lydia Hart who disappeared around that time. It is possible that all three women were slain by the same hand. If so then the killer was certainly not the ripper but a second stalking ghoul.

The first victim who can actually be linked with the ripper crimes was a young woman named Ada Wilson. An earlier alleged victim, known only as "Fairy Fay" and supposedly found dead near Commercial Road in December, 1887, seems to have been pure invention. No record of this crime has ever been located. Ada Wilson, who described herself as a sempstress, lived at 19, Maidman Street, Mile End. On March 28th, 1888 she was attacked in her room by a man who demanded money and stabbed her twice in the throat. Fortunately she survived the assault and described her assailant as about thirty, 5ft 6 inches tall will a sunburnt face and a fair moustache. He was wearing a dark coat, light trousers and a wideawake hat. This is a passable description of the man later seen with three of the established ripper victims. An interesting feature of the crime was the demand for money. Although Jack the ripper was primarily a sexual killer he was obsessed by money, without doubt robbed his victims and was to forfeit his own life through avariciousness.

The Police never linked the attack on Ada Wilson with the ripper murders. Nor can they be blamed for this. Only time and bitter experience would show that serial killers often work their way up to killing through lesser assaults. Peter Sutcliffe, the Yorkshire Ripper, is a prime example. Although Ada Wilson cannot positively be listed as a ripper victim all the hallmarks are there. This assault may have been the catalyst, the moment when violent fantasy turned to reality leading inexorably to the murders four months later.

Less than a week after the stabbing of Ada Wilson a forty five year old prostitute was struck down in the streets of Whitechapel. Little is known about Emma Smith, except that she had seen better times. In the early hours of April 3rd, she was stalked by a group of men who attacked her on the corner of Brick Lane and Wentworth Street. She was robbed, beaten and raped. Finally one of her assailants rammed a stick into her vagina rupturing her perineum. Afterwards she picked herself up and staggered home. There is a desperate sadness about the plight of this lonely middle aged woman reeling through the streets, trying to staunch the blood from her wounds and refusing to tell any passer-by what had happened to her. Only when she reached her lodgings was she persuaded to go to Hospital. She died two days later from peritonitis. The Police did not learn of the assault until after her death. Later this murder was to be attributed to Jack the ripper but at the time the Police concluded that Emma's killers were members of a street gang, based in Brick Lane, called the "Old Nichol" who preyed on women of the streets. They were undoubtedly right. Smith was assaulted by at least three and probably four men, one of whom was apparently only eighteen or nineteen. She was not murdered by the ripper. She was however sadly typical of the victims to come.

July 1888 was a bitterly cold month. Snow fell and in the East End homeless people died of exposure in the streets. The Autumn bank holiday that year fell on August 6th and after such an awful summer must have been keenly anticipated. Little did anybody know that it was to mark the beginning of a reign of terror unparalleled in criminal history. The pubs were busy throughout the day as people celebrated their holiday with a drinking spree. Amongst the revellers in the East End were many soldiers from the nearby army barracks at the Tower of London. Late that evening a Corporal and a Private from the Coldstream Guards picked up two prostitutes at the "Two Brewers" in Brick Lane. One of them, who paired off with the Corporal, was Mary Ann Connolly. Her companion was thirty nine years old Martha Tabram.

The quartet left the "Two Brewers" and moved on to the "White Swan" in

Whitechapel High Street. There prices were agreed and the couples separated. It was now 11.45. Connolly took her client to nearby Angel Alley, serviced him and parted from him. Tabrum took hers to George Yard, now Gunthorpe Street, a mean little thoroughfare situated between Commercial Street and Osborn Street. She was never seen alive again.

Sometime during the early hours of August 7th a Mrs Hewitt, Wife of the Caretaker of George Yard Buildings, was woken by a cry of 'oh murder'. In this area, where poverty begat so much violence and couples even fought on their wedding day, such cries were all too commonplace. Mrs Hewitt turned over and went back to sleep. At 2 a.m. a couple named Mahoney returned home to George Buildings. They saw nothing on the darkened landings. A few minutes later Mrs Mahoney went out again for fish and chips. Again, nothing. At about this time a Police Constable named Barrett encountered a young Grenadier Guardsman, apparently a Private, on the corner of Georges Yard and Wentworth Street. The soldier told him that he was waiting for a friend who had gone into the yard with a girl. 3.30 a.m. and Alfred Crow trudged wearily up to his apartment in the Buildings. In the grey, pre-dawn light he could make out a figure lying on the first floor landing. Drunks often used George Buildings to sleep it off. Crow passed by and went to bed. At 4.45 another tenant, John Reeves, came down on his way to work. On the first floor landing he slipped over in the pool of blood in which Martha Tabram lay. She had been stabbed thirty nine times, nine wounds in the throat, seventeen in the breast and thirteen in the abdomen and vaginal area. Both lungs, her heart, liver, spleen and sternum had been punctured. The nightmare autumn had begun.

Martha Tabram was the first fatal victim of this ghoulish death hunt. She was flotsam and jetsam, cared about for a few minutes in back alleys. A human being, she was worth more but humanity was not the code of Victorian England. Her mortuary photograph shows a flabby faced woman, not pretty, just homely. She seems to have come originally from Greenwich. Around the late 1860's she married Henry Tabram, a Foreman Packer. They had two sons the eldest of whom was eighteen at the time of her death. The couple separated around 1875 but never divorced. Henry Tabram was to tell Martha's inquest that he had left her because of her drinking. That she was a heavy drinker, probably an alcoholic, there can be no doubt. But in these cases who speaks for the dead? What made Martha drink?

Henry Tabram initially paid her 60 pence[*] a week in maintenance but reduced it to 12 ½ pence[*] when he found out that she had turned to prostitution. Martha promptly had him arrested. Later she herself served a gaol sentence for repeatedly annoying Henry's sister. Around 1879 she took up with William Turner, a Carpenter, and Henry stopped the payments altogether. The relation-

[*]   Decimal currency

ship with Turner, who may have been somewhat younger than Martha, was stormy. They parted several times, the last shortly before her death. Like Henry Tabram, Turner blamed her drinking habits. At the time of her murder Martha was living in a common lodging house in George Street, Spitalfields, having absconded from her previous lodgings owing two weeks' rent. She last saw William Turner on the Saturday before her death. He gave her 7½pence*, in today's terms around £5. Despite their ups and downs the couple seem to have been genuinely fond of each other. Now their relationship had been severed by a madman's knife.

Martha Tabram's post mortem was carried out by a Doctor with the eerie name of Timothy Killeen. Dr Killeen put the time of death at approximately 3.30 a.m. This squares with the evidence of Alfred Crow and the Mahoneys. Crow noticed a figure lying on the landing at 3.30. The Mahoney's saw nothing at 2.00 or afterwards although of course the landing was in pitch darkness at that time. However, Mrs Mahoney had crossed the landing three times and if a body had been lying there then it is rather unlikely that she would not have come across it.

Dr Killeen noted several other points. Thirty eight of the wounds had been made by what he thought could be a penknife. The other, the wound in the sternum, had been caused by a longer bladed weapon, a dagger or a bayonet. The murderer was right handed and possessed surgical skill, knowing where and how to cut. This last assessment was a foretaste of confusions which were to bedevil the search for Jack the ripper for many years.

The Police investigation into the murder of Martha Tabram was led by Inspector Edmund Reid, Divisional Head of H Division C.I.D. which served Whitechapel. Reid was a colourful and interesting character. A talented singer and actor, he held the record height for ascent in a balloon and had made Britain's first parachute jump. He was a good policeman too and his men quickly ferreted out Mary Ann Connolly. On August 13th and 15th she attended identity parades at the Tower of London. On the second one she picked out two men as Tabram and her clients on Bank Holiday Monday. Both soldiers were able to prove alibis. Barrett also attended two identity parades and on the second selected a man whom he thought might have been the Grenadier he had spoken to. He too demonstrated an alibi. In fact whilst these charades were taking place Jack the ripper may well have been on holiday.

In all probability Reid thought it unlikely that Martha Tabram had been murdered by a soldier. The evidence put the time of death between 3.00 and 3.30. Tabram had gone off with her Guardsman at 11.45 and would have been through with him by 12.15 at the latest. It is not unknown for a prostitute to linger with a client she has taken a liking to but not on one of the most promising nights of the year. Whether she was the girl who later went off with the

---

*   Decimal currency

Grenadier's friend we do not know but George Yard Buildings was commonly used by many prostitutes. A bayonet may have been one of the murder weapons but these were freely sold in nearby Petticoat Lane. The police decided that Tabram, like Emma Smith, had been murdered by a street gang, the motive robbery. Reid did not share Killeen's opinion that medical skill had been shown.

Whether Martha Tabram was a victim of Jack the ripper has vexed historians for years. I have no real hesitation in saying that she was. My only reservation is that the Ripper was in Wolverhampton during part of August. Martha has been dismissed as his victim for two main reasons. The first is modus operandi. Tabram was repeatedly stabbed whilst the later victims had their bodies ripped open. But there can be no doubt that the assault on Tabram was sexual in nature. The killer's targets were her breasts, stomach and vagina. What is probable is that he later varied his mode of butchery because he did not reap enough satisfaction from Tabram's murder. What is improbable is that there were two sexual psychopaths haunting the same small collection of streets at the same time, one who killed once but never again and one who then took over from him.

The second objection stems from Sir Melville Macnaghten afterwards Assistant Commissioner in charge of the C.I.D. Macnaghten, whom we shall meet again later, was a meddlesome mattie, an ex-tea planter and 'Gentleman Amateur' Detective possessing neither the training or the ability for his rank. He was not with the police in 1888 but later became involved in the aftermath of the ripper murders. Macnaghten's view, rather sourly expressed, was that Martha had indeed been murdered by her Guardsman client but that Connolly thwarted the police by refusing to identify him. As we shall see, Macnaghten did not enjoy a very close relationship with factual detail. It is sufficient to say that his views were not shared by other senior Detectives who did work on the Whitechapel murders. Edmund Reid came to believe that Tabram was a ripper victim, a view shared by Inspector Frederick Abberline and endorsed by the Head of the C.I.D. Sir Robert Anderson.

Two factors, one hitherto unknown, the other generally unperceived*, really put the issue beyond doubt. All save one of Martha Tabram's wounds were probably inflicted with a penknife. Jack the ripper slept with a penknife under his pillow. And the Tabram killing established a pattern of murder. She was slain on August 7th, the next crime occurred on the last day of August. Then Annie Chapman was murdered on the eighth day of September followed by the murders of Elizabeth Stride and Catharine Eddowes on the final day of that month. The pattern was broken in October and for a very good reason, but resumed again in November with Mary Kelly on the 9th. Martha Tabram was the first major link in this gruesome chain. Almost certainly, she was a victim of Jack the ripper.

---

*   Martin Fido, 'The crimes, detection and death of Jack the Ripper', seems to be the only other writer to have noticed it.

August 30th/31st, 1888 the night of the fires. And of blood in the streets. At 8.30 p.m. on the 30th, South Dock burst into flames. It took fireman three hours to bring the blaze under control. No sooner had they done so than Shadwell Dock erupted. It was as if the East End was determined to burn that night; to make a sad funeral pyre for Mary Ann Nichols.

Mary Ann, known affectionately as "Polly", was a forty three year old prostitute with a drink problem. That night she had been drinking in the "Frying Pan", a cosy little pub in Brick Lane*. She left at 12.30** and weaved her way to a lodging house in nearby Thrawl Street where she was turned away because she did not have the price of a bed. Not in the least put out she laughingly told the attendant: 'I'll soon get my doss money. See what a jolly bonnet I've got now.' What she did for the next hour or so is unknown but at 2.30 a.m. she bumped into her friend and room mate Emily Holland in Whitechapel High Street. Holland had been down to Shadwell to gawp at the fire which was still burning brightly and could be seen as far away as Finsbury Park. Clearly tipsy, Polly repeated her intention of earning her doss money and again showed off her new hat. Little things mean a lot to poor people. When they parted at 2.40 a.m. Polly had just under an hour left to live.

Whitechapel tube station is an approximate fifteen minutes walk from the spot where Polly Nichols and Emily Holland had their last conversation. Being rather drunk Polly probably took a little longer to reach it. Just past the station on the left is Brady Street and a little way down Brady Street, second on the left, is Durward Street then called Bucks Row. At 3.45 a.m. a carman named Charles Cross was walking to work along Bucks Row when he spied what looked like a tarpaulin on the other side of the road. Cross went to investigate. The 'tarpauline' turned out to be the dead body of Mary Ann Nichols.

Almost immediately, Cross was joined by another carman, Robert Paul. Together the two men set off to find a policeman. They could not have been gone for more than a few seconds when one turned up, P.C. John Neil. By lantern light Neil could see that the dead woman had had her throat cut. Other injuries were not then apparent. Straightening up, Neil winked his lantern for assistance. From the top of the street came the comforting flash of an answer and within seconds he was joined by P.C. John Thain whom he despatched to fetch a Doctor. At about this time a third Constable, Jonas Mizen, alerted by Cross and Paul arrived. Neil sent him for an ambulance (actually a wheeled stretcher).

Thain returned with Dr Rees Llewellyn who made a very perfunctory examination of the body, pronounced life extinct and went home to bed. Llewellyn did however notice that there was not a lot of blood on the ground; only a wine glass and a half by his estimation. Had he stayed then he would have

---

*   Now an Indian Restaurant
**   Under the then Licensing Laws Pubs stayed open until 1:00 a.m.

seen that there was considerably more on the back of the body. Helping to load the corpse onto the Ambulance P.C. Thain got his hands covered in blood. The mortal remains of Mary Ann Nichols, who only a short time before had been happily joking with her friend, were now wheeled in silence through the semi-darkened streets to Old Montague Street Mortuary. Behind them, in the gutter, an obscene parody of her earlier high spirits; the jolly new bonnet of which she had been so pathetically proud. Away in the distance the flames from the Shadwell fire seemed almost to reach the sky.

Mary Ann was born into a respectable working class family in 1845. Her father, Edward Walker, was originally a locksmith. They lived initially in Dean Street, off Fetter Lane, the area which used to be the heart of the Newspaper Industry. She married young (eighteen) and may well have grown up with her husband. He was William Nichols, a printer of Bouverie Street which is very close to Dean Street. Polly Nichols was apparently a very pretty young woman with dark hair, delicate features and high cheek-bones. Most writers on the case have depicted her as a toothless hag[*] but at the time of her death her father told Reporters that she looked ten years younger than her real age. There is probably some truth in this. According to Emily Holland Polly claimed to have had three clients on August 30th. Prostitutes are notorious for exaggerating the number of their clients, but Polly had earned enough money that day to buy her new hat and get drunk, and it was a Thursday, traditionally the Prostitute's leanest day of the week. It therefore seems likely that she did retain some vestige of her youthful good looks.

The marriage between Polly and William Nichols appears to have been happy at first. Children arrived at regular intervals, Edward 1866, Percy two years later, Alice 1870, Eliza 1877 and Henry in 1879. But at some point things began to go wrong and Polly started to drink heavily. She and William split up several times. Not that the fault was all on her side. At one point William had an affair with another woman, the Nurse who attended Polly when she gave birth to Eliza. Although Polly took him back their eldest son, Edward, refused to forgive him and went to live with Polly's father.

By the time of her death the youngest boy Henry was also living with his grandfather.

The final separation came in September 1880. For the next two and a half years Polly lived mainly in the bleak and depressing environment of Lambeth workhouse. Such surroundings were not conducive to helping a woman with a drink problem. Nor was the niggardly 25 pence[**] a week she received in maintenance from William (about £15 on today's values). This was less than half the sum which Henry Tabram initially settled on Martha. It was therefore

[*]   she had several teeth missing by 1888
[**] decimal currency

hardly surprising that Polly drifted into prostitution. On discovering this William ceased her maintenance entirely. In March 1883 she went to live with her father; now a blacksmith, in Camberwell. Two months later she left after a row over her drinking but they remained on good terms. Another short spell in Lambeth workhouse was followed by an upturn in her life. She moved in with a man named Thomas Drew and stayed with him for the next four years. As Drew was also a Blacksmith it is possible that she met him through her father. The relationship ended in October 1887 — why we do not know — and Polly's life now went into the downward spiral which ended with her miserable death ten months later. Until the middle of April she either lived in workhouses or slept rough in the streets. From April to mid July she made a desperate effort to pull herself together and found work as a housemaid with a family named Cowdry in Wandsworth. From there she wrote to her father:

> *"I just write to say you will be glad to know that I am settled in my new place and going all right up to now. My people went out yesterday and have not returned, so I am left in charge. It is a grand place inside, with trees and gardens back and front. All has been newly done up. They are teetotallers and very religious, so I ought to get on. They are very nice people and I have not much to do. I hope you are all right and the boy has work. So goodbye now for the present. Yours truly, Polly. Answer soon please and let me know how you are."*

Polly Nichols has traditionally been portrayed as a near moron. This little letter disproves that image. Although short (most people are not long letter writers) it is neatly put together and well expressed.

Sadly, Polly's sojourn with respectability did not last long. The craving for drink again laid hands on her and in July she absconded with clothes worth £3.50 (about £200 today). Her final descent into hell was swift and sure. On August 2nd she arrived in Spitalfields and went to stay at the lodging house from which she was turned away on the night of her murder. Some semblance of pride still remained. The room which she shared with Emily Holland (and two other women) was kept neat and tidy and she was very clean in her person, a point noted during her autopsy. However on August 24th she commenced sleeping at another lodging house in Flower and Dean Street which was to all intents and purposes a brothel. Polly Nichols' was a wasted life. Married at eighteen without experience of life or men she dutifully produced five children and lapsed into alcoholism. She was the product of a society which regarded woman as simply the property of their husbands. Unhappiness and unfullfilment ending in the solace of the bottle is a sadly recurring theme in the ripper Murders.

The full extent of Polly's injuries did not become known until after her corpse reached the mortuary (in reality a large shed). According to P.C. Neil, Inspector John Spratling pulled up her skirt to inspect the body and discovered to his horror that she had been disembowelled. Later the body was stripped and washed by two mortuary attendants, James Hatfield and Robert Mann, an action which caused considerable annoyance because the police had told them not to touch it. Dr Llewellyn performed a post mortem the following morning. His findings can be summarised as follows. There were two bruises on Nichols' face, one on the lower right jaw, the other on the left. These could have been caused either by a fist or pressure from a thumb. Her throat had been cut twice, very deeply, from left to right. In fact these cuts had gone right through to the vertebrae and had very nearly decapitated the poor woman. Her lower abdomen had been savagely mutilated. There was a deep, jagged wound two to three inches from the left side, several incisions running across the abdomen and three or four cuts on the right side which ran on a downward axis.

These were Polly Nichols actual injuries. Llewellyn did not fix a time of death but this can reliably be put at around 3.30 a.m. The body was discovered at 3.45. Constable Neil had last patrolled Bucks Row at 3.15 and the body was not there then. Fanciful theories, which were already being floated by the Press, suggested that she might have been killed elsewhere and dumped in Bucks Row, thereby accounting for the paucity of blood on the ground. However, both the police and Dr Llewellyn were adamant that she had been killed where she was found, and most of the blood had anyway been absorbed by her clothing.

Llewellyn thought that the murderer 'must have had some rough anatomical knowledge'. All the cuts had been inflicted by the same weapon, a sharp knife. The killer appeared to him to have been left handed. This last point, although it was perfectly proper to make it, has also led to much confusion about the ripper.

An item which Dr Llewellyn did not mention, he probably thought it of no consequence, was that one of Polly's fingers bore the impression of a ring. Whether this had been pulled off by her killer we do not know for certain but it fits the pattern of Jack the ripper, not only a revolting sadist but a mean, grasping little man who stole what valuables his victims had. Finding that Polly had no money he probably took the ring instead. The pattern was to be repeated with his next victim. The Police may well have concluded that the ring had been stolen because their initial theory was that Polly Nichols, like Martha Tabram and Emma Smith, had been murdered by the 'Old Nichol' gang.

The Inquest on Mary Ann Nichols commenced that afternoon, Saturday, September 1st. It was preceded by a brief and poignant reunion between three of the men in Polly's life. Arriving at the mortuary to view his wife's remains William encountered her Father and his own estranged son, Edward. Edward Walker told his son-in-law, 'Well, here is your son, you see. I have taken care of him and made a man of him.' William replied: 'Well, I really did not know him; he has so grown and altered.' This chance meeting may have rankled with William Nichols because on being shown Polly's body he rather unctuously declared: 'Seeing you as you are now, I forgive you for what you have done to me.' Polly's family clearly thought that he could have been a better husband. Afterwards William emerged from the mortuary, pale and shaken, to tell Reporters that his Wife had come to a bad end at last. He was nothing if not constant in his self-righteousness.

The inquest itself was held at the Working Lads' Institute, situated next to Whitechapel Station. The Coroner was Wynne Baxter, a dandified forty-four year old Solicitor who clearly believed that he, and only he, was going to be the dominant force in his Court Room. Baxter was to hold the inquests on the next two ripper victims as well. Although a thorough man he seems to have wanted to inject himself into the case and to have enjoyed the publicity. Polly's inquest was to drag on well into September and involved Baxter in some quite unnecessary clashes with the police. Meanwhile, behind the scenes, it was the police who were doing the real work.

Although Bucks Row was a part of Whitechapel it fell (just) within the precincts of J Division of the Metropolitan Police. This meant that the investigation into Mary Ann Nichols murder would be carried out by J Division Detectives led by their Divisional Inspector, Joseph Helson.

The initial police theory, that Polly was a victim of the Old Nichol gang, was swiftly discarded. It was from this point on that the police began to hunt for a lone killer. It was also at this time that the police decided that all three prostitutes deaths, Emma Smith, Martha Tabram and Mary Ann Nichols, were the work of the same man. This was somewhat unfortunate in Emma's case because whatever inquiry was still going on into her death was now switched away from the real murderers with the result that they were never caught.

The murder of Mary Ann Nichols was conspicuous by the lack of clues. Nobody remembered seeing her after she left Emily Holland and nobody in Bucks Row had seen or heard anything. Waiter Purkiss, who lived opposite the murder site, was awake during various times of what had been an unusually quiet night. He heard nothing. His wife had been awake most of the night, certainly at 3.30; — she was quite adamant about that. Again, nothing. And there was Mrs Emma Green, whose bedroom window almost overlooked the murder site. Green was a light sleeper but the first she had heard was the police knocking at her door.

Between Whitechapel Road and Bucks Row lies Winthrop Street which actually converges with Bucks Row near the spot where Polly Nichols was struck down. In Winthrop Street was a slaughter house (long since demolished). Three of the slaughtermen, Henry Tomkins, James Mumford and Charles Brittain had wandered across to Bucks Row to look at the human slaughter after it was discovered, but neither they nor any of their workmates had heard or seen anything. Patrick Mulshaw, a night watchman in Winthrop Street, had spoken to a man who told him that a woman had been found murdered but this was after the body had been discovered and the man was certainly just a passer-by.

The only witness who did claim to have heard anything lived in Brady Street. She was Mrs Sarah Colwell who said that she had been woken up in the small hours of August 31st by the sound of a woman running and crying out 'Police, Murder'. Colwell thought that she had also heard blows being struck but, rather strangely, no sound of any other footsteps. As the murder was committed in Bucks Row the police — and subsequent writers on the case — have dismissed Mrs Colwell's statement as fantasy but this is remarkably unimaginative. Polly Nichols had bruises on her face which *could* have been fist marks. One possible scenario of the murder is that the ripper approached Polly in Brady Street with a demand for money, caught her and punched her when she tried to escape and then forced her into Bucks Row with his knife at her throat to ensure her silence. Then he strangled her, cut her throat and mutilated her. This would explain the very silent death of Mary Ann Nichols.

But this of course is all hypothesis. What the police were faced with at the beginning of September, 1888 was a murder as perplexing as it was silent. And a press which was now anything but silent. A gruesome killer had to be caught and stopped. But what sort of man were the police looking for? By the beginning of the following week they thought they had found the answer.

Chapter Three: Leather Apron & Dark Annie

His sobriquet was leather apron and according to popular myth he walked half man, half beast, a mixture of quilp and Poe's Baboon. He stomped the streets of London in a leather apron robbing and terrorising prostitutes at knife point. He was the Jew conjured up by Goebbels, short, squat and ugly and within whom no human heart beat. And in all probability he never existed.

How 'Leather Apron' came into the case is sketchy. Xenophobia, anti semitism, the fear of an unknown killer with a knife, perhaps a combination of all three. He seems to have arrived on the scene at the same time that the Police discarded their gang theory. Apparently word had begun to percolate through to them about a grim visaged, knife wielding Jew who menaced and robbed prostitutes in various parts of the capital. If so, then it is strange that they had not heard of him before. Equally strange, he was allowed to operate by gangs like the 'Old Nichol' who made their living from robbing prostitutes. Of this more later. By the beginning of the week of September 2nd the Police were looking for this man. Two days later the Press took the cry up with a vengeance and in Shakespeare's words, judgment fled to brutish beasts.

Stanley Baldwin once summed up the Press as having: "power without responsibility, the prerogative of the harlot down through the ages". Their performance during the ripper murders provides a striking example of this. Fleet Street, which is only thirty minutes walking distance from Whitechapel, had ignored Emma Smith and Martha Tabram. Now reporters descended on the East End in droves, pens poised to pass instant judgments on matters which they knew little or nothing about. An early example is this gem of analysis sent by the 'New York Times' London stringer to his Newspaper.

> *'He has just slaughtered his third victim, and all the women in White-chapel are terrified, whilst the stupidest detectives in the civilised world stand aghast and say they have no clue.'*

In fact, the 'stupidest detectives in the civilised world' were led by a Commissioner who was a gifted Mathematician, had already written three books on Archaeology and would later publish definitive works on weights and measures. Under him, the Assistant Commissioner in charge of C.I.D. was a Doctor of Law and a Biblical Scholar of renown, whilst the man running the day to day investigation of the ripper murders was a Latin and Greek Scholar. As for 'standing aghast', neither clues nor suspects can be manufactured out of thin air. If they do not exist then they cannot be made to exist.

There is an old journalist maxim that lies are halfway around the world before the truth has got its boots on. How closely this applied to Newspaper coverage of the ripper murders has been aptly described by William Le Queux, then a young journalist for the now defunct 'Globe'. Le Queux enjoys the unenviable reputation of being the least reliable journalist in history. Later, his strictly dubious talents were employed by the British Government to manufacture anti-German spy stories. Writing about the ripper crimes he confessed:

> *'... as each murder was committed we wrote up picturesque and lurid details while we stood on the very spot where the tragedy had occurred. One evening Spingfield... would publish a theory of how the murders had been done...; next night Charlie Hands would have a far better theory.... and then I would weigh in with another theory in "The Globe".'*

Clearly, not all of the ghouls had knives in their hands. Le Queux and his charming cohorts were however to be eclipsed by at least one other journalist, a reporter named Best who worked for 'The Star'*. It was in fact 'The Star' (and possibly Mr Best) which was initially responsible for whipping up the 'Leather Apron' hysteria. On September 5th the Newspaper published a blood curdling description of him which it claimed had been based on interviews with fifty women. For what it is worth, which is precisely nothing, 'The Star's' description of its little bogey man ran as follows: of Jewish appearance, short and thickset with a tree-trunk neck, glinty eyes and a horrible smile; black hair and moustache, late thirties and wearing a tight fitting cap and a leather apron. His movements were silent and sinister and he carried a knife with which he threatened to "rip women up". He had served a (fictitious) prison sentence for attacking a woman and, giving it the illusion of authenticity, had a friend and soulmate called 'mickeldy Joe'. That this was all simply a highly embellished version of Dickens Quilp from 'The old curiosity shop' was lost amidst the clamour it created. For good measure 'The Star's' reporter must have been a singularly expeditious man because he claimed to have conducted his fifty interviews in just three hours (three and a half minutes each unless he interviewed the women in batches)!

With the rest of Fleet Street swiftly following suit the floodgates of fear and prejudice were opened. Somebody was decimating the female population of East London and (so the quaint notion ran) he could not be an Englishman or a Christian. The Jews, particularly those of foreign extraction, were the obvious scapegoats. Feared because they were of an alien religion and culture, hated because they were willing to work for less money than their gentile counterparts, anti semitism now ran rife. Matters were not helped by a sensational story about a Polish Jew named Ritter who was said to have murdered and mutilated a women in Cracow**. The East End quickly became a pogrom waiting to happen. That it did not was a tribute to the good sense of the Jewish Community who made themselves as inconspicuous as possible.

* Not the same 'Star' in circulation today.
** in fact he was acquitted

22

In the midst of all this passion the police were indeed searching for a foreign born Jew, one John Pizer whom, it was alleged, was the dreaded 'Leather Apron'. On September 7th Inspector Helson reported to Scotland Yard that Pizer had been "ill using" prostitutes throughout London for some time. At a glance Pizer was worth looking at. In 1887 he had served a six month jail sentence for stabbing a man in the hand and in August 1888 he had been arraigned for indecent assault. However, the stabbing was in a row over work and the assault charge was dismissed. On what basis Helson asserted that Pizer had been mistreating prostitutes is unknown. The suspicion must be that this was an attempt to inculcate Pizer with leather apron and not the other way around.

John Pizer would soon become the target for libellous attacks in the press. But before that happened another murder took place.

*****

In the early hours of September 8th a dumpy, middle aged woman with dark curly hair sat huddled close to the stove of a common lodging house in Dorset Street, Spitalfields. She was Annie Chapman sometimes known as Annie Sievey, or 'Dark Annie'. Annie was forty-seven years old and she was dying (although she did not know this) of a disease of the lungs which was far advanced. Because her body was dying and it was a cool night she needed the warmth from the stove and she desperately hoped that she might be allowed to stay where she was because she did not have the price of her bed. But at about 2 a.m. Tim Donovan, the lodging house Deputy, came into the kitchen. He found Annie eating a baked potato and asked her if she would be going up to bed that night. Annie confessed that she did not have the money. Donovan, who may have been the same Timothy Donovan who died two months later of cirrhosis of the liver, told her that in that case she would have to leave. She obeyed, rather pathetically asking him not to let her bed. And so a possibly dying man turned a dying woman out into the street. The exigencies of the economic system had triumphed over common humanity.

What Annie did during the next three and a half hours we do not know. Shortly before half past five she was seen talking to a man in Hanbury Street (two minutes walk from Dorset Street). A minute or so later Albert Cadosch, who lived at No 27, Hanbury Street, went out into the backyard and heard a voice say "no" followed by the sound of something thudding against the fence which separated No 27 from No 29. The backyard of No 29 could be entered from the street through an unlocked passageway and was frequently used by prostitutes to entertain their clients. It being none of Albert Cadosch's business he turned and went back inside. Just before six John Davis, a tenant at No 29, walked blearily out into his backyard. What he saw woke him up with a start. Lying on her back next to the fence was the dead body of Annie Chapman. Her tongue was protruding from her mouth, her throat had been cut and her stomach ripped open. Part of her intestines had been laid out across one of her shoulders. Shocked and stunned Davis staggered back through the house and out into Hanbury Street where two men who worked nearby, James Kent and James Green, were waiting for the 'Black Swan' pub to open. To them Davis blurted out the dreadful news that a woman had been murdered. Kent and Green and a third man named Henry Holland who had been passing by on his way to work went into the backyard of No 29 to see what was amiss. They returned with alacrity and went charging off in all directions, Green to his workplace, Kent to the 'Black Swan' for a brandy and Holland to fetch a Policeman. He found one in Spitalfields Market but the Officer refused to return with him because he was on fixed point duty. Under the circumstances the refusal was clearly obtuse. Somehow the police were summoned, whether by Davis or Holland is unclear, and Inspector Joseph Chandler hurried to the scene from Commercial Street Police Station. When he arrived at No 29 he found that a small crowd had already formed in the passageway.

Chandler immediately sent for Dr George Bagster Phillips, the divisional police surgeon. Phillips arrived at 6.30. The body was already cool to the touch and he decided that Annie had been dead for approximately two hours. By now a crowd estimated at several hundred had gathered in Hanbury Street and the tenants of No 29 were charging the most ghoulish onlookers sixpence a time to look down into the yard from their back windows. Anxious to put a stop to this nauseating behaviour Phillips had the body removed to the Whitechapel Work-house Mortuary.

Chandler made a thorough search of the backyard of No 29. There were splashes of blood on the fence and a large quantity on the ground. Also lying on the ground were the meagre contents of Annie Chapman's pocket which the murderer had cut through with his knife. Later a story was to gain acceptance that three brass rings, torn from Annie's fingers, had been laid out at her feet. It was a myth. The autopsy revealed that three rings had indeed been pulled off one of her fingers but they were not found with the body.

In a corner of the Yard Chandler made an electrifying discovery. There on the ground wet and laid out to dry was a leather apron!

Meanwhile, Annie Chapman's mutilated corpse was already stiffening at the mortuary. Hers had been a sad life. She was born in Paddington in 1841 the daughter of a soldier named Smith who christened her Eliza Anne. Clearly she did not like Eliza because she never used it. When she was fifteen the Smith family uprooted to Windsor where, at the rather late age of 28, she married a coachman named John Chapman who was related to her mother and two years Annie's junior. As with all of the ripper victims there were no photographs taken of her during life so we do not know what Annie looked like when young. Her mortuary photograph shows a rather motherly face neither older nor younger than her age.

After the wedding Annie and John Chapman made their home in West London. They had three children, two daughters, one of whom died in childhood, and a son who was a cripple. Shortly before the death of Annie's daughter in 1882 the family broke up. Annie left John, the boy was put into a cripples home and the other daughter was sent to an institution in France. Exactly what prompted the break up is unknown. The image portrayed of Annie by most writers is of a drunken sot who slept with other men. In fact this is all assumption and not very good assumption at that. She did enjoy a drink and had been arrested (but not prosecuted) for drunkenness in Windsor. She was not however an alcoholic. John Chapman on the other hand certainly was and died of cirrhosis of the liver four years after Annie left him.

After leaving home Annie seems to have spent most of her time in the East End. She lived by selling matches and doing crochet work and on 50p a week* which John Chapman sent her until his death on Christmas Day, 1886. Sometimes she prostituted herself but only when necessity forced her to.

In 1886 she lived for a while with a sievemaker who was known as Jack Sivvy, hence her own nom de plume of Annie Sievey (or Sivvy). In the months leading up to her death she had another boyfriend of sorts, a labourer named Edward Stanley whom she saw at weekends. According to friends Annie generally got drunk on a Saturday night, but did not imbibe much during the rest of the week. Tim Donovan and two other men were later to state that she appeared to be tipsy on the night of her death but the autopsy, which found very little trace of alcohol in her body, refutes this. It is possible that she seemed drunk because of her illness.

Her last week on earth was a particularly miserable one. She complained of constantly feeling ill and tired and at some point probably visited a workhouse infirmary because amongst the possessions found by her body were two pills. Sometime during that week she had a fight with another woman, Eliza Cooper. There are several versions of what caused it. The one generally given most credence is that Cooper attempted to swindle a friend of Annie's, a man who went by the prosaic name of "Harry the Hawker". Chapman objected and the two woman came to blows, Annie getting the worst of it. She was noticeably down on Friday, telling her friend Amelia Palmer: 'It's no good my giving way. I must pull myself together and go out and get some money or I shall have no lodgings.'

She did not pull herself together and she did not get lodgings. Instead she went out into the night and a heartless creature destroyed her in Hanbury Street.

As the attending physician it fell to Dr Phillips to perform the autopsy. Like Polly Nichols, the corpse had already been stripped and washed when he arrived. Robert Mann was once again dancing attendance and may have been responsible but the task itself fell to two Nurses from the workhouse infirmary. On this occasion the police made no complaint and Dr Phillips was more concerned with the conditions in which he had to work.

---

* Decimal Currency

Annie Chapman's injuries were barbarous. There were bruises on her temple, forehead, chin, jaw and chest, although only those to the chin and jaw were recent. The others had been sustained in the fight with Eliza Cooper. She had been strangled as evidenced by her tongue protruding from her mouth and her fists being clenched, both signs of strangulation. Replicating Polly Nichols' murder, Chapman's throat had been cut twice very deeply from left to right almost cutting her head off. The wounds to the lower part of her body were different from Nichols: deeper and more penetrating. If anyone had previously doubted the sexual nature of the attacks on Tabram and Nichols then those doubts were stilled now. Annie Chapman's sexual organs had been very deliberately attacked and mutilated. Her abdomen had been ripped open and her intestines pulled out and placed on her shoulder. Then the killer had cut out her uterus, the upper portion of her vagina and two thirds of her bladder. These he had taken away with him as though they were some hideous trophy. Perhaps they were. However, as we shall see, there was another theory about them.

Like Rees Llewellyn, Dr Phillips had no doubt whatsoever that the murder had taken place where the body was found. He gave no opinion as to whether the murderer was left handed or right handed. He decided that the killer had used a knife with a thin blade at least 6–8 inches long. It was not a bayonet or a leather worker's knife but could have been of the type used by a slaughterman or a Doctor during post mortems. This reference to Doctors presaged the two most controversial parts of the autopsy report, the murderer's anatomical knowledge and the time of death.

Phillips presented his findings to Annie's inquest on two separate days, September 12th and September 19th. This was because he was extremely reluctant to detail the abdominal wounds in open court. Whilst his reticence does him credit he was in fact obliged by law to provide details of all the injuries and therefore had to return on the 19th to complete his evidence. Then he described the mutilations as the work of an expert, a man used to anatomical or pathological examinations and possessing the skill to remove the organs with single sweeps of the knife. He, Phillips, did not think he could have performed the mutilations in under fifteen minutes and in the deliberate calm of the operating theatre he would have taken the better part of an hour. However, as we shall see, Phillips was not always quite so emphatic about the degree of knowledge shown by Annie Chapman's murderer.

The time of death was a poser. Phillips put it at 4.30, perhaps even earlier. However the evidence of three witnesses, Cadosch, a Mrs Elizabeth Long and a market porter named John Richardson made it an hour later at 5.30. In the end the Police came down on Phillips' side, presumably because his was a professional judgment. But in 1888 estimation of the time of death was in its infancy. It relied mainly on touch and this was the method which Phillips had used. The morning of September 8th was a chilly one and the mutilated condition of the corpse (its wounds were exposed to the air) would have caused it to cool even more rapidly. There can be no doubt that in this instance Phillips was wrong and the witnesses right. Cadosch had heard the sounds of the scuffle at 5.30. He had then left for work and on passing nearby Spitalfields Church had noted that the time was 5.32. Mrs Long had seen a woman, whom she later identified at the mortuary as Annie Chapman, talking to a man outside No 29 just before 5.30. She heard him ask "Will you?" and Chapman's reply "Yes". John Richardson had called in at No 29 on his way to work at 4.45. His mother, a rather religious lady, lived at No 29 and Richardson was in the habit of popping in to see that the backyard was not being used by prostitutes. That morning he had sat down on the back doorstep and attempted to trim some leather from a boot that was hurting him. It was already getting light and if Annie's body had been lying in the Yard then he could not have failed to see it. Somewhat disgruntled the police suggested that the open backdoor would have obscured his view but in fact they were wrong, and very badly wrong at that because by accepting Phillips time of death they made their single greatest blunder of the entire investigation. Mrs Long's evidence was discarded and along with it her description of the man she had seen with Chapman. It was only scanty — he had kept his back to her — and ran as follows:— 'shabby genteel' appearance, deerstalker hat, dark coat, about 40, dark complexion, foreign looking and only a little taller than Annie who stood an even five foot. Given that Mrs Long never really saw him facially then her estimate of his age and origin cannot really be relied upon, but her impression of his height — short — and of his clothes, 'shabby genteel', fit Jack the ripper exactly. There can be no doubt that she, and she alone, saw Annie Chapman with her murderer.

Unfortunately, in addition to their mistake over Elizabeth Long, the police were also wandering off on several other tangents all of which were to prove blind alleys. One was the leather apron found in the backyard of No 29. At first this appeared to be of momentous consequence. In fact it was anything but. The apron belonged to John Richardson and his mother had washed it for him and left it in the yard to dry on the day before the murder. Exit one red herring. The next was an itinerant boot finisher named Emmanuel Violenia who claimed to have seen two men quarrelling with a woman — one threatened to knife her — in Hanbury Street during the early hours of September 8th. Violenia was also destined to make an early exit from the case. Another who should have done was Emily Walters who spoke of being accosted by a sinister man in black in Hanbury Street at 2.00 on the morning of the murder. Having spurned his advances (or so she said) Walters then saw him pick up another woman and take her into No 29. But Walters story was gravely suspect. It took her 48 hours to come forward and she went not to the police but 'The Star'. The description she gave of this black garbed foreigner is too close for comfort to an artist's impression of Leather Apron which had appeared in the Newspaper. Unfortunately, because Emily Walters' story dovetailed with their own notions about the man they were seeking, the police accepted it and issued the following notice:-

> *'Description of a man who entered a passage of a house where the murder was committed of a prostitute at 2.00 a.m. on 8 September. Age 37, height 5ft 7in. Rather dark beard and moustache; dress — dark jacket, dark vest and trousers, black scarf and black felt hat. Spoke with a foreign accent.'*

The police investigation was effectively in disarray. They had chosen the wrong time of death, the wrong description and the wrong witnesses. This was to have particularly tragic consequences in the weeks and months to come. They had married their mistakes to a Newspaper led creation and were hopelessly on the wrong track. Although the police performance was to greatly improve as the hunt progressed they were to remain wedded to these errors throughout. In consequence, when Jack the ripper did come to their attention they missed out on him.

✳✳✳✳✳

In 1888 the Metropolitan Police Force was less than sixty years old and its relationship with the Public it served was an uneasy one. Set up in 1829 by Sir Robert Peel to tackle the capital's horrendous crime rate (in the 1780s it reached heights comparable to present day New York), the Met was not overtly welcomed by Londoners. A populace which fifty years earlier had championed the cause of the American Colonists and individual liberty, was fearful that its own freedoms might be eroded by this new, militaristic style of policing. Just how deeply ingrained this fear was can be seen from an incident which occurred a few years after the Met had been formed. When a Police Constable was stabbed to death during a political demonstration the coroner's jury exonerated the culprit on the grounds that he had been defending political freedom! Another major worry was that out of uniform the police might act as spies on the community. Consequently, there was initially no Detective Branch and Officers were forbidden to wear mufti off duty. But the most protracted opposition came from the square mile of the City of London which by Royal prerogative ran its own courts and policing apparatus under the auspices of the city aldermen. The city spurned the Met's embrace and was eventually allowed to create its own police force in 1839. The result was an absurd anomaly. London had — and still does have — two completely separate police bodies each with its own Commissioner, ranks and departments, one, the Met, answerable to the Home Office, the other to the City of London Corporation. This was to prove anything but helpful in the search for Jack the ripper.

By 1842 fears had eased sufficiently for the Met to create a small and much needed Detective Branch. This grew both in size and prestige until 1876 when the Criminal Investigation Department, as it subsequently became known, was torn apart by a major corruption scandal involving high ranking Detectives. Some were sent to prison and others left the force. Three men who survived unscathed were Superintendent Frederick Williamson and Inspectors Donald Swanson and Frederick Abberline. Swanson and Abberline were later to lead the hunt for the ripper.

Despite these teething troubles the C.I.D. continued to expand. By 1884 its establishment had risen to approximately 800. That year it also acquired a new Chief, Assistant Commissioner James Monro, formally Head of the Bombay Police Department. Monro was something of a paradox: sternly disciplinarian but approachable, deeply religious yet secretive, a model of integrity but ambitious and not adrift in the political in-fighting.

The Met's next big scandal was one of efficiency, not corruption. On February 8th, 1886 an inadequately policed demonstration in Trafalgar Square got out of hand. A small section of the crowd rioted and then looted their way through the West End even — horror of horrors — breaking the windows of the Carlton Club, Bastion of high Toryism. The following morning the Commissioner, Sir Edmund Henderson, awoke to a uniformly hostile press and the wrath of Queen Victoria. On the 10th a rumour reached Scotland Yard that a large mob was gathering to attack the West End again. The Police ordered the shops to close but the mob proved fictitious and yet another paroxysm of rage descended upon the hapless Sir Edmund. The upshot of it all was that Henderson was sacked. The man who replaced him was to be even more controversial.

Sir Charles Warren. Bete noir of the Ripperphiles. Depending on which writer one reads, Warren was: 'Autocratic... a "reds under the beds" man[1]; 'a none to modern Major-General' who 'handled policemen as if they were soldiers and demonstrators as if they were the enemy[2]; a toadying Freemason whose: 'sole function (during the ripper murders) was to operate a cover up'; and who 'confronted the poor with his new-style military police force[3]; 'A most unsuitable choice for the office,... in manner and mentality the nineteenth century counterpart of Colonel Blimp[4]; 'A man whose: 'middle and later years seemed marred by promotions for which his qualities of military leadership were inadequate[5]; and, more concisely, 'a rigid, slightly comic figure[6];. There is much more in similar vein. Victorian dramas needed their Jasper Stoneyheart and by 1888 the radical press had already cast Sir Charles in this role. Subsequent writers have regurgitated their spiteful portrayals with far less justification.

1   Elwyn Jones & John Lloyd 'The Ripper File' (PBK) p106
2   Daniel Farson 'Jack the Ripper' (PBK) p30
3   Stephen Knight 'Jack the Ripper': The final solution pp158 & 83
4   Donald McConnick 'The Identity of Jack the Ripper' (1970 Edition) p69
5   Terence Sharkey 'Jack the Ripper: 100 yrs of investigation' p51
6   Melvin Harris 'Jack the Ripper, the Bloody Truth' p13

By 1885 Sir Charles Warren had earned himself a glowing reputation as a soldier, administrator and archaeologist. At the youthful age of 45 he was not a coming man but a man who had already arrived. A knighthood, a garter and the rank of Major General marked his accomplishments.

Had he died heroically defending some beleaguered outpost of empire then he would have gone down to posterity as a great Victorian hero. Instead that honour fell to his close friend, Gordon of Khartoum. The sun shines its golden rays on some but not on others. Gordon was the martyred hero of colonial self sacrifice: his friend the bumbling incompetent driven from office by Jack the ripper.

Gordon's blood had hardly dried before Warren's career began to turn sour. He stood for Parliament in the 1885 General Election as a Liberal but went down to defeat along with his Party. Generals were not supposed to involve themselves in Politics — certainly not Liberal Politics — and it was made known to Warren that his Army career was over. But within months came an unexpected reprieve, possibly because he was a high ranking freemason, possibly because the Liberals regained power early in 1886. Whatever the reason, Warren found himself in Suakin as Military Governor and Commander of the British Forces there. He had barely unpacked when a telegram arrived offering him Henderson's job. Once again fortune seemed to be smiling. But behind the smile lurked a gargoyle. Had Warren stayed put then he and not Kitchener might have been the man who avenged Gordon and liberated the Sudan. Instead he accepted the job as Police Commissioner and the fateful dye was cast.

Warren's regime began auspiciously. He earned praise for his handling of two demonstrations and tightened up on discipline. Administratively, he made the far sighted decision to create a new rank of Chief Constable, below Assistant Commissioner, to which Career Police Officers might aspire*. Unfortunately he then marred this wisdom by appointing army officers to two of the three available positions. Only Superintendent Williamson of the Detective Branch gained promotion. Worse followed.

Jubilee Day 1887. Policing of the celebrations had been firm but fair. It all appeared to have gone off well and it did until late that evening. At first it was a trivial enough affair; a Police Constable named Endacott arresting a seamstress named Cass for soliciting in Regent Street. Miss Cass however very volubly protested her innocence and her employer backed it with a private prosecution against Endacott for wrongful arrest. The Cass affair quickly became front page news. In retrospect it was an accident waiting to happen, Cass and Endacott the victims of a stupid and vindictive piece of legislation. Warren paid the price handling an inquiry rather clumsily and offending supporters of both parties.

The new Commissioner's mind may well have been on other things.

*   See Appendix One

Relations with James Monro were severely strained. Monro was angling to make the C.I.D. autonomous of Warren's control. And he had just scored a notable victory. Surveillance and infiltration of Fenian and Anarchist groups, hitherto the function of the Home Office, had now been placed in Monro's hands. The result was a new Department (Special Branch) made up of hand picked Detectives based at Scotland Yard but paid for by separate fundings and answerable only to Monro who in turn reported directly to the Home Office about its activities. Warren was excluded and outraged. Ironically, in view of the criticism to come, one of his complaints was that he disliked policemen being used as spies. The disputes between the Commissioner and his Chief of Detectives were to rumble on until well into 1888 effectively splitting and demoralising the police force. For this neither Warren nor Monro can be blamed. The fault lay fairly and squarely with the Home Secretary, the weak and vacillating Henry Mathews, who should have ensured that the new unit was properly integrated into the police force (as it is now) and made it clear that an autonomous Detective Force was out of the question. Mathews, who disliked Warren (and almost everybody else for that matter), did neither and the situation drifted on detrimentally.

The Autumn of 1887 was a particularly brutal one for the unemployed. Thousands of homeless and jobless people took over Trafalgar Square and turned it into a vast open air squat (Polly Nichols stayed there for a time). Their plight elicited no sympathy from West End shopkeepers who complained that the ragged hordes frequently stole from their shops. No doubt they did. They had a right to live and if Society could not and would not provide them with either jobs or subsistence then they had little recourse other than to steal. This was not however a view which the Police could take. Whatever the private sympathies of police officers their job was to uphold the law. Warren sought approval from the Home Office to clear Trafalgar Square. Vacillating as usual, Mathews first gave it and them promptly rescinded it. This provoked a new danger. Shopkeepers threatened to raise their own private *lumpenproleterian* army to clear the square. The potential for anarchy and bloodshed was obvious and Warren again asked for permission to act. It was granted and notice given to the army of vagrants that the police intended to close Trafalgar Square and move them on. Socialist groups, led by the Marxist Social Democratic Federation, proposed to march on the square on Sunday, November 13th, 1887. The stage was now set for bloody Sunday.

To read a book on the ripper murders is to gain the impression that "Bloody Sunday" was an historic event in Labour history rivalling the Tolpuddle martyrs. In fact the Labour movement, including the far left, completely forgot about it many decades ago and never regarded it as anything more than a trivial, passing incident. Warren correctly forecast a massive turn out and detailed 4,000 police backed up by 600 Cavalry and Grenadier Guards to prevent the demonstrators getting into the square. In view of the fact that 100,000 people turned up such a force was hardly excessive. Predictably, violence flared. One demonstrator was killed and 150 injured. Again, in view of the numbers involved the casualties were not excessive. The object of the exercise, to maintain law and order, was achieved. But for Warren it was a pyrrhic victory. Criticism descended upon him from all sides. Depending on your political beliefs he was a red hating martinet who had ridden down the poor in their own blood, a blinkered reactionary destroying personal freedom or simply a fool who had over reacted. The irony was almost gothic. Warren was a moderate Liberal, mace bearer of the wing of his party which for years had been attacked as the respectable face of anarchy and socialism. In a private memo written before bloody Sunday he had made it clear that his concern was not with the socialists but the thieves and trouble makers who attached themselves to political demonstrations. But objective truths like these were thrust aside as demonology took over. He had become the man you love to hate.

The simmering row with Monro erupted again in the summer of 1888. Complaining of being overworked, Monro wanted to bring in his friend, Sir Melville Macnaghten, as Assistant Chief Constable of the C.I.D.. Warren vetoed Macnaghten; Monro resigned. Mathews had no option but to back his Commissioner but gave Monro a desk at the Home Office with the title 'Head of Detectives Services'[*]. Meanwhile a 47 year old Irish lawyer, Sir Robert Anderson, made the journey the other way, leaving the Home Office to replace Monro at Scotland Yard.

Anderson took up his post on September 1st the day after Polly Nichols murder. He too has been roughly handled by historians of the ripper murders, 'an Irish fool on the make'[1] according to one source. Sir Robert was a long way from being a fool. His tenure as head of the C.I.D. was to last until retirement thirteen years later. During that period Scotland Yard regained its self respect following the ripper debacle. But in 1888 Anderson was the wrong man in the wrong place at the wrong time.

For a start he was tired and needed a holiday. He had accepted his new job on the understanding that he would take a two month vacation commencing September 8th. This would not have mattered very much if Williamson had been able to deputise for him but the Chief Constable was ill with heart trouble. The outset of the ripper's reign of terror therefore found the C.I.D. leaderless. Beneath Williamson, the most senior Scotland Yard Detective was Chief Inspector Donald Swanson. A former schoolteacher well read in Latin, Greek

1   The Ripper File (pbk edition) p107

*   He retained control of Special Branch

and Philosophy, Swanson was entrusted with the day to day running of the ripper investigation by Anderson. His dictate has survived.

> *"I am convinced the Whitechapel murder case... can be successfully grappled with if it is systematically taken in hand... I could myself in a few days unravel the mystery provided I could spare the time... I therefore put it in the hands of Chief Inspector Swanson who must be acquainted with every detail...*
>
> *"He must have a room to himself and every paper, document, report, telegram must pass through his hands. He must be consulted on every subject. I would not send any directions... without consulting him. I give him the whole responsibility...*
>
> *"All the papers must be kept in his room and plans of the positions etc...*
>
> *"Everything depends upon a careful compliance with these directions"*

It was clearly a going on holiday memo. Without doubt Anderson expected the murderer to be under lock and key by the time he got back. Fond hope, harsh reality.

Swanson's first action was to appoint a yard man to run the investigation on the ground. Whitechapel kept divided Councils. H Division was investigating Smith and Tabram; J Division Nichols. Clearly somebody was needed to co-ordinate their efforts. The obvious choice was Inspector Frederick Abberline, Head of H Division C.I.D. until he was promoted to the Yard's purple in 1887. Abberline was a Dorset man who had joined the police in 1863. Unquestionably, he was one of the most able detectives in the Met, specially picked out for advancement by Monro and Williamson. Now he was back in Whitechapel tasked with catching an unknown killer. He was not to report directly to Swanson but through the Yard's other Detective Chief Inspector, Henry Moore, presumably because Moore was his superior and the matter one of protocol. Abberline took with him only one aide from Scotland Yard, Detective Constable John McCarthy, later an Inspector with Special Branch. In the East End Abberline worked with a small team of detectives who were continuously engaged on the case, Reid, an Inspector named Nairn and three Sergeants, Pierce, Thick and Godley. Nothing is really known about Nairn or Pierce. William Thick, nicknamed 'Johnny Upright', was a colourful local character whose loud check suits belied the fact that he was a very determined thief taker. George Godley rose to the rank of Inspector and is remembered as the man who arrested the poisoner, Severin Klosowski[*]. This then was the nub of the ripper murder squad[**]. It had begun to operate by the time Annie Chapman was killed. Unfortunately, despite

---

[*]   See Chapter Seven
[**] scores of other detectives were also employed on the investigation at their direction.

all the undoubted talents of these men, it was they who had blundered so badly in the wake of her death.

*****

On September 14th a small funeral party gathered at Manor Park Cemetery, Wanstead, there to commit the mortal remains of Annie Chapman to the earth. Her epitaph was movingly written by the 'Daily Telegraph' on October 6th. There were few moments during the Whitechapel murders when Fleet Street distinguished itself. This was one of them:-

> *"Dark Annie's spirit still walks Whitechapel unavenged by justice. Yet even this forlorn, despised citizeness cannot be said to have suffered in vain. Dark Annie's dreadful end has compelled Londoners to reflect what it must be like to have no home except the kitchen of a low lodging house; to sit there, sick and weak, bruised and wretched; to be turned out after midnight to earn the requisite pence, anywhere and anyhow; to come across your murderer and caress your assassin. She has affected more by her death than many long speeches in Parliament. She has forced people to realise how and where our vast floating population — the waifs and strays of our thoroughfares — live and sleep at night, what sort of accommodation our rich and enlightened capital provides for them. "Dark Annie" will effect what fifty secretaries of state could never accomplish."*[*]

Meanwhile the Police had finally located John Pizer.

---

[*] condensed by the author.

Chapter Four: The Swedish Femme Fatale & The Little Sparrow

On Monday morning, September 10th, 'Johnny Upright' turned up on Pizer's doorstep and arrested him with the words "You're just the man I want". Pizer went very pale and began to tremble. Aware of the suspicions against him, he had kept to his house in Mulberry Street, Whitechapel, since September 6th. He was a Jew of Polish origin and a boot finisher by trade although he had not worked for some time. Without doubt, he carried knives around with him and was of a quarrelsome disposition. There was not, however, any evidence that he was a menace to women.

Sergeant Thick took Pizer to Leman Street Police Station where he was put on an identity parade in front of Emmanuel Violenia. Violenia picked him out as one of the men he had seen threatening the woman in Hanbury Street. At this point things looked a little bleak for Pizer but the situation changed abruptly when Violenia announced that he also knew him as Leather Apron. This caused consternation. Violenia was en-route to Australia from Manchester and had only been in London for a few days. That afternoon Violenia was subjected to a vigorous interrogation and contradicted himself over and over again. He was also taken to see Chapman's corpse and failed to identify it. The Police concluded that his story was a pack of lies concocted out of a morbid desire to see the body. They kicked him out that evening with a caution for wasting police time.

Pizer was also questioned. On the night of Polly Nichols' death he had stayed at a lodging house in Holloway[*]. He had been out and about in Seven Sisters Road from 11.00 p.m. to 1.30 a.m. The London Docks' fires were burning brightly in the distance and he had spoken about them to a passing constable. Both the Policeman and the Lodging House Deputy corroborated his story. His family confirmed that he had not left the house since September 6th. Plainly John Pizer was not the man the police were looking for. On September 12th they took him to Annie's Inquest to clear himself. Afterwards they released him. Pizer then sued a number of Newspapers who had named him as the killer.

At this point both Pizer and Leather Apron should have disappeared from the story. Pizer did but not Leather Apron. The will of the wisp Polish Jew became an idée fixe with the police. They ought to have been asking whether he really existed in the first place.

The first note of doubt had already been struck by the 'Guardian' on September 10th. Others should have been posing the same question. Here was a

[*]   North London

35

strange tale indeed. A pug ugly little man in a leather apron terrorising women the length and breadth of London and whom by now half the East End claimed to know. Yet the police had never heard of him, could never lay hands on him, and, Pizer aside, nobody knew his name or where he lived. There is an air of unreality about the whole thing. Nobody can say it with absolute certainty but Leather Apron was probably a myth, one of the many which surrounds Jack the ripper. Perhaps he was a composite of many low brutes who had held knives at prostitutes' throats and robbed them (then as now an occupational hazard), perhaps an anti semitic hob goblin created by fear and prejudice, even, perhaps, a story circulated by the 'Old Nichol' to take the heat off of them. Possibly a mixture of all three. Once the seeds were sown the press and mass hysteria took over. There is an interesting parallel here with the kidnap-murder of the Lindbergh baby in America. Experimentally, a team of journalists showed photographs of alleged suspects to local New Jersey residents. Invariably one or other of the photographs was identified as a man seen prowling around the neighbourhood at the time of the kidnapping. The so called 'suspects' were in fact eminent politicians and Judges! Some elements of Jack the ripper's character were present in Leather Apron but as a separate entity he cannot be taken seriously. Unfortunately the police never relinquished their belief in him. The result was failure.

*****

To examine Annie Chapman's Inquest would be tedious and unnecessary. It was a protracted affair which ended on a note of pitiful low farce. During his summing up Coroner Baxter (who was simultaneously still conducting the Nichols' Inquest) caused a sensation by claiming that there had been a market for the missing organs, an American buyer in London. The story had no real basis in fact and seems to have been one of Baxter's devices for grabbing the headlines. By now the police were heartily sick of him, his publicity seeking (at their expense), his hectoring cross examinations, his sometimes obtuse observations (incredibly he thought that Pizer had been ill advised to stay indoors), above all, the sheer length of his Inquests. But this to was too have unfortunate consequences.

*****

The disappointing conclusion to the Pizer affair meant that the police were now back to square one. But a picture was beginning to emerge. Martha Tabram had been slain at around 3.30 on a Tuesday morning, Polly Nichols' fifteen minutes walking distance at the same time on a Friday morning; Annie Chapman five minutes walk from Tabram's murder site, fifteen from Nichols', in the early hours of a Saturday morning. Logic suggested that the killer lived either in the immediate vicinity of the crimes or at least within easy distance of Whitechapel and Spitalfields. Equally, logic suggested that he was either a night worker or unemployed. There was however a third possibility, that he was self-employed. The police do not seem to have considered this. They should have done.

The question of the murderer's medical knowledge was a perplexing one. Three surgeons had concluded that it was there in one degree or another. The police were sceptical but not being medical men themselves they could hardly ignore the Doctors' opinions. Possibly then the killer might be a slaughterman, a butcher or a medical student. Teams of Detectives combed the slaughterhouses in the district, taking statements, checking movements, making inquiries. The results were negative. A Holloway Butcher named Joseph Issenschmidt seemed briefly to be an interesting possibility. Local gossip portrayed Issenschmidt as a man of somewhat uncertain temperament, much given to terrorising rent collectors, and waving knives at customers and threatening to "put their lights out". Not surprisingly his business had failed and Issenschmidt had spent some time in a lunatic asylum. He was not, however, the man the police were seeking. Nor were three medical students who had been diagnosed as insane. Two were traced and eliminated. The third, John Sanders, could never be pinned down but latter day research suggests that he was in an asylum during 1888. Equally elusive were a Russian born criminal named Michael Ostrog said (without foundation) to be a homicidal maniac and a deranged surgeon called Puckridge who, interestingly enough, had been released from an asylum only three days before Martha Tabram's death. Neither Ostrog or Puckridge were ever found.

Two men who were detained and caused hopes to flicker briefly, were Charles Ludwig and William Pigott. On September 18th a city police constable, John Johnson, found Ludwig in an alley in the Minories with a terrified young prostitute named Elizabeth Burns who cried out, "Oh policeman, do take me out of this". Johnson sent Ludwig on his way and walked with Burns to the end of his beat. As they parted Burns told him: "he frightened me so much when he pulled that big knife out." Pausing only to admonish her for not telling him sooner, Johnson set off in pursuit. Ludwig meanwhile had gotten himself into more trouble and was arrested for threatening a man with his knife in Whitechapel High Street. He was still in custody twelve days later when the Ripper struck again.

William Pigott was a former Publican from Gravesend who was arrested there on September 9th with blood on his clothes. He had expressed a violent hatred of women. However, Abberline's inquiries satisfied him that Pigott was not the murderer. Something which comes over very strongly about the police investigations into these crimes is how scrupulous and fair they were. William Pigott was simply a wandering misogynist who was slowly going off his head. Whilst in custody his sanity gave way altogether and he was committed to an asylum.

The sum total of all this police activity was nil. The press meanwhile was having a field day, the 'Star' hugely enjoying itself. According to one of its leaders:

'London lies today under the spell of a great terror. A nameless reprob-ate — half beast, half man ... daily satisfying his murderous instincts...

'Hideous malice, deadly cunning, insatiable thirst for blood... a pawnee Indian simply drunk with blood and he will have more'

On reading this a Mrs Mary Burridge collapsed and died. Which is what happens when the office boy is allowed to write the editorials.

It was at this time that an old friend made his all too predictable entrance into the fray; — the media scapegoat. 'Punch' started it with a serious editorial (or perhaps not) opining that the killer was acting under the influence of lurid picture posters. Other Newspapers quickly joined in pointing accusing fingers at a stage play of 'Jeckyll & Hyde' then performing at the Lyceum theatre (it was taken off). Before the murders were over 'Penny Dreadful' magazines and French novels had also been indicted. Innuendo is shouted from the roof top; correction whispered from the cellar.

Other, more flesh and blood scapegoats, were also being targeted. Sir Charles Warren was the obvious one. 'A maladroit martinet' according to the 'Star', whilst the 'Pall Mail Gazette', whose contribution to the ripper hunt was a theory that he was a black magician*, wanted Sir Charles removed from Scotland Yard and posted to upper Zambesi. Presumably the Gazette imagined that he might fare better against witch doctors than magicians. Behind Warren was the somewhat shadowy figure of Home Secretary Mathews who, as the Autumn wore on, came increasingly under fire himself. The 'Star' again, with its usual schoolboy jibes, described him as: 'A feeble mountebank who would pose and simper over the brink of a volcano', whilst the 'Daily Telegraph', then a far more radical tome than it is today, assured its readers that Mathews: 'knows nothing, has heard nothing and does not intend to do anything'; and was: 'a source of miserable weakness and discredit to the present administration'. A week later the 'Telegraph' was rather repetitiously savaging Mathews again as an anonymous figure who: 'does not know, is not aware and does not remember.'

Politicians in their ivory towers and maybe even Commissioners were arguably fair game, but not ordinary police officers and the 'Telegraph' was way below the belt when it described the C.I.D. as being: 'in an utterly hopeless and worthless condition', their performance: 'a scandalous exhibition of stupidity'. The 'New York Times' correspondent also sallied forth again: 'The London Police and Detective force is probably the stupidest in the world'. Whatever the merits of his argument, his choice of adjectives was remarkably limited.

In the face of all this ill judged, uninformed criticism Swanson and his team were trying to come to grips with a situation which no British Police Officer had ever encountered before. Mistakes had been made and would be again but

* See Chapter Seven

they were of inexperience, not stupidity. Even the law was against them. Policeman and prostitutes were on opposite sides of its divide, a situation which hindered the police and helped the ripper. Ninety years later the West Yorkshire police were to encounter the same difficulty during the hunt for Peter Sutcliffe.

On the ground in the East End the police were daily having to cope with an hysterical population drive almost mad with fear. Walter Dew, then a young detective constable, later the man who caught the murderer Crippen, has left this account of the wildfire panic surging through Whitechapel:

> *'The whole area was in a panic after they found Annie Chapman's body. The day after the murder I was in Hanbury Street when I saw a man called 'Squibby' who was wanted. Every time he was arrested it took half a dozen policeman to bring him in and usually half the police weren't fit for duty for a while again.*

> *'I was with another Detective called Stacey when I saw Squibby. He (Squibby) dashed across the road and ran off down Commercial Street. Stacey and I went after him. But seeing us dash off, the crowd started shouting "Jack the Ripper! Jack the Ripper".*

> *'Soon there were hundreds of people yelling out and coming after us. Squibby got into a house in Flower and Dean Street with Stacey and me after him. Finally we grabbed him. We were both done in by now and I thought we were going to be really in for it, trying to take Squibby in.*

> *'But instead of starting to fight, he was shaking like a leaf. It wasn't us he was scared of it was the crowd. They were shouting that the ripper was in there and for us to bring him out so they could lynch him. Eventually scores of policeman cleared a space in front of the house.*

> *'But when we got Squibby out, the crowd went mad. They rushed us and tried to break through the cordon and get at Squibby. In the end we put him in a four wheeler with the police forming a cordon all around it. But that wasn't any good either and they almost turned the cab over several times.*

> *'Finally an Inspector said we would be better off on foot.*

> *'The whole of Commercial Street was filled with a yelling mob by now but the police formed a cordon all the way to Commercial Street police station. In the end we managed to fight our way into the station. The doors were shut but the mob stayed outside for hours trying to get in.'*[1][*]

This tranch of murders had now reduced the poorest quarter of London to a state bordering on anarchy. Even worse, an image had been created of the serial

---

1   Dew was either mistaken about the date of this incident or the name the crowd was chanting. The nickname 'Jack the ripper' did not come into usage until October.

*   Condensed by the Author

killer as superman, an omnipotent assassin able to brush the police aside and strike with impunity. It is a myth still perpetuated today in films such as 'The Silence of the Lambs'. This illusion began with Jack the ripper and is demonstrably false. However, the events of September 30th, 1888 did nothing to dispel it.

✶✶✶✶✶

The hop picking season had not been kind to Catharine Eddowes and John Kelly. Let Kelly describe it in his own words:

> *'We didn't get on any too well and started to hoof it home... we did not have enough money to keep us going till we got to town, but we did get there... luck was dead against us... we were both done up for cash.'*

'Hoofing it home' actually means walking all the way from Maidstone in Kent to London's East End. Neither Kelly or Eddowes was in good health. Both suffered from kidney complaints. Sadly, it was to be their last journey together.

Catharine Eddowes was forty six. She was born in Wolverhampton, the daughter of a tinplate worker who not long after her birth uprooted the family to Bermondsey. George Eddowes seems to have kept his wife in an almost permanent state of pregnancy; according to one report she bore him no less than twelve children. She died in 1855, probably worn out, and the family was splintered, Catharine returning to Wolverhampton to live with an Aunt. She grew up there, friends and relatives describing her as "intelligent and scholarly" but of "fiery temperament", and "very good looking and very jolly". She was a tiny little woman, only 4 foot 11 inches tall on reaching maturity.

Sometime in the early sixties Cathy met an Army Pensioner named Thomas Conway who made his living by writing "chap" books[*]. Conway was later described as "old" which suggests that there was a considerable age gap between them. Despite this she took up with Conway and spent sixteen or seventeen years with him, bearing him a daughter and two sons. The relationship seems to have deteriorated as time wore on. Cathy left Conway several times and finally parted from him in 1880 taking her daughter Annie with her. There are two versions of what caused the break up. Annie Conway blamed her mother's heavy drinking: Cathy's sister claimed that Thomas Conway frequently drank and beat her up.

It is not clear where Cathy was living when she separated from Conway, but she ended up in a lodging house in Spitalfields where she met John Kelly. Their relationship is again best told in Kelly's own words:

> *"We got throwed together a good bit here in the lodging house and the*

[*]   Books of lives

result was we made a regular bargain.... Kate got a job charring now
and then and I picked up all the odd jobs I could get in the market. She
would take a drop to drink but she was never troublesome."

They were to be together for seven years. According to those who knew
them John Kelly was a quiet inoffensive man with fine features and intelligent
eyes, Cathy a cockney sparrow type of character, gregarious and popular, fond
of the bottle but not an alcoholic. There is no reliable evidence that she was ever
a prostitute or that she had any other boyfriends than Kelly. Indeed, their
relationship seems to have been a close and happy one summed up, probably
correctly, by Begg, Fido and Skinner as: 'appealingly loyal and mutually
supportive'.[1] Other writers on the ripper have certainly done Cathy a disservice
describing her as a bag lady who looked in her sixties. Her horrific mortuary
photographs are not recommended viewing but her face still manages to convey
the impression of a likeable, good natured soul. She was not close to her daughter
who took pains to avoid her as a persistent scrounger, but only months earlier
Cathy had nursed her through her first confinement.

John Kelly and Catharine Eddowes trudged wearily into London on Friday,
September 28th. Kelly earned sixpence that afternoon which was not quite
enough for a bed for the pair of them, so Cathy told him to take fourpence and
go to their usual lodging house in Flower and Dean Street whilst she went to the
"spike"* in Shoe Lane. There, for tuppence, she slept on the floor with her arm
draped over a rope. In that manner, cold lonely and uncomfortable she passed
her last night on earth.

✻✻✻✻✻

Whilst Eddowes and Kelly were on the hoof back to London a bizarre encounter
took place in a Spitalfields lodging house. Dr Thomas Barnardo, the philan-
thropist and founder of the Barnardo Childrens' Homes, was making his rounds
of the lodging houses, urging prostitutes to let him take their children into care,
when he stopped to talk to a group of women about the murders. One of them,
described by writer Tom Cullen as a 'gaunt, sharp faced creature' told him: 'No
one cares what becomes of us. Perhaps one of us will be killed next'[2]. Four days
later Barnardo would see those same features again on a mortuary slab.

Elizabeth Stride, known to her friends as 'Long Liz', was not in fact gaunt
or sharp faced. She in particular has suffered at the hand of the myth makers,

---

1   The Jack the Ripper A to Z p219 (First edition)
2   Autumn of Terror (PBK) p93

*   Casual Ward

generally being portrayed as an ugly, angular woman addicted to beating up other woman and sometimes men too. There is no evidence that she was of a violent nature and her mortuary photograph is almost startlingly different from the granite faced harridan normally depicted by ripperphiles. A few weeks away from her forty fifth birthday, Liz Stride was still an attractive woman with gentleness in her features.

'Long Liz' (she was tall by 1880's Whitechapel standards) was Swedish. Born Elizabeth Gustafsdotter (daughter of Gustaf) at Torslanda, Sweden, in November, 1843, she grew up in a farming community which was clearly too restrictive for her because at the age of seventeen she moved to Gothenburg as a domestic servant. Beyond doubt she was of a romantic nature much given to living in dream worlds and inventing stories about herself. Five years later she was officially registered as a prostitute, twice underwent treatment for venereal disease and gave birth to a stillborn daughter. What led to her descent into the nether world of vice and disease can only be guessed at but with a head full of fantasies and looks which men found appealing she was an easy target for the sort of men who use and then abandon impressionable woman.

1866 found her in London trying to put the misery of her early life behind her. Three years later she married John Stride a Ship's Carpenter who was over twenty years older than her. For a while the couple kept a Coffee house in Poplar but details of their lives together are scanty. We do know that Liz never lost her taste for mythologising. Amongst her stories was one that she had lost her husband and children when the pleasure steamer 'Princess Alice' capsized in the Thames in 1878. In fact she was not one of the passengers, had no children and John Stride died of heart trouble in 1884.

The marriage seems to have been over well before then. Perhaps she was unable to cope with domesticity, perhaps she was still too susceptible to the attentions of other men. Whatever the cause, the sad pattern of her early life was repeated. By the age of forty Liz was living in doss houses and begging hand outs from the Swedish Church in London. Almost certainly she had reverted to her earlier trade of prostitution.

1885 found a new man in her life, a rough-hewn Waterside labourer named Michael Kidney, nine years her junior. Although they were to remain a couple for most of the remaining three years of Stride's life, the relationship was not a stable one. Liz began to drink heavily. In 1887 and 1888 she was fined no less than eight times for being drunk and disorderly. Kidney was also prosecuted and went to prison. In April, 1887 she had him arrested for assaulting her but did not press the charge. She left him several times and undoubtedly supported herself by prostitution during these absences. Kidney was later to tell her inquest that Liz came from a good family and spoke Yiddish fluently. These were probably more of her fictions. Overall the impression which lingers is of a woman who wanted more from life than nineteenth century society had to offer, made too many mistakes, and became increasingly more unhappy and frustrated as the years went by. In the end she was to gain immortality but in a way no one could want.

*****

Saturday, September 29th, 1888. Cathy Eddowes spent the last full morning of her life pursuing the depressingly familiar routine of trying to keep body and soul together. She left the Shoe Lane casual ward early, with a little bee buzzing around inside her bonnet. She told the ward superintendents: 'I have come back to earn the reward offered for the apprehension of the Whitechapel Murderer. I think I know him.'

It is just conceivable that she did.

Possibly humouring her the Superintendent warned Cathy about being murdered herself. She replied: 'Oh, no fear of that.' Those words were to die ashes in her mouth.

From Shoe Lane she rejoined Kelly at the Flower and Dean lodging house. Later that morning the couple pawned a pair of his boots for half a crown (about £8 today), had breakfast and bought some food. By lunchtime they were penniless again and parted, Cathy telling Kelly that she was going to Bermondsey to get some money from her daughter. In fact Annie was no longer living there. What Cathy actually did during the next few hours is unknown, but at 8.30 that evening she was arrested in Aldgate by the City Police for being drunk and disorderly. She spent the next four and half hours in the cells at Bishopsgate Police Station.

*****

It was perhaps in the nature of her life that Liz Stride chose that week to walk out on Michael Kidney yet again. Saturday found her alone and broke. That afternoon she earned a few pennies from charring. In the evening she spent them in the 'Queen's Head', Commercial Street. The pub and the alcohol cast their rosy glow over her, the prophecy to Barnardo was forgotten, and she went in search of more drink.

Liz was next seen in 'The Bricklayer's Arms', Settles Street at 11 o'clock. People remembered her that night. She was wearing a dress with a red and white flower pinned to it. And she was no longer alone. Her escort was a young man with a black moustache and 'sandy' eyebrows, dressed in a morning suit and a billycock hat. He was about 5 foot 5 inches tall. Rain was beginning to fall and the couple were reluctant to leave the pub. Instead they stood near the doorway kissing and cuddling until two labourer named Best and Gardner began to poke fun at them. They stood it for a while and then left.

Another labourer, William Marshall, saw them next at 11.45. Marshall was catching a breath of fresh air outside his home, No 64 Berners Street*. Stride and her man friend were standing on the pavement opposite. The man gave Marshall the impression of being a clerk. He was about 5ft 6ins, stout and neatly dressed in a small black cutaway coat, dark trousers and a peaked, sailors type hat. Marshall heard him tell her: 'You would say anything but your prayers.' It sounded innocuous: in reality it was spine chilling. After about ten minutes the couple moved off down the street.

A Fruiterer named Matthew Packer next laid claim to have seen them, at midnight when they came into his shop in Berners Street and bought some grapes. Afterwards they crossed over the road and stood outside the International Working Man's Club, No 40 Berners Street. Packer then saw them walk up to the corner of Berners and Fairclough Streets. They were still there half an hour later when he closed up his shop. Packer also thought the man looked 'clerkly' (although he may have been influenced by Marshall who lived close by). He described him as between 25 and 30, about 5ft 7ins, broad shouldered and wearing a long black frock coat and a soft felt 'kind of hunter' hat.

12.30 and Police Constable William Smith passed by on his beat. He barely noticed the couple who were now standing outside Dutfields Yard which adjoined the International Working Man's Club. Why should he? The man bore no resemblance to the suspect the police were hunting. He was around 28, about 5ft 7ins, appeared respectable and wore a dark cutaway jacket, dark trousers and a dark felt deerstalker hat. He did not appear to have whiskers.

The next sighting we have is around ten or twelve minutes later, back again on the corner of Berners and Fairclough Streets. James Brown was en route to his home in Fairclough Street. On the corner he saw Stride with a stoutish man, approximately 5ft 7ins, wearing a long coat almost down to his heels. Brown heard Liz say: 'No, not tonight: some other night.' He put the time at 12.45 but in all probability it was a few minutes earlier than this.

Israel Schwartz was a Hungarian Jew. Shortly after Brown had spotted the couple, Schwartz encountered them at Dutfield's Yard again. Only now they were doing more than talking. As he watched the man attempted to pull Stride into the Street and then spun her round and threw her onto the pavement. She screamed three times but not very loudly. Turning from her, Stride's assailant called out the word "Lipski" to Schwartz although at the time Schwartz thought it was directed at a second man who was standing on the other side of the street. Schwartz hurried away and then broke into a run because it appeared that the second man was following him. His descriptions of the two men were as follows:

> *Stride's attacker: about 30, 5ft 5ins, fair complexion, dark hair, small brown moustache, full face, broad shoulders. Dress: dark jacket and trousers, black cap with peak. Second man: about 35, 5ft 11ins, fresh*

* Now Henriques Street

complexion, light brown hair.

Dress: dark overcoat, old black hard felt hat with a wide   brim. Had a clay pipe in his hand.

There is a measure of confusion about what happened next, but it seems that a Mrs Fanny Mortimer emerged from her house, three doors away from Dutfield's, and stood outside for about ten minutes. She had not heard Stride's screams but she had heard what she described as the measured tread of a Policeman (P.C. Smith). Later, her ten minutes became a full half an hour between 12.30 and 1.00. Whilst in the Street she saw nobody other than a man named Goldstein who walked past the Club. Shortly after going back indoors Mrs Mortimer heard the sound of Louis Diemshutz's horse and cart driving up to the Yard.

Diemshutz was the steward of the International Working Man's Club. The Club itself was a meeting place for Jewish socialists and anarchists. That night there had been a debate on the need for socialism amongst jews followed by music and singing. The sounds of the latter were still audible when Diemshutz drove up to the Club at 1.00 a.m. He had been to Crystal Palace to sell trinkets. The side door of the Club opened out into Dutfield's Yard and Diemshutz wanted to take his horse and cart into the Yard. But something was wrong. The horse stopped in the entrance way to the Yard and refused to go any further. Diemshutz got down and discovered a woman lying just behind the gate. Even the darkest tragedies have their moments of unintentional humour and Diemshutz's first thought was that it was his wife lying there drunk (what Mrs Diemshutz thought about this is not recorded). He went into the Club to summon help.

Behind him, her only companion now a frightened horse, he left the dead body of Elizabeth Stride.

*****

Vicissitudes of fate. Had Cathy Eddowes been taken in by the Metropolitan Police, who had a stodgy attitude towards drunks and hauled them up before the Magistrates, then her life would have gone on, pauperish no doubt, hard and grinding certainly, but life is sweet for all that. Instead she had been arrested by the City Police who did not believe in wasting their Courts' time with inebriates. They discharged them as soon as they were reasonably sober.

Constable George Hutt decided at 1.00 a.m. that Cathy was fit enough to leave. There was some light hearted banter, 'I shall get a damn fine hiding when I get home', she told him. 'Serves you right,'he chided. The memory of this encounter may have preyed on poor Hutt's mind because he left the police the following year. The last he saw of Cathy Eddowes was her turning left outside the station.

Cathy did not go home. Perhaps she did sometimes earn her doss by prostitution. Perhaps on the other hand she was still too befuddled to find her bearings properly. We shall never know. What we do know is that 1.30 found her at Church passage, a bare eight minutes walk from the Police station. There she met Jack the ripper.

Joseph Lawende and his friends Harry Harris and Joseph Levy were late in leaving the Imperial Club because of the rain. Their route home took them through Church Passage and across Mitre Square. They reached the passage at 1.35 and passed Eddowes and a man in deep conversation. Levy made a remark about the couple signifying disapproval and Lawende turned to look at them. He judged the man to be about 30, 5ft 7-8ins tall and medium build with a fair complexion and a moustache. He was wearing a loose fitting salt and pepper coloured jacket, a grey peaked cap and a red neckerchief. It was only a cursory glance and Lawende did not think he would be able to recognise him again. Neither Harris or Levy took any notice of the man's features or attire.

Church Passage leads into Mitre Square, a dark, brooding place with an evil reputation. Three centuries earlier a Church had stood there and inside it a woman had been kicked to death by a deranged Priest as she prayed at the Alter. The Square's reputation did not bother George Morris the night watchman of the Kearly and Tonge warehouse there. That night Morris, an ex-policeman, had the Warehouse door ajar, in all probability expecting the beat Constable, Edward Watkins, to drop in for a mug of tea. Morris heard nothing until 1.45 when Watkins appeared at the door. But not the normal Watkins. He was deathly white and shaking like a leaf. He gasped out: 'For God's sake mate, come out and help me. There's another woman been cut to pieces.'

*****

Mitre Square lies within the precincts of the City Police Force and the murder of Catharine Eddowes brought them fully into the case. According to their acting Commissioner, Major Henry Smith, the City Police were already playing an active role in the investigation. They had visited every Butcher's shop in the City and Smith had placed a third of his men in plain clothes with instructions to mingle with the public and keep their eyes and ears open. It was, he says 'subversive of discipline but I had them well supervised by senior officers'.

Unhappily, it did not achieve anything. Until recently Smith has keen something of a favourite son with Ripperphiles, a laughing Cavalier to Sir Charles Warren's austere roundhead. Tom Cullen is positively eulogistic:

> '*In contrast to the General, who was inclined to panic, the Major displayed coolness, imagination and wit.*'[1]

---

1   Autumn of Terror p108 (PBK)

In fact, Smith's greatest feats of imagination were reserved for publicising himself. He was indeed a contrast to Warren who was a man of genuine distinction. There has always been something slightly bogus about Smith. He derived his military rank not from the regular Army (in which he had never served) but the Suffolk Militia. Although he entitled his memoirs 'From Constable to Commissioner' he joined the Police with the rank of Chief Superintendent and was really one of the Gentleman amateurs who infested the higher echelons of the police at this time. Smith's only job prior to the police force was book-keeping in Glasgow. Although this may have come in useful in the City, — its police were mainly engaged on fraud cases, — there is a suspicion that Smith owed his position to string pulling. He was a close personal friend of Godfrey Lushington, a fast rising Civil Servant at the time of Smith's appointment and the permanent Under Secretary at the Home Office by 1888. All in all the Major comes across as the sort of man who eases his way through life with doors being opened for him by the right contacts.

Smith was asleep at Cloak Lane Police Station when word came through that the murderer had struck in the City. By 2.30 he was at Mitre Square taking personal charge of the investigation. Later, he was to boast that he had been: 'within five minutes of the perpetrator'. This convinced the gullible Cullen:

> *'All during this Saturday night (sic) the Major was to find himself exactly one jump behind Jack the ripper, who was fleeing for his life through the back streets of Spitalfields. In fact the Major could trace the route which the killer had taken.'*[1]

All of which can fairly be described as moonshine.

Another of Smith's claims and a very tawdry one at that because it meant belittling his own men, was that if only his instructions had been obeyed (where have we all heard that one before) the murderer would have been taken. According to Smith, orders had been given that any couples out after dark were to be stopped and questioned. He wrote:

> *'The beat of Catherine (sic) Eddowes was a small one. She was known to a good many Constables, but known or not known, she was in the streets late at night, and must have been seen making for Mitre Square... Had she been followed... the murderer would... have been taken red handed.'*[2]

Smith seems to have had a penchant for tall stories rivalling that of Liz Stride! There is no evidence that Cathy Eddowes was known to anybody as a

---

1   Autumn of Terror p109 (PBK)
2   From Constable to Commissioner

prostitute and no police officer saw her after she left Bishopsgate Police Station (perhaps Smith had too many of them gossiping in pubs). Smith's instruction applied to *couples* and no officer came across Cathy with her killer. On the other hand she had been released in accordance with the City Police's standing instructions on drunks and as Deputy Commissioner Smith presumably bore some responsibility for policy.

The events of that Sunday morning did not end with the bloodbath in Mitre Square. Goulston Street is on the Met's ground and lies about five minutes due east of the Square. In 1888 it was home to a series of rather pretentious apartment blocks called Wentworth model dwellings. Patrolling them at 2.55 that morning Constable Alfred Long made a highly controversial discovery. Inside the open doorway of No's 118–119 he found what appeared to be a blood stained piece of rag. On the passage wall above it was a message written in chalk:

> 'The juwes are
> the men that
> will not be blamed
> for nothing'

Long's first thought was that the murderer had struck again.

After summoning assistance he searched the block landing by landing, thankfully finding nothing.

Meanwhile, over in Mitre Square, the City Police had been alerted to his discovery. Detective Constable Daniel Halse, who had earlier traversed Goulston Street in pursuit of Cathy Eddowes murderer, now returned there and identified the piece of rag as part of her apron. Rivalry seems to have flared, Halse criticising Long for searching the block rather than setting off in pursuit. At this point, according to his somewhat unreliable memoirs, Smith arrived and gave orders that the writing on the wall should be guarded until it was light enough to be photographed. He then tore off on a wild goose chase of the surrounding streets summed up very aptly by Martin Fido as: 'Inspector Clousseau after the Pink Panther'[1].

In Dorset Street, soon to be the scene of the worst of all the ripper's atrocities, Smith claimed to have come across a communal sink with blood still gurgling down the plughole. Whether this is true is a moot point and is of no consequence anyway because it had nothing to do with the murders. Jack the ripper was long gone.

Whilst Smith was allegedly gyrating around Spitalfields, Detective Halse was having problems back in Goulston Street. A message had been sent to

1   'The Crimes, Detection & Death of Jack the Ripper' p50

Superintendent Thomas Arnold at Berners Street apprising him of the Goulston Street discoveries. Arnold, the Divisional Commander of H Division, was directing the inquiries into Elizabeth Stride's murder. He had only just returned from holiday and September 30th marked his baptism of fire in the ripper murders. He went hotfoot to Goulston Street and seems to have panicked on seeing the writing. First he decided that the message would have to be erased lest it cause an anti semitic riot and then he had second thoughts and decided to consult Sir Charles Warren.

We now first make the acquaintance of Dr Thomas Dutton. Dutton resembles no one so much as Cyrus Trask, the mythologising private in John Steinbeck's 'East of Eden' who is forever being consulted on how to fight tomorrow's battle. The good Doctor assists at the ripper post mortems, Abberline is constantly racing round to his surgery to sit at his font of wisdom and the police are forever turning to him on subjects as diverse as micro-photography and graphology as they strain to catch the killer. That morning, according to Dutton, he was summoned to Goulston Street, there to take micro-photographs of the writing. Later, he averred, Warren personally destroyed the prints. In reality Dutton was of course tucked up in bed and catching murderers only in his dreams. Later, ripperology would be seduced by his fictions. It is perhaps in the nature of the beast.

5.30 a.m. back in the real world. Dawn's creeping pallor arrived with Sir Charles Warren. He had decided to make his one and only excursion to Whitechapel. He should have stayed in bed. Warren conferred with Arnold and announced that the message would be obliterated without further delay. Halse protested. He made a number of counter suggestions: cover the writing up, erase only the top line or even just the word 'Juwes' itself. It would have been helpful if his own Commissioner had been on hand but, according to Halse, Smith only visited Goulston Street *after* the wording had been erased. So much for Clousseau! Having spent his adult life in hierarchical chains of command Warren was unlikely to favour a mere private's opinion over that of a divisional commander, especially one from a different force. At the Commissioner's direction (Smith later said vengefully by his own hand) the 'Juwes' message was sponged from the wall.

Was it from Jack the ripper? That we shall never know. Probably not. Long, at Eddowes Inquest, and later Walter Dew in his memoirs, both stressed that the Goulston Street graffiti was only one of many scrawled on walls around the East End. According to Long the apron had not been there on his previous patrol at 2.20. The writing he could not be sure about. But Long may not have been altogether reliable; ten months later he was sacked for being drunk on duty and there is a hint that he may have been slightly befuddled that morning[*] Halse saw nothing at around the same time but there is no suggestion that he checked

---

[*] Fido describes him as confused and slow witted.

any of the apartment blocks. He was, anyway, returning to Mitre Square via Goulston Street and would have been on the opposite side of the road. All the evidence that we have about Jack the ripper suggests that he made his escape as quickly and as expeditiously as possible. We know that he left Mitre Square at about 1.43 which means that he probably reached Goulston Street at 1.48, just missing Long who would have been patrolling there at 1.45. In all probability the ripper simply tossed the piece of apron through the open doorway as he hurried past. It is highly unlikely that he would have stopped to chalk up a message; even more unlikely that he would have attempted it in the dark.

Having said this, the police were certainly wrong in erasing the writing before it could be photographed. Although there was no dissenting Met voice that night Sir Robert Anderson would later denounce it as 'crass stupidity'. No anti semitic riots broke out when the text of the message became public knowledge a few days later. Halse had made some credible suggestions and it would shortly have been light enough to take photographs anyway. On balance, it is extremely doubtful that the ripper wrote those words but the police were wrong to destroy what *could* have been a valuable clue, *particularly as they had just received a letter purporting to come from the murderer.*

By that letter he was christened Jack the ripper.

Chapter Five: The Worst Sight This Side Of Hell

The letter was dated September 25th and sent to the Central News Agency. The Yard received it on the 29th. It was written in red ink and ran:

> Dear Boss,
>
> I keep on hearing the police have caught me but they wont fix me just yet. I have laughed when they look so clever and talk about being on the right track. That joke about Leather Apron gave me real fits. I am down on whores and I shant quit ripping them till I do get buckled. Grand work the last job was. I gave the lady no time to squeal. How can they catch me now. I love my work and want to start again. You will soon hear of me with my funny little games. I saved some of the proper red stuff in a ginger beer bottle over the last job to write with but it went thick like glue and I cant use it. Red ink is fit enough I hope ha ha. The next job I do I shall clip the Ladys ears off and send to the Police Officers just for jolly wouldn't you. Keep this letter back till I do a bit more work, then give it out straight. My knife's so nice and sharp I want to get to work right away if I get a chance. Good luck.
>
> Yours truly
> Jack the Ripper
>
> Dont mind me giving the trade name.
> Wasnt good enough to post this before I got all the red ink off my hands curse it no luck yet. They say I'm a Doctor now ha ha.[*]

Grisly humour indeed. The letter was published in the newspapers on October 1st and immediately produced a second missive. Written in crayon on a postcard this read:

> I was not codding dear old Boss when I gave you the tip, youll hear about Saucy Jackys work tomorrow double event this time number one squealed a bit couldnt finish straight off had not time to get ears for police thanks for keeping last letter back till I got to work again,
>
> Jack the Ripper

A third, and mercifully much shorter letter, was also received.

> Beware, I shall be at work on 1st and 2nd Inst, in Minories at twelve midnight, and I give the authorities a good chance, but there is never a

---

[*]   the second postscript was written in red crayon

51

policeman near when I am at work.

Yours,
Jack the Ripper *

These three communications were to spawn scores of imitatory letters and postcards. Some were prose, others garish forms of verse. To examine them all would simply be a waste of time. We need only look at the three quoted above and, a little further on, two more which were received in mid October.

First the 'Dear Boss' letter. It was plainly written by a literate man pretending to be uneducated. At three points the mask slips and he gives himself away. Having written the rest of the letter without apostrophes he includes them in "wouldn't", "knife's" and "I'm". Sir Robert Anderson and Donald Swanson were convinced that the letter was a hoax written by a journalist, in my view probably to keep the pot boiling. Latter day research points to a 'Star' reporter named Best. ** Plainly Ben Bates the obnoxious reporter in Thames T.V.'s 'Jack the Ripper', is based on him. Best may also have been partly responsible for the 'Leather Apron' myth (see Chapter Three) and it is interesting that the letter states:

'That joke about Leather Apron gave me real fits'.

Those who believe that this letter might be genuine have pointed to the threat to 'clip the Ladys ears off'. As we shall see, Catharine Eddowes right ear was cut through (part of it was found in her clothes) and Mary Kelly's ears were severed and left beside her corpse. But in both cases these wounds were part of a general disfigurement of the face. There is no reason to think that the ears were singled out specially.

The postcard for years caused great excitement amongst Ripperphiles. Although the handwriting is clearly different it seems to be a follow up to the letter, and from a superficial reading appears to know that Eddowes ears had been tampered with. It was generally believed that the postcard was posted on the Sunday and received on October 1st. If all this were correct then it would indeed pinpoint both communications as coming from the same source, possibly the killer or a close confidant. But it is not correct.

The postmark shows that it was posted on October 1st, i.e. *after* the letter had appeared in the press. As for the ears, the writer says:

'had not got time to get ears for police.'

Viewed properly it seems clear that the writer was *not* aware that one of Cathy's ears had been sliced through. There is just a hint that the correspondent might have been a woman. A female would be more likely to slip into "Jacky" rather than "Jack"***.

---

*　Postmarked East London
**　The letter was postmarked 'EC' which is the Fleet Street area
***　a young Bradford woman was later prosecuted for writing a hoax letter

The third letter, posted from Liverpool, is a puzzle. It is claimed to have been sent September 29th but there is no verification of this and the use of 'Inst' strongly suggests October 1st, once again, after the Dear Boss letter had been published. Almost certainly it was unrelated to either of the other; equally certain, they were all hoaxes. However, there is a caveat to this. It is a pity that the Police did not photograph the Goulston Street graffiti. Had the handwriting matched either of the letters or the postcard then it would have established their mutual authenticity.[*]

It is however extremely unlikely. Asked in 1988 to a prepare a psychological profile of the ripper for a Television Documentary[**], the F.B.I. were categoric that he was not the sort of exhibitionist killer who enjoys drawing attention to himself. We shall see later that they were absolutely right (and in virtually all of their deductions). The man who was Jack the ripper craved no notoriety. He sought to distance himself from his crimes, not write, joke or even talk about them.

From the grotesque to the ridiculous. Dr Dutton saunters back into our story again, this time claiming to have photographed 128 items of 'ripper' correspondence from which he deduced that 34 were in the same hand. Foreshadowing his fictional soulmate Trask, he never awards himself any exalted status, just your everyday expert on everything whom Scotland Yard consults at every turn. There is of course no record of him ever having photographed or analysed anything.

The importance of the Jack the ripper correspondence lies in one thing only; — the name. Leather Apron was altogether too mundane (imagine a book entitled 'The Identity of Leather Apron' or 'The Leather Apron Legacy'), and now vanished like the early morning dew (except in police minds). An alternative suggestion by 'The East London Advertiser', 'The Red Terror', caught nobody's imagination. 'Jack the ripper' did and became the symbol of the serial killer worldwide. It conjures up an image of mutilated corpses, swirling fog and silent assassins in the night; above all, fear. If the Ripper had meant to run the streets of Whitechapel with blood and terror then he had succeeded. In fact he didn't. He was a wretched sexual degenerate who shrank from his own infamy.

*****

On Sunday morning, September 30th, huge crowds descended on Berners Street and Mitre Square. Amongst the onlookers was John Kelly. He had been told by friends that Cathy had been picked up drunk the previous evening and fondly imagined that she was still sleeping it off in a cell. The horrible truth would come

---

[*]   See Appendix Two
[**]   The Secret Identity of Jack the Ripper

tomorrow. On that day, he identified her body at Golden Lane Mortuary. He stood looking down at her for a long time. Then, the silent farewells said, he examined her clothing for money. It was not mercenary; simply necessity.

Michael Kidney's reaction was as different as the two men were. That Monday he staggered into Leman Street Police Station, drunk and bruised from a fight, and made one of the strangest expressions of grief ever uttered. 'If Long Liz had been killed on my beat', he assured the Sergeant, 'I would shoot myself.' His life seems to have gone to pieces after Liz' death. During the following year he was in and out of hospital with lumbago, dyspepsia and syphilis.

Liz Stride's Inquest opened on October 1st, Coroner Baxter presiding. Hopes that it might be farce free were soon dashed. Mrs Mary Malcolm turned up claiming that the victim was in fact her sister, an Elizabeth Watts. Truth to tell, Mrs Malcolm did resemble Stride and the matter was not resolved until the real Mrs Watts, very much alive and highly indignant, was wheeled into court. This miniature Tichborne affair took up a lot of time and trouble and peeved Mr Baxter who in turn took it out on Sven Olsson, a clerk to the Swedish Church in London. Or maybe Baxter simply didn't like Swedes.

The important evidence was given by the witnesses who had seen Stride during the hours before her death, and Dr Phillips and Dr William Blackwell both of whom examined her body. We have already seen what the eyewitnesses had to say; we can now turn to the medical evidence.

Dr Blackwell was first on the scene at 1.16. He decided that Stride had been dead for no more than twenty minutes, which put her demise at no earlier than 12.56. Nobody can time death with such exactitude and in all probability she was murdered between 12.45 and 12.50, when Mrs Mortimer came out into the Street. Stride's throat had been cut from left to right and there was blood on her right hand which to Blackwell indicated a struggle. He thought, originally, that she had been pulled backwards by a scarf she was wearing and then killed whilst still on her feet. Later he was not so sure.

The wound in the throat was her only major injury. There was no mutilation of the body whatsoever.

Bagster Phillips arrived at 2 a.m. He concurred with Blackwell about the time of death, deciding that Stride had been dead for not more than an hour. Once again, he was probably out by about ten minutes. Phillips noted a packet of cachous* clutched in her left hand. There was a considerable amount of blood. It had streamed (his word) out of the left side of her throat. The following afternoon Phillips carried out a post mortem with Blackwell in attendance. Death had been caused by the throat wound which was deep but not as deep as those in Annie Chapman's neck (or Nichols). The murder weapon was a knife with a rounded blade an inch in diameter. There was bruising on both shoulders and

---

* Breath Sweeteners

the front of the chest. Phillips' opinion, and here he differed completely from Blackwell, was that the murderer had seized Liz by the shoulders, pressed her down on the ground and then cut her throat from her left side. Phillips was the older man by seventeen years and Blackwell seems to have bowed to his judgement. Somewhat improbably, Phillips did not think the killer would necessarily have been splattered with blood. He thought that whoever did it had 'A knowledge of where to cut the throat'. The blood on Stride's right hand was 'a mystery'.

The murder of Liz Stride brings the Ripper into focus more clearly than any of his other homicides. An ordinary man, able to melt into the backcloth of his killing ground, he drank in the same pubs as his victims, shrank in fear from capture and exploded with hate at rejection.

Liz Stride escaped mutilation not because Louis Diemshutz interrupted the Ripper — the assumption usually made — but because he lost his nerve. Two men, Israel Schwartz and the onlooker with the clay pipe had seen him attack her and had then scuttled off possibly to find a policeman. Staying to mutilate risked capture and the hangman. Serial killers do not court disaster, a point made by Dr David Abrahamsen in the most recent study of the murders.[1] Abrahamsen reminds us that David Berkowitz, the 'Son of Sam' killer, sometimes gave up looking for a victim altogether when the chances of being caught became too great. In Berners Street that night Jack the ripper was faced with a similar situation. He killed and ran. But the rage was still upon him, his abnormal lusts unabated. How he satiated them we shall see later. For the moment we stay with the Stride murder.

The consensus has been that she was with two, possibly three or four men that night. But the evidence points in a different direction as the following table of descriptions shows (see next page, figure 1)

Marshall and Packer both described the man they saw as 'clerkly', Marshall added that he was decently dressed and P.C. Smith thought he looked respectable. Smith also noticed that he had what appeared to be a parcel, 18 inches long and 6-8 inches wide, in his hand. In fact, this was certainly the paper in which Packer had wrapped the grapes. Packers evidence was criticised by the police as unreliable. He was first interviewed by them on September 30th and apparently said that he had seen and heard nothing. Two days later a pair of Private Detectives in the employ of the 'Evening News' found a discarded grapestalk in Dutfields Yard and Packer told them his story of the couple buying grapes. He repeated it to the 'Evening News' who published it along with a statement, purportedly in Packer's own words, that no policeman had questioned

---

1   Murder and Madness: The Secret Life of Jack the Ripper.

	Best	Packer	Marshall	Smith	Brown	Schwartz
Age	–	25–30	–	28	–	30
Height	5.5	5.7	5.6	5.7	5.7	5.5
Build	–	Broad Shouldered	Rather Stout	–	Stoutish	Broad Shouldered
Features	Black moustache	–	No whiskers	No whiskers	–	Small Brown moustache
Coat	moming suit	Long black frock	small black cutaway	dark	Long cutaway	dark jacket
Trousers	"	dark	dark	dark	dark	
Cap	billycock	soft felt 'hunter'	peaked sailorly	dark felt deerstalker	–	black peaked

fig 1

him about the grapes. Not surprisingly, this angered the police. On October 4th Packer was interviewed by Sir Charles Warren, no less. Afterwards the police issued a counterblast of their own: No grapestalk had been found in Stride's hand, the autopsy showed that she had not been eating grapes and Packer had contradicted himself.

The real villain of this rather sad little contretemps was the 'Evening News'. The way in which Packer's statement was worded and indeed the whole thrust of the story, was meant to imply that the police had been sloppy. In the usual style of tabloid journalism this petty debating point, along with some preening at having unearthed the evidence themselves, was more important than catching the murderer, i.e. power without responsibility. Unfortunately, the police chose to respond in kind. There were contradictions in Packer's evidence but not of a serious nature.[*] His description of the man who had bought the grapes was not, as the police inferred, culled from P.C. Smith's Inquest testimony. He was right in saying that he had not been questioned about the grapes until October 2nd. In order to test his veracity Packer was first taken to see Cathy Eddowes body and immediately said she was not the woman he had seen. Confronted with Liz Stride's corpse he identified her without hesitation. Although Liz had not been eating grapes, a handkerchief found on her body was stained with fruit juice. Had cooler heads prevailed then the simple explanation, that the ripper had eaten the grapes and borrowed her hankie to wipe his hands on, might have occurred to somebody.

The debate about Packer has tended to obscure the fact that he was the one witness who actually spoke to Jack the ripper. And the Ripper it was without

---

[*]   See Appendix Three

any doubt. There are minor differences in the six descriptions. Given the fallibility of human recollection it would be astonishing if there were not. Recalling an experiment in which thirty policeman, lawyers and law students were asked to describe a man they had seen, the American writer Anthony Scaduto catalogues the results as follows:

> *'colour of hair ranged from black to blond, height varied by as much as twelve inches and weight by fifty pounds. Some said he had been a German, others Italian, and two described him as Oriental.'*[1]

What is remarkable about the descriptions of the man seen with Liz Stride is not their slight variations but how closely they tally with each other. There can be no doubt that all six witnesses are describing the same man. And that man in turn dovetails with Mrs Long's description of Chapman's murderer; 'shabby genteel' and wearing a dark coat and a deerstalker hat.[*]

Now let us pull it all together. Exactly where and how Stride met the ripper we shall never know. The first sighting of them was at the 'Bricklayers Arms' where Best and Gardner enjoyed some light hearted humour at their expense. For a while they took it in good part but then, significantly, Best called out: 'That's Leather Apron getting round you.' At this the couple left.

Where they spent the next 40-45 minutes we do not know but certainly in another pub. It was raining quite heavily at this time, but when Dr Blackwell examined Liz' body at 1.16 he found: 'the clothes were not wet with rain.'[2]

The rain seems to have eased off quite considerably by 11.45, probably by now just a light drizzle. Morris Eagle, who had chaired the debate at the International Working Men's Club, left to take his girlfriend home. Down the street aways Stride and her deadly escort were standing opposite William Marshall's house where they remained for about ten minutes before moving off in the direction of Packer's fruit shop. After buying the grapes they crossed the road and stood outside the club, ostensibly listening to the singing. They then moved up to the corner.

By 12.30 the rain appears to have stopped altogether. Give or take a minute or so either side of the half hour, several things now happened in rapid succession. First Packer closed his shop and noted that the couple were still on the corner, standing outside a school. Then, a little later, P.C. Smith passed them outside Dutfield's Yard after which they peripitated back to the corner again.

Just afterwards a William West left the club through Dutfields Yard and

---

1   'Scapegoat' p329
2   Inquest Testimony

*   See also Appendix Three

delivered some literature to a Printers nearby, returning immediately. There was nobody outside the Yard. He would not have seen the couple further up the street because he was short sighted. Around this same time Charles Letchworth also traversed Berners Street noting that 'everything was going on as usual'. At 12.30 Morris Eagle returned to the club and a few minutes after this a club resident named Joseph Lave took a stroll in the Yard. Neither noticed anybody standing about outside.

Meanwhile, up on the corner, Liz had changed her mind about her prospective client. Why can only be guessed at, but prostitutes develop a sixth sense over the years and it is probable that he had reacted nervously to P C Smith's appearance. She may have coupled this with their hasty departure from the pub after Best's remark about 'Leather Apron'. Whatever the reason, when James Brown passed them he overheard Liz say: 'No not tonight: some other night', and noticed that the man had his arm against the wall more or less hemming her in.

When Liz was next sighted she was back yet again at Dutfields Yard, apparently hoping to entice the man with the pipe who was standing on the other side of the street. Exactly where the ripper was at this point is unclear. He may have followed her; on the other hand he may have walked past the Yard then turned and gone back. What is clear is that he was seething with rage. Jack the ripper was the last man able to cope with rejection. He hated women and was particularly contemptuous of prostitutes. He had lived in a brothel, suffered from V.D. and was actually married to an ex-prostitute.

Outside Dutfields, and in full view of the man with the pipe and Israel Schwartz who had now arrived on the scene, he attacked Liz and threw her to the ground. Then he shouted 'Lipski' and after Schwartz and the other man had scurried off, he forced her into the yard and cut her throat.

The insane revenge had been extracted. For once Jack the ripper had risked capture. And had either Schwartz or the second man possessed an ounce of altruism then he might actually have been caught, his miserable career of murder put an end to. There were policemen in the area: in addition to Smith two other constables, Lamb and Collins. But, like so many other serial killers since, the ripper's luck held that night. His perversions thwarted, he went in search of a second victim.

✳✳✳✳✳

All deaths are sad but some sadder than others. The murder of Cathy Eddowes, a tiny, inoffensive woman is an appalling example of just how badly one human being can treat another.

Her post mortem was carried out on September 30th by Dr Frederick Brown, the City Police Surgeon, and was observed by a whole panel of Doctors, William Saunders, George Sequeira and the omnipresent Bagster Phillips who attended on behalf of the Met.

Summarising the injuries as briefly as possible, Cathy's face had been extensively mutilated, particularly her nose which had almost been hacked off. Three oblique cuts running from left to right had severed the tip of the nose, penetrated the bone and extended across to her cheek and upper mouth. A separate wound had been inflicted on her lower mouth. Both eyelids were punctured, both cheeks slashed triangularly and a small part of her right ear cut off. Minor by comparison were two abrasions on her left cheek.

The throat had been cut twice, once superficially, the other very deeply. There was some evidence of strangulation, her face was congested and her fingers slightly bent.

Eddowes body had been mutilated in the most sickening manner. The catalogue of horrors commenced at the abdomen which had been ripped open from the pubes to the breast bone. The liver had been stabbed three times, the groin, the perineum, the spleen and the pancreas. Both the uterus and the left kidney had been removed entirely and taken away along with part of the left renal artery. The intestines had been pulled out and draped over the right shoulder except for a small particle which had been severed and placed between Cathy's left arm and body. Both thighs were mutilated. A curious feature of the attack was that the murderer had carefully cut around the naval leaving it, in Dr Brown's words, "a tongue of skin" amidst the carnage. In contrast to Annie Chapman's murder, neither the vagina or the bladder had been damaged.

Many writers have portrayed Cathy as a gin sodden wreck. It is therefore interesting to note what Dr Saunders later said:

'The liver was healthy and gave no indication that the woman drank.'

Brown also described her liver as healthy.

The Doctors found no evidence of recent sexual intercourse. Precisely what "recent" means is unclear, but it may suggest that Cathy did not obtain her drinking money the previous day by prostitution.

The abrasions on her cheek point in this case to punch marks. There was also a bruise on the back of her left hand as though she had raised it to block somebody hitting her.

The question of medical knowledge assumed its usual significance. Brown thought that the murderer had displayed "considerable" anatomical knowledge but would venture no opinion about his surgical skill. However, Brown's view of the anatomical knowledge was coloured by the fact that he thought the killer had been specifically seeking the kidney and knew where to find it. The perpetrator might, he decided be a man familiar with cutting up animals. Both Saunders and Sequeira disagreed with him. They thought that the murderer was not seeking any particular organ and that he possessed no anatomical knowledge whatsoever.

Which all leaves Dr Phillips rather out in the cold, particularly as he thought Annie Chapman's injuries could not have been inflicted in under a quarter of an hour, whereas Brown ascribed five minutes for Eddowes' more extensive mutilations. (Five minutes was in fact all the ripper would have had in Mitre Square that night.) But nil desperandum. Phillips circumvented the difficulty by describing the injuries as "unskilful" and probably the work of an imitator! Which leaves him in a minority of precisely two along with our other old friend, Coroner Baxter, who accepted his judgement.[*]

The inquest was held on October 4th and 11th. Joseph Lawende gave his evidence. His description of the ripper's clothing differs quite considerably from the Berners Street witnesses. However, Lawende shot him only a very quick glance in the darkness and the point has already been made about the frailty of human recollection.

Elizabeth Stride was interred at Bow in a sad paupers grave. Few attended. She was buried as she had lived and died, the end of an unhappy could-have-been life with all the wrong turnings taken.

By contrast Catharine Eddowes received an almost royal East End funeral, a phalanx of policemen accompanying her to her final resting place at Ilford Cemetery. The 'East London Advertiser', coughing discreetly behind its hand, described the female mourners as dressed in a style not altogether befitting the occasion. Cathy, one feels, would have been amused.

✶✶✶✶✶

Early that October fog descended on London. Whitechapel became an eerie derelict, drifting through mists of terror. Few ventured out after dark; those who did dreaded every footfall behind them. But in fact the fog earned Londoners a much needed respite from the ripper's activities. The pattern established on August 7th was broken: no murder occurred on either October 6th or 31st. The fog was without doubt the major reason. This should have led the police to an important deduction. It didn't. Unhappily they were in a fog of their own.

On October 6th Sir Robert Anderson returned to duty. The termination of his holiday, only half completed, was to placate public opinion. Noting his absence the 'Pall Mall Gazette' had mocked him as a sort of scarlet pimpernel in reverse, never to be found where he was most needed:

> 'You may seek Dr Anderson in Scotland Yard, you may look for him in Whitehall Place, but you will not find him.'

Anderson spent the next thirty six hours 'reinvestigating' the crimes. He discovered that in his absence Abberline and his men had carried out house to house inquiries in a designated area where they believed the killer was living.

---

[*]   At Stride's inquest. Eddowes' was conducted by the City Coroner Samuel Langham.

The zone was astonishingly limited. To the West the City Police Boundary; to the north Buxton Street thereby excluding Bethnal Green, Hoxton, Shoreditch, Old Ford, and even part of Brick Lane. The invisible boundary line then meandered on down through Deal, Dunk and Great Garden Streets to the East, effectively cutting Whitechapel in half, before coming to rest at its southernmost tip, Whitechapel Road. From there it ran in a straight line to the city boundary, ignoring the southern portion of Whitechapel and the whole of St Georges-in-the-East, Shadwell and Wapping. Further to the east Stepney, Limehouse, Mile End, Bow, Bromley and Poplar were not thought worthy of consideration. In short, the police had confined themselves to Spitalfields and the North Western sector of Whitechapel. Sad but true, even the man who Anderson and Swanson later came to believe was the ripper lived outside their area of search.* As for the ripper himself, he was quite safe.

Anderson seems to have been satisfied with this performance. He decided, along with the rest of his team, that the ripper was a Polish Jew. This verdict was set in stone.

Equally convinced that the killer was a Jew was the Home Secretary, Henry Matthews. Matthews was a political makeweight. Almost everybody seems to have disliked him. The left regarded him as somewhat to the right of Atilla the Hun, he was unpopular with his own party and very few people could get on with him. The Press, in particular, held him in contempt. 'The never at home secretary' sneered the 'Star' whilst the 'Telegraph', in a wincingly cruel attack, categorised him as 'a dead weight' which the Government had to drag along with it. Much of the criticism centred around his refusal to offer a reward for the ripper's capture. The City of London Corporation had offered £500 (around £30,000 in today's terms), and private sources at least another £300.

Matthews had declined to offer a reward on the advice of his officials. Sir Charles Warren, on the other hand, had suggested the quite staggering sum of £5,000; — well over a quarter of a million today. Matthews himself was not adverse to a reward and the fact that £800 (£50,000) was already on offer made Home Office objections redundant. Unhappily the Home Secretary allowed himself to be ruled by his Mandarins.

He was also at sea in assessing operational matters, pestering the Police with comments about the ripper's shouted remark of "Lipski" which, said Matthews, strengthened his conviction that the killer was Jewish. The previous year Matthews had signed the death warrant of Israel Lipski, a young Polish Jew convicted of murdering a woman he was infatuated with. The case released a wave of anti semitism and "Lipski" became a popular term of abuse in the East End. Matthews very largely ignored this and appears to have convinced himself that the remark had been addressed to the man with the clay pipe who might be

---

*   Almost comically, John Pizer also lived outside the interviewing zone.

an accomplice. In vain, Abberline, Anderson and even Warren tried to point out that the shout was probably directed at Schwartz. Here was a classic dialogue of the deaf: neither side was listening to the other and both were missing the real point. The ripper's shout was clearly meant for Schwartz who in appearance was very obviously semitic. Lipski had lived in the street adjacent to Berners Street, and one Jew was hardly likely to shout anti semitic slogans at another. Lost amidst this kerfuffle was the fact that Schwartz's descriptions strongly implied that both men were Anglo Saxon, a point resolutely ignored by all concerned. The Home Secretary and the Head of C.I.D. were futilely debating something they were in error about in the first place!

Equally sterile was George Bernard Shaw's contribution to the ripper debate. In a letter entitled 'Blood money to Whitechapel'* Shaw wrote:

> *'whilst we conventional social democrats were wasting our time on education, agitation and organisation some independent genius has taken the matter in hand, and by simply murdering and disembowelling four women, converted the proprietary press to an inept sort of communism.*
>
> *If the habits of Duchesses only admitted of their being decoyed into Whitechapel backyards a single experiment in slaughter house anatomy might fetch in a round half million and save the necessity of sacrificing foure women of the people'*

One thing Jack the ripper was not was a social reformer. As for Shaw, he was the type of socialist who cares endlessly about the poor from the comfort of a West End apartment. There is something terrible about anyone, Duchess or Commoner, dying alone in the darkness, torn apart by a nightmare creature. Apparently human life was cheap to Shaw if it benefited the cause.

*****

On the evening of October 16th a small parcel was delivered in the post to George Lusk, a builder and chairman of an action group called the Whitechapel vigilance committee. It contained half a human kidney and was accompanied by the following letter:

> *From Hell*
> *Mr Lusk , Sor*
> *I send you half the kidne I took from one woman prasarved it for you tother piece I fried and ate it was very nise I may send you the bloody knif that took it out if only you only wate a whil longer.*
>
> *signed   Catch me when   you can*
> *Mishter Lusk*

---

* Published in the 'Star'

Opinions are divided on whether this letter, and the kidney, were sent by Jack the ripper. The kidney was examined by Dr Thomas Openshaw, curator of the London Hospital's Anatomical Museum, who declared that it was human and had been preserved in spirit of wine. The old game of chinese whispers then began and Openshaw was mistakenly quoted in the press as saying that the kidney was that of a 45 year old woman suffering from Bright's disease and removed during the previous three weeks. On October 29th he received a letter signed Jack the ripper which read in part:

'Old Boss you was rite it was the lift Kidny'.

Openshaw wrote to the Newspapers repeating what he had actually said and there the matter should have ended. But others, Dr Saunders at the time and Major Smith, much later, became involved. Saunders correctly observed that it was impossible to determine the kidney's age and sex from the portion received but then added, doubtless from faulty memory, that Eddowes' other kidney had been healthy whereas the autopsy had noted signs of Bright's disease. Smith, in his memoirs was convinced that the kidney was genuine; that it bore traces of Bright's disease, the length of renal artery attached tied in with what had been left in Eddowes body and that it had not been charged with fluid as it would if it had come from a body passed to a hospital for dissection, the theory current at the time.

He seems to have been right in the last assertion because Swanson made the same comment in a report on the kidney. However, this is not an 'all shall have prizes' essay and both Saunders and Smith would have been wisest to stay out of the matter. The plain fact is that all we really know about the kidney is that it was human and had been immersed in spirit. There is no reliable evidence that it was part of Cathy Eddowes' missing kidney. As for the letters, both were in a different hand, the ripper was not the sort of murderer to display exhibitionist tendencies, and although the 'from hell' letter appears to have been written by a poorly educated man, there are two points which seemingly give the game away. One is the correct form of address "Mr", and the second, much more significantly, the correct spelling of "signed". One would have expected it to match the literal spelling in the rest of the letter and be minus the "g". In short, the whole thing was almost certainly another tiresome hoax, probably a medical student's prank.

*****

October and the fog dragged on. The ripper remained in his lair. The police beavered away manfully, got nowhere, and were disgracefully lampooned in the Press. A typical example portrayed the week of a Detective, engaged on the ripper hunt, who ends up arresting himself. As humour it is best described as turgid.

The tale of the Bloodhounds has been told many times before. Two dogs,

Barnaby and Burgho, were tried out, found to be unsuitable for work in the East End and returned to their owner. Inaccurate stories in the Press suggested they had been lost and Sir Charles Warren was held up to ridicule.

Bloodhounds were the least of his problems. As the weeks went by he found himself increasingly isolated, a sure sign of drawing the short straw in the fall guy competition. Behind his back Anderson was liaising with James Monro about the murders, sometimes taking Swanson and Moore to the Home Office to help brief their Old Chief. Monro in turn briefed Matthews. Warren by contrast found himself supplied with only the sketchiest details and his access to the Home Secretary was limited by Godfrey Lushington, a man who liked him not. In the classic syndrome of the Fall Guy it also fell to Warren to explain to his superiors why pet schemes would not work. One involved house to house searches which, as the Commissioner explained, the police had not the power to carry out.

Next the palace put the boot in. Victoria was fond of airing her views and the ripper was no exception. Her first letter began:

> *'The Queen fears that the Detective Department is not so efficient as it might be'*

A later missive ended that the Detective Branch was: 'not what it should be'.

Whether Warren was aware of his sovereign's disapproval is unclear but the path to his sacking was being made ever more smooth.

The axe fell on November 8th. He had been asked by 'Murrays' Magazine' to contribute an article on policing the metropolis and used it to counter some of the criticisms. Retribution came very quickly in the shape of a stern Home Office rebuke for publishing the article without permission. Sir Charles declined to accept such a limitation and submitted his resignation which was accepted.[*]

Less than twenty four hours later the most hideously mutilated of all the Ripper's victims lay cold and dead in a Spitalfields hovel.

✳✳✳✳✳

Mary Jane Kelly A.K.A. Marie Jeanette Kelly, 'Ginger', 'Fair Emma' and 'Black Mary'. Apart from the ripper himself, more legends have been woven around this young woman than any other character in criminal history. On screen she has been played by a procession of beautiful and alluring women, Louise Brooks (Pandora's Box), Edina Ronay[**] (A Study in Terror), Susan Clark (Murder By Decree) and Lysette Anthony (Jack the Ripper). Writers have created endless fantasies about her; femme fatale extraordinaire, Ripper's accomplice, Blackmailer, Mythomaniac, Lesbian, and so on. One recent study calls her a police informer, another suggests that she may have prostituted herself

---

[*]   See Appendix Four
[**] Now a top fashion designer. Barbara Windsor plays a chirpy Annie Chapman in the same film.

with women as well as men. As befits her status as a woman of mystery we know very little about her.

Mary's own story of her life can be told in a few sentences. She was born in Limerick, raised in Wales and at sixteen married a miner named Davies who was killed in a pit explosion two years later. After this she went to stay with a cousin in Cardiff, spent several months in hospital there and later drifted into prostitution. Around 1883, when she was allegedly twenty, Mary moved to London and worked for a while in a West End brothel. The high point of this period seems to have been a trip to France with a client. Circa 1885 she decamped to the East End, living first in lodgings and later with a man called Morganstone whom she left for a Stonemason or Plasterer named Joseph Fleming. Her family had disowned her save for a brother, Henry, a private in the Scots Guards.

Very little of this can be factually established. Researchers have struggled in vain to discover any trace of Mary in Wales or the West End, although according to one East End source she spoke fluent Welsh, a detail unlikely to be invented. There is reliable evidence of her lodging in Shadwell around 1886. Her Landlady, a Mrs Carthy, spoke highly of her as well educated, artistic and coming from a good family. However, there is anecdotal evidence that Carthy's house was a brothel which means that it was in her interest to portray Mary as respectable. That having been said, her depiction of Mary's artistic ability is again an unlikely flight of imagination. Nobody has ever traced Morganstone but there is valid evidence of the liaison with Fleming, also of her brother's existence.

Easter 1887 found Mary living in a lodging house in Thrawl Street. That Good Friday she met Joseph Barnett, a Billingsgate fish porter and begun to live with him as his common law wife. According to Barnett, Fleming was still on the scene and visited her. He later described Mary as being very fond of him. She told other acquaintances that Fleming still gave her money and had struck her for living with Barnett. Barnett spoke of her brother visiting her and of her corresponding with her mother in Dublin. There is independent corroboration of her receiving letters from Ireland.

Mary Kelly and Joe Barnett lived together at various addresses in Spital-fields from April 1887 to October 1888. They were normally obliged to move on though non payment of rent and drunkenness. This aside, they appear to have been a likeable couple, Kelly in particular. Echoing Carthy, a prostitute friend named Maria Harvey described Mary as being 'much superior'. That she was noisy and aggressive when drunk is well attested to but all sources agree that she was otherwise a charming, vivacious and good looking young woman. Walter Dew, who knew her by sight, states that she was "attractive" and generally surrounded by friends. Whatever the truth of her earlier years she seems to have been only an occasional prostitute in the East End, resorting to it when she was without a man to provide for her.

That was the situation on the night of November 8th. A few months earlier she and Barnett had moved into No 13, Miller's Court a tiny room in a cul-de-sac off Dorset Street. Here the relationship faltered. Barnett lost his job and the rent was again considerably in arrears, about seven weeks owing. There was a fight on October 30th which ended in a window being broken. Afterwards he moved out but continued to visit her regularly although she confided to a friend that she could no longer bear him. Barnett's version of the break up was that she had been bringing prostitutes home to stay with them, first a Julia Venturney, then Maria Harvey. Inevitably, this has let to speculation that Mary was bi-sexual but the truth is probably much simpler; —they were a device to get rid of Barnett whom she was bored with. The overall impression of Mary Kelly is of a rather charismatic young woman — possibly intelligent and talented — who needed more from life than the East End and its Flemings and Barnetts had to offer. In the most horrible and sad manner possible those aspirations were only to be realised through her death.

Barnett called in to see Mary that evening and found her talking to a young woman named Lizzie Allbright. Allbright described his visit as amicable, but Mary was sad that night, telling her that she was sick of London and longed to go back to Ireland. She also lectured her friend against following the path of prostitution she had trodden. But the rent was far behind and due tomorrow and so after Lizzie had departed she set out to walk that arid path again. Her mood of depression deepened: when she bumped into another friend she spoke of suicide, a terrible irony in view of what was to come.

The fog had lifted and it was now cold and clear. A tailor named Maurice Lewis claimed to have seen Mary in a pub on the corner of Dorset Street drinking with Barnett and Venturney. Although neither confirmed this later it may be true. Another source places her in a second pub at 11.00 p.m. in the company of a young man with a moustache and about 45 minutes later Mary Ann Cox, a Miller's Court resident, saw her take a man into No 13. He is described as thirties, stout, blotchy faced with a carroty moustache, and wearing shabby clothes and a billycock hat. He was carrying a beer pail.

This client seems to have been serviced quite quickly because between 12.00 and 1.00 a.m. Mary was singing loudly in her room to the annoyance of neighbours. 2.00 a.m. found her in the streets again according to a Labourer named George Hutchinson who knew her. She asked him for sixpence and when he disappointed her turned away and picked up an ornately garbed man in his thirties, about 5ft 6ins tall with a small moustache curled up at both ends. Hutchinson thought he looked jewish. He followed the couple back to Miller's Court and waited outside the Court for three quarters of an hour. Neither emerged.

Sarah Lewis had stormed out after a row with her husband and made her way to Miller's Court, there to stay with a Mrs Keyler at No 2. She arrived at 2.30 and noticed a man outside the Court, probably Hutchinson. She also saw two couples. One passed along Dorset Street, the other were standing outside a pub. She decided that the male in this second duo was a man who had frightened her two days earlier.

Shortly before 4 a.m. Lewis and a Mrs Elizabeth Prater who lived in the room above No 13, heard a cry of "murder". Lewis heard it loudly, Prater faintly.

Circa 8.00 a.m. Mrs Caroline Maxwell encountered Mary on the corner of Miller's Court. They had a short conversation the gist of which was that Kelly had a hangover and had just been sick. About an hour later Maxwell saw her again, this time outside a pub talking to a stout man in dark clothes and a plaid coat. At around this same time another, unidentified woman, also reported seeing Kelly.

The sequence of events which had began with Maurice Lewis' claims now ends with more of them. At 10 o'clock, said Lewis, he saw Mary Kelly drinking in the 'Britannia' pub, apparently in company.

Tom Bowyer was not Spitalfields most popular man on Friday morning. It was his job to collect the rent in Miller's Court and that morning he had been given strict instructions to get something out of Mary Jane. At 10.45 he knocked on the door. No answer. Perhaps she was pretending to be out. He pushed aside a coat hung over the broken window pane, pulled back the curtain and peered into the gloomy little room. What he saw would remain with him for the rest of his days.

Lying on the bed was what appeared to be a butchered animal. They were the remains of Mary Jane Kelly. Her face no longer existed. Her nose, ears, eyebrows and cheeks had been slashed off and lay in a sickening little pile next to her head. The rest of her face had been cut to ribbons, the lips virtually torn off. Only the eyes, two terrified orbs in a ruined head, remained undamaged.

Mary's throat had been cut right the way through to the spinal column. Below that the injuries almost defy coherent description. Both breasts had been cut off, one placed by her right foot, the other under her head where it had been joined by the uterus and both kidneys, a dreadful Butcher's display of bloody organs. Her liver lay between her feet and her spleen by her left side. On the other side of her body were her intestines. Part of her right lung had been hacked through, her heart removed in its entirety and taken away by the murderer. Next to the body on a bedside table, lay a small amount of flesh congealing in its own blood.

The horror was unrelenting. The photograph makes it appear that she is wearing britches. In fact the thighs have been stripped of skin, the right torn away to the bone, the left savaged down to the knee. Below it the calf had been ripped open. Part of her right buttock had also been mutilated.

Not even her arms had been spared, as several deep gashes testified. Abrasions on the back of Mary's right hand bore mute evidence of a struggle but it must have been pitifully brief.

We can leave now this scene as Bowyer recoils in shock. There are no words adequate to describe it. Walter Dew, who saw the body, could never bear to think of it again.

In the words of one writer, it was quite simply the worst sight this side of hell.

Chapter Six: Bloody Aftermath

November 9th was the day of the Lord Mayor's show and by eleven people were already lining the streets to watch the procession. A holiday atmosphere prevailed. But as news of the latest atrocity rippled through the crowd so the mood changed and many of the spectators made their way across to Spitalfields. By noon Dorset Street was under siege, Cordons of Police holding back a sombre, heaving mass of people at both ends.

In truth the police had little else to do. The murderer had locked the door of No 13 behind him and taken away the key. Unaware that the Bloodhounds had been cancelled, Abberline and his men decided not to enter the room until they arrived. At 1.30 they were finally told that the dogs would not be coming and John McCarthy, the Landlord, broke the door down with a pick axe. At 2 o'clock Bagster Phillips and Dr Thomas Bond examined the body. Bond was the Divisional Police Surgeon for 'A' Division and probably the nearest the police had to a Forensic Pathologist in 1888. He had been specially brought into the case by Anderson. Bond decided that Mary had been murdered at around 2 o'clock that morning and that her killer had demonstrated no surgical or anatomical knowledge whatsoever. Phillips seems to have endorsed the first point of view but it is unlikely that he agreed with the second.

At 3 o'clock Mary Kelly's body was removed to Shoreditch Mortuary. The remains were wrapped in several parcels and drawn through the streets in a public death cart driven by a pauper. At the Mortuary it took six hours to re-arrange her into a semblance of a human being.

No 13 raised many seeming puzzles. According to Barnett the key had been missing for some time. In the grate were the charred remains of some clothing and a bonnet. There was also a burnt out kettle. It all had echoes of the 'Mary Celest' and over the years many erstwhile Solly Floods have created their own little fantasies from these so called clues. All are capable of simple explanations. Barnett had moved out ten days earlier and lost keys do have a habit of turning up, particularly in a tiny room only 12 foot by 10. Mary's clothes were found on a chair and those in the grate probably some outworn items which she had burnt to keep the room warm. As for the kettle, there is no reason to think that it was not already damaged.

The inquest was a hurried affair, conducted by Dr Roderick Macdonald, a Liberal M.P., Police Surgeon and Coroner for the Shoreditch area. The murder had been committed in Spitalfields, Baxter's domain, and it is plain that the police had had enough of him. A favourite debating topic amongst Ripperphiles is whether Macdonald had the right to hold it. The Law is in fact quite simple and dates back to 1887: An inquest can be held either where the body lies or where death has taken place.

Unfortunately, a word which the Ripper Inquiry abounds with, Macdonald went to the opposite extreme to Baxter, both opening and closing the inquest on November 12th. Bond did not give evidence and Bagster Phillips was allowed to get away with giving the cause of death only. This was illegal but done for a very laudable reason. It was common knowledge that the ripper had taken away one of the organs, the general assumption being the uterus. Only the real killer would know that it was the heart.

The inquest closed too quickly for the evidence of at least one material witness, George Hutchinson the Labourer who had followed Mary and her client home. Hutchinson did not come forward until the evening of the 12th. His statement impressed Abberline. The time of the encounter slotted in reasonably well with the medical evidence about the time of death and the reported cry of 'murder' overheard by Sarah Lewis and Elizabeth Prater. Mary Ann Cox had heard somebody leaving the court at 6 a.m. and at 7.30 Catherine Picket, a friend of Mary's, had knocked at her door and received no answer. For good measure Hutchinson described the man he had seen as being of Jewish appearance, another point which recommended him to the police.

But there are serious problems with George Hutchinson. Why did it take him so long to come forward? And can we really take his minutely detailed description of the man's clothing seriously? He described him as though he had spent the evening with him. Hutchinson's statement, which is given in Appendix Five, is too elaborate by half. But for the fact that Mrs Lewis saw a man loitering outside Miller's Court at the relevant time I would be inclined to dismiss it as fiction. As it is, I think most of the details were invented but that like many concoctions it has a basis in fact.

Whether or not George Hutchinson saw Jack the ripper has no particular relevance in establishing his identity. Nor does the actual time of Mary Kelly's death. But the latter is a mystery in its own right, one which has spawned many myths about the case. It is time to end those myths. We turn now to the testimony of Caroline Maxwell.

Mrs Maxwell is seemingly a square Peg in a round hole. According to her, Mary Kelly was still very much alive five hours after the Doctors and other witnesses have her dead. But, as we shall see, Maxwell was not alone.

She was an impressive witness who came forward on the discovery of the body, never varied her evidence and refused to budge in the face of police skepticism and some almost intimidatory remarks by Coroner Macdonald who told her: 'You must be very careful; your evidence is different from the rest.'

Her story was that she had come across Mary standing outside Miller's Court between 8 and 8.30 that morning. She was wearing a green bodice, dark skirt and maroon shawl. Mary told her: 'I have the horrors of drink on me'. She had been to the pub for a liverner but had brought it up and indicated some vomit on the pavement. Maxwell replied: 'I pity your feelings' and left her. An hour later she saw her again, this time outside the 'Britannia' Pub, Dorset Street, talking to a short, stout man in a plaid coat who looked like a market porter.

Two other persons also claimed to have seen Mary Kelly that morning. One was an unidentified woman. The other is Maurice Lewis. There is a temptation to discard Lewis as unreliable. But was he? He said that he saw Mary fleetingly in Miller's Court at about eight, which ties in with Maxwell's evidence, and later in the 'Britannia' at ten when she appeared to be in company. The time must really be wrong but Maxwell saw her outside the pub with a man half an hour to an hour earlier and if they went in for a drink then Lewis's sighting could well be valid. It has not been appreciated just how Caroline Maxwell and Maurice Lewis's accounts compliment each other; in particular how Maxwell's resolute testimony gives credence to Lewis's.

There are other points of corroboration for Mrs Maxwell. One is the maroon shawl Mary was wearing. Mary Ann Cox also noticed that she had on a red shawl the previous evening. A second is that Maxwell had a specific reason for being out and about that morning. She was returning some crockery to a friend and was able to verify this. Another impressive point: Maxwell claimed no great intimacy with Kelly. She knew her by sight but had only spoken to her twice before. The conversation which she recounted is exactly the sort of conversation anyone might have with a casual acquaintance suffering from a hangover. And Mary had been drinking the previous evening. That is well documented. She was seen in several pubs and appeared tipsy to Mary Ann Cox when she took home the client with the beer pail at 11.45. Afterwards she annoyed the neighbours by singing loudly in her room.

Temporarily discarding the medical evidence, what facts pinpoint Mary's demise as the early hours of the morning? Simply these. Hutchinson saw her with a client. That does not mean he was the ripper. Cox heard a man leave the Court. He could have been anybody; the client, a beat constable (as she admitted at the inquest) or just a resident on his way to work. Picket got no answer at 7.30 but if Maxwell was right then Mary would have been having her early morning drink in the pub at that time. Sarah Lewis heard a loud scream of 'Murder', Elizabeth Prater only heard it very faintly. But if it came from No 13 then Prater should have heard it loudly too; more loudly than Lewis who was staying at No 2. *Prater occupied the room immediately above Kelly's. To all intents and purposes they were living in the same house.* Neither woman took any notice and for a very simple reason. Dorset Street was the worst street in the worst slum in Europe and such cries were commonplace. It could have come from anywhere in Miller's Court or Dorset Street and Prater's evidence actually points away from Kelly at No 13.

What we are left with is only the medical evidence and this was outlined very succinctly by Dr Bond.

"Rigor Mortis had set in (by 2 p. m.), but increased during the progress of the examination. From this it is difficult to say with any degree of certainty the exact time that had elapsed since death as the period varies from 6 to 12 hours before rigidity sets in. The body was comparatively cold at 2 o'clock and the remains of a recently taken meal were found in the stomach and scattered about over the intestines. It is, therefore, pretty certain that the woman must have been dead about twelve hours and the partly digested food would indicate that death took place about three or four hours after the food was taken, so 1 or 2 o'clock in the morning would be the probable time of the murder."

As remarked earlier, estimating the time of death in 1888 was not an established science. It was done by the crudest procedures imaginable. No rectal temperature was taken, no room temperature, no allowance made for the subject's build, the condition of the body, outside influences and so on. Crucially, there was no way of determining the rate at which the body cools which 'Taylors Principles and Practice of Medical jurisprudence' describes as: 'The most important early phenomenon in the estimation of time of death'. Determination was made by touch, the presence of rigor mortis and in this case at least, the digestion process of food in the body.

In assessing when Mary Kelly died we have to take into account several factors which at the time Bond and Phillips, in ignorance of the subject, overlooked. It was a bitterly cold day and cold air was billowing into the room. The window of No 13 had been broken since Kelly and Barnett's final row and whatever protection the old coat over it afforded was removed from the time Bowyer pulled it back. Later, in order to photograph the body, the police took the window out altogether. Once again, 'Taylors Medical Jurisprudence' sums it up:

'A body lying exposed in a well ventilated room will cool more rapidly than one in a sealed room, as the freely circulating air will rapidly carry away the air warmed by the body.'

There was now no fire and the appallingly mutilated state of the corpse, naked except for a chemise, meant that it would have cooled very rapidly leading much more quickly to rigor mortis than Bond allowed for. In this case 6 to 12 hours was out by a long way. Rigor would certainly have set in in 4 hours, probably less. And at 2 p.m. rigor was still commencing, the muscles not yet fixed, as Bond makes clear:

'Rigor Mortis had set in but increased during the progress of the examination'.

The body was only "comparatively" cold.

Highly pertinent was the rate of digestion, Bond estimating that Mary had consumed her last meal three to four hours before her death. I have no argument with this. But, and here is the 'but', Bond was basing his analysis on an erroneous cooling rate which suggested to him that she had last eaten on the previous evening. In reality, her final meal was probably breakfast partaken between six and seven in the morning which in turn hinges with rigor mortis having set in three to four hours after her death. In short, modern day expertise suggests that Mary Kelly actually died around 10a.m. which in turn dovetails with the evidence of those witnesses who saw her alive up to this time. Dr Bond cannot be criticised for getting it wrong. His findings were based on the best available knowledge at that time. He can in fact be praised for providing the very comprehensive details which enable us to determine, in all probability, the correct time of death a century later. We do not know, specifically, how long the mutilations took to inflict. Bond made no estimate, but those on Cathy Eddowes took five minutes. Mary's were very much more extensive and thirty minutes would be a reasonable assumption.

Cutting the gordian knot of the mythmakers, Mary Kelly was probably slain by the man whom Caroline Maxwell saw her with and at about 10 a.m. on Friday morning.

*****

November 19th. The East End buried its dead in the way that only the East End can. At noon the bell of St Leonard's Church began to toll. A huge crowd had already assembled lining the streets many deep. This was no gathering of the upper classes muttering pious hypocrisies about one of their own but a vast throng of real people, crying real tears. Raggedy men who had been kicked like dogs all their lives and women who had often been forced to do the same things as the tragic young woman they were burying that day.

Faithful to the last, Joe Barnett had had her coffin inscribed with the name she liked to call herself, 'Marie Jeanette'. As it appeared, borne by four men, the crowd surged forward many struggling desperately to touch it, tears streaming down their faces and calling out 'God Forgive Her'. Every man was bareheaded.

Then the final sad procession to Leytonstone, the crowd following on behind and becoming ever more swollen as the cortege passed through the streets and more and more people joined its wake. The mourners' coaches were almost engulfed by a sea of humanity. And emotion. A large body of police struggled manfully to keep order, protecting Mary in death as they had not been able to in life, restraining her friends in the way they had not been able to restrain her assassin.

The final resting place was St Patrick's Catholic Cemetery. Here the official mourners, a bare eight, none family, stood in prayer whilst the coffin was lowered into the ground. The grave remained uninscribed for almost a century before a tombstone was erected. Today it has gone, only a sad little plinth remaining with the words 'Marie Jeanette Kelly murdered 9/11/88'. But there is perhaps a more heartwarming story. When I visited the grave in 1988 I was unable to find it at first. It was a grey, mournful November afternoon and the cemetery was about to close. Finally, I asked a young gravedigger where I might find a grave 100 years old. He smiled and asked 'Mary Kelly?' He knew its location exactly and was clearly used to being asked about it. In all that vast cemetery with its thousands upon thousands of graves this was the one which stood out, the one visited by people who had never known Mary Kelly in life. It is not how she would have wanted to be remembered but it is an epitaph of sorts and in a way her victory over the man who so fouly slew her.

*****

Whilst Mary Kelly's funeral was taking place Scotland Yard was playing musical chairs. Warren had forced Monro out. Now he had been sacked. His successor was... James Monro! Within eighteen months he too would lose the support of the Home Secretary and follow Warren into the wilderness.

Matthews himself barely survived. There was an emergency cabinet meeting on November 10th. Saturday cabinet meetings normally only take place at times of grave national crisis and this, more than anything else, illustrates the way in which Jack the ripper had traumatised the country. Shortly afterwards the following proclamation was issued:

> '*MURDER PARDON. Whereas on 8 or 9 November in Miller's Court, Dorset Street, Spitalfields, Mary Jane Kelly was murdered by some person or persons unknown, the Secretary of State will advise the grant of Her Majesty's pardon to any accomplice not being a person who contrived or actually committed the murder who shall give such information and evidence as shall lead to the discovery and conviction of the person or persons who committed the murder.*'

Matthews, as the Home Office files make clear, had long favoured such an offer. Even so, he sheltered behind his sacked Commissioner and issued it in Warren's name. As an exercise in political survival it showed Matthews as a sort of twelfth rate Talleyrand. In terms of catching Jack the ripper it achieved nothing whatsoever. Nor was it ever likely to. An unhappy House of Commons, which cheered Warren's resignation, thought that it was also time for a new Home Secretary but the Prime Minister, Lord Salisbury, supported him, rather as, in Lenin's classic phrase, the rope supports the hanged man. For the Government there were more important long term issues than the murders of East London prostitutes, most notably Ireland where Matthews was an integral piece of Salisbury's jigsaw puzzle. So the arguably lamest Home Secretary in history clung on to Office.

Monro had whispered advice into Matthew's ear but was untainted by Scotland Yard's failure to put an end to the ripper's depredations. The new Commissioner produced no particular initiatives to catch the killer. Throughout the Autumn an increasing number of police had been drafted into the East End from other areas. In so far as the uniformed branch was concerned this policy was now halted and men began to be transferred back to their regular divisions. The decision was a sound one. Swamping Whitechapel with beat Constables had not achieved anything and had left other areas dangerously denuded of policemen. Conversely, more Detectives were filtered into the East End to join the hunt. As the former head of the C.I.D. Monro was clearly relying on investigation rather than foot slogging to catch the murderer. This shift in emphasis did not work either, but it might have if the police had had unfettered minds.

✳✳✳✳✳

Had Jack the ripper stuck to his established pattern then London could have expected another atrocity on November 30th. He did not. Nor was there one on December 7th. The mood of terror which had gripped Londoners since the end of August now began to abate. Today's fear is tomorrow's ennui and the populace was tiring of the ripper. Nothing was likely to surpass the sheer horror of Mary Kelly's murder and there was a feeling that he had done his worst. When the next murder occurred it was not associated with the ripper. In fact, according to the Police, it was not a murder at all.

Rose Mylett, a.k.a. Catherine Millett, 'Fair Alice' Downey and 'Drunken Lizzie' Davis, was twenty six. Her nicknames imply an attractive young woman who drank heavily. She was probably a prostitute although this is not definitely established.

Davis was Mylett's married name. Little is known of her background. Her husband was an upholsterer and they had one son, born around 1881. Sometime afterwards the relationship folded and she became yet another sad denizen of the Spitalfields lodging houses.

Early on the morning of December 20th, death came and took Rose Mylett. At 4.15 a.m. Police Constable Robert Goulding discovered her lifeless body in Clarke's Yard, Poplar High Street. There were no apparent marks of injury aside from some bruising on her throat and face. The Police decided that she had choked to death on her own vomit and that the marks on her neck had been caused by a stiff collar. A women with the somewhat ill timed name of Graves claimed to have seen Rose, apparently the worse for drink, outside a Pub in Commercial Road at 2.30 a.m. The Autopsy report then came as something of a shock.

The first Doctor to examine the body was Matthew Brownfield, a 'K' Division (Poplar) Police Surgeon. Later, with his Assistant, a Dr Harris, Brownfield carried out the Post Mortem examination. His conclusion, firmly endorsed by Harris, was that Mylett had been strangled from behind with a ligature. A mark on her throat could have been — and according to Brownfield was — a rope mark. Other bruises on the neck he decided, had been caused by pressure from fingers and thumbs. There was an abrasion on her face as though she had been punched. Exploding completely the Police theory that she had been drinking and choked on her own vomit, Brownfield and Harris found no trace of alcohol in her body. The rope mark was only a faint one but what convinced the Doctors was congealed blood under the skin.

The police, and in particular Sir Robert Anderson, were appalled at these findings. The ripper scare had begun to die down and Rose Mylett's murder threatened to rekindle it. Their reaction was a very simple one. They refused to accept the Doctors' verdict and sent Dr Alexander MacKellar, the Police Surgeon General, down to Poplar to examine the body. The result was hardly what they had hoped for. MacKellar supported Brownfield and Harris.

Three Police Surgeons had now categorically stated that Rose Mylett had been murdered. But rather like a donkey caught up in its own obstinacy, Anderson refused to accept their conclusions. He turned once again to Dr Bond. Yet more shocks were in store. Bond sent his Assistant to view the body. He concurred with Brownfield, Harris and MacKellar. Four-nil. Finally Bond was persuaded to go to Poplar himself only to report that he agreed with the previous verdicts.[*] With all this weight of opinion against them one would reasonably have expected the Police to have changed their minds but not a bit of it. Instead Bond was cajoled into changing his mind.

Police objections notwithstanding, there can be no real doubt that Rose Mylett was murdered[**], a view shared by her inquest on January 9th. The real question is whether she was murdered by Jack the ripper.

On the face of it, no. Her throat had not been cut, there were no mutilations, strangulation had been by ligature and Poplar was some way off the ripper's beaten track. Nor was she robbed. 1s/2d (6 pence today but around £4 in actual value), was found on her body. However, as I shall suggest in the final Chapter, there are grounds for believing that Rose was slain by the ripper, and a very definite link with what was to be his final murder.

That later. Although London could not know it the Ripper's East End blood bath was over. Four weeks after Rose Mylett's murder he left England for good.

*****

Behind him he left a floundering Police Force. The deep rooted obsession with Polish Jews had surfaced again, this time in the shape of Joseph Isaacs a cigar maker who fell prey to his landlady's suspicions after pacing his room at nights and leaving his lodgings the day after Mary Kelly's murder. Isaacs was arrested for stealing a watch on December 6th and taken, in what was described as a "strongly escorted" cab, by Abberline to Commercial Street Police Station. He proved to have no connection with the murders. The grounds for suspecting

---

[*]   Bagster Phillips — who did not see the body — also seems to have concluded that
      Mylett was strangled.
[**] For the Police arguments see Appendix Six

Isaacs were virtually non existent, save for his origin. Two months later Abberline was to find himself investigating the real Jack the ripper, the murderer in the palm of his hand. But he wasn't Polish and he wasn't Jewish and so he was discarded.

Throughout 1889 there were to be various scares that the ripper had recommenced his activities. In the Spring parts of a female corpse began to turn up in the Thames. They belonged to a Knightsbridge prostitute named Elizabeth Jackson. She was speedily discounted as a Ripper victim but a similarly dismembered corpse, unidentified but possibly a prostitute calling herself Lydia Hart and found in Pinchin Street, St Georges in the East, on September 10th, received more serious attention, Monro speculating in a report to the Home Office whether she might be a ripper victim. His conclusion was that she was not and he was right although it is possible that "Hart" and Jackson were both murdered by the same man[*].

On the face of it Alice McKenzie was a far more likely candidate to join the ripper's list. A forty year old occasional prostitute, McKenzie was found dead in Castle Alley[**], Whitechapel in the early hours of July 17th. She had been stabbed twice in the throat and there were some minor injuries to the body. A long cut ran down from her breasts to the navel and a second wound and some scratches formed a series of tributaries running down towards her genitals.

Briefly it seemed as though the ripper might have returned. The murder found Scotland Yard in a state of flux. Anderson was on holiday and Williamson a sick man with only a few months left to live. Monro had just pushed through the appointment of his friend Sir Melville MacNaghten as Assistant Chief Constable but as Macnaghten had no knowledge or experience of Police work the investigation was placed in the hands of Colonel Bolton Monsell, Chief Constable of the Uniformed Branch. It was a situation bordering on the Keystone Cops. Scotland Yard had appointed a Deputy who was unable to deputise to a post meant for a career Police Officer over the head of a career Policeman (Swanson) who was ideally suited for the job. Not surprisingly the result was a confused mess. Bagster Phillips, who performed the Autopsy, decided that McKenzie was not a ripper victim; Bond summoned for his third and final appearance concluded the opposite. Monro, reporting to the Home Office thought that she might be, a view not shared by the majority of his subordinates, least of all his friend Macnaghten.

Lost in the middle of all this was poor Alice McKenzie whose murderer was never caught. As for the ripper himself, he had been dead for exactly twelve weeks when her body was discovered.

The final victim to be attributed to Jack the ripper was Frances Coles, a good looking young prostitute of twenty five. A former packer, Coles had been

[*]   See Chapter Two
[**]   Now Castle Street

a prostitute since the age of nineteen. Shortly after 2 a.m. on February 14th, 1891 she was found with her throat cut in Swallow Gardens, a very dark and menacing alleyway near the Royal Mint. She was still alive when discovered but died on the way to Hospital. Her murder immediately set up the cry that the ripper was back and brought Scotland Yard out in force, Anderson and Macnaghten accompanying Superintendent Arnold and Inspector Reid to the murder site*. For once an arrest was made, a ship's Fireman named Thomas Sadler who had slept with Coles the previous night and spent most of the 13th in her company. But the case against Sadler did not get very far. He was found to be telling the truth about his movements at the time of the murder and was discharged at the Magistrates Court. This did not prevent Macnaghten from later branding Sadler as not only Coles' murderer but McKenzie's as well, a proposition for which there was not the slightest shred of proof. As we shall see, Macnaghten was very prone to making allegations without evidence.

*****

Excluding Rose Mylett, the nightmare Autumn ended with Mary Kelly's murder. Along with his identity, the ripper left several unanswered questions, his motives, his domicile, whether he was left or right handed and the extent of his medical knowledge.

Jack the ripper was clearly a sexual pervert of the most virulent type. Because of the nature of Victorian England that was not always admitted at the time. A society which covered the legs of tables from prudish hypocrisy saw but refused to see. It was fashionable, and comforting, to ascribe other motives to his crimes. Religious mania, revenge, megalomania and simple dementia were all popular. The police on the other hand (after discarding their initial theory) were in no doubt. They were used to dealing with the seamy side of a Society which refused to acknowledge its existence. They correctly diagnosed the ripper as a gross sexual deviant with homicidal tendencies, what we today call a sexual serial killer.

Exactly how the ripper gained his satisfaction we do not know for certain. Only in one instance, Catharine Eddowes, was the body examined for sexual connection. There was no evidence of recent intercourse which means that he did not penetrate her naturally as part of the attack. Nor were there any semen stains on her clothes which means that he did not masturbate over the body. Apparently he gained his release whilst inflicting the mutilations themselves, a process chillingly summed up by Colin Wilson as: 'rape with a knife'.

Prostitutes were an obvious target. They were easily available, conducted their business away from prying eyes and had already been cast in the role of victims by the dehumanised Society which created them. But in the Ripper's

---

* Abberline had left the Force the previous year

twisted mind prostitutes were also endowed with an extra dimension for hatred. He had contracted Venereal Disease from one of them.

Robbing them was part of his make-up, a subject, hitherto ignored. Two farthings were found by Annie Chapman's body, but apart from that none of the victims had any money on them. Nichols and Chapman were both trying to earn their doss money. Had they succeeded then they would not have ended up with their murderer. But both apparently had rings pulled off their fingers, in Chapman's case three of them. Keith Skinner, Co-Author of 'The Ripper Legacy' and 'The Jack the Ripper A to Z', has made the credible suggestion that the rings could have been stolen in the Mortuary and we note that the Pauper attendant Robert Mann was present on both occasions. However the Mortuary was swarming with Police Officers and it seems unlikely that anybody would have risked looting the corpses. For good measure, Chapman's body was stripped and washed by two Nurses. Chapman's killer also cut her pocket through, apparently deliberately, and left the contents scattered around her body.

Both Eddowes and Stride had spent what money they had on drink. In Stride's case the ripper would not have stopped to ransack the body anyway. Which leaves us with Martha Tabram and Mary Kelly. No money was found but both had earlier picked up clients. Tabram might have spent the money from her soldier on drink; equally she may have gone in search of more clients and been the prostitute who went into George Yard with the Grenadier two hours later. The likelihood is that she did have some money and was robbed. Mary Kelly had two and possibly three clients. Some of the money may have been spent on breakfast and her drink in the pub but not all of it. Yet no money was found at No 13, a clear indication that it was taken by her murderer.

Robbery of course was only a distant secondary motive for the ripper but it is possible that he sheltered behind it in his own mind, unwilling to accept his abnormality, in much the same way that Peter Sutcliffe, the Yorkshire Ripper, has always refused to accept the sexual nature of his crimes[*]. And whilst Jack the ripper was a long way from being destitute in 1888, he was a slave to money, in the same way that misers are, a fact which ultimately proved his undoing.

The Police believed, at least in 1888, that he lived in the immediate vicinity of his crimes, the collection of mean little streets called the 'Evil Quarter of a Mile', the slums of Whitechapel and Spitalfields. But his failure to strike during the fog bound days of October should have led them to a different conclusion. He was neither close enough to home, or sufficiently familiar with the maze of streets, warrens and alleys that was Spitalfields to risk striking in the fog. It meant that the ripper lived farther afield and that whilst he had a knowledge of the area he was not a native Eastender.

Whether he was left handed, right handed or ambidextrous has intrigued historians for years. Only two of the Doctors who examined the ripper victims

[*] See 'Voices From an Evil God' by Barbara Jones

ventured an opinion. Killeen (Martha Tabram) decided that he was right handed: Llewellyn (Polly Nicholls) opted left. But Llewellyn did not commit himself beyond the word "might", and his left handed theory has been sharply criticised by Begg, Fido and Skinner.

> *'...it has not proved persuasive to subsequent researchers. The M.O. (Modus Operandi) proposed is clumsy, would be almost impossible to carry out silently, and would probably rip the murderer's own sleeve.'*[1]

Although no other Doctor of the time was prepared to venture an opinion, Professor James Cameron, the eminent Pathologist, has recently placed on record his belief that the ripper was right handed. Analysing the drawings and photographs of Catharine Eddowes' corpse, Cameron noted that the incisions dragged to the right and became progressively deeper.

Whilst the evidence does not preclude the possibility that the ripper was ambidextrous, there can be no doubt that he favoured his right hand.

By far the most controversial question surrounding the ripper (aside from his identity) is that of his medical skills. Doctor Killeen (Tabram) thought he knew where and how to cut, but this judgment must be set against the fact that Tabram was not deliberately mutilated but stabbed repeatedly. It is very difficult to understand why Killeen attributed skill to what was really a frenzied attack.

Rees Llewellyn (Nichols) endowed her murderer with: 'some rough anatomical knowledge. He seems to have attacked all the vital parts'. But in fact no organ was attacked. Nichols belly was simply ripped open in a number of places which is hardly a sound basis for accrediting her assailant with anatomical ability.

It is plausible to suggest that neither Killeen or Llewellyn fully appreciated the sexual designs of the attacks.

William Blackwell (Stride) offered no opinion in the absence of mutilations. Frederick Brown (Eddowes) decided that: 'It required a great deal of medical knowledge to have removed the Kidney and to know where it was placed. Such a knowledge might be possessed by some one in the habit of cutting up animals'. But Brown's view was distorted by the fact that he thought that the ripper was deliberately seeking the Kidney. Even here he attributed to him only the anatomical knowledge of a slaughterman. Pressed by the Coroner on whether actual surgical skill had been shown, Brown answered only that the killer had shown anatomical knowledge.

His colleagues who assisted him at the Post Mortem, Doctors George Sequeira, William Saunders and George Bagster Phillips, all sharply disagreed with him. None of them thought that Eddowes' murderer had displayed any

1   The Jack the Ripper A to 2 page 296 (first edition)

medical expertise whatsoever.

The firmest opinion in favour of the ripper's medical skill was voiced by Bagster Phillips. He told the inquest on Annie Chapman's murder that her mutilations were: 'the work of an expert... one who had such knowledge of anatomical or pathological examinations as to be enabled to secure the pelvic organs with one sweep of the knife (which) seemed to indicate great anatomical knowledge*'.

But he was not always so positive. At the same inquest a week earlier he had spoken only of '*indications* of anatomical knowledge' and '*some* anatomical knowledge'. His views seem to have expanded as time went on.

Bagster Phillips was the only medical man to actually credit the killer with *surgical* skill and this judgment, along with "great" anatomical knowledge, only developed later. On what was it based? Purely on the fact that the ripper had cut out Chapman's uterus in its entirety, apparently with a single cut. The injuries to other organs were by no means as impressive. Only the upper portion of the vagina and two thirds of the bladder had been removed.

Having gone out on a limb at Chapman's inquest, Phillips then found himself in difficulties. Forced to agree with Sequeira and Saunders that Eddowes killer had displayed no medical craft he quite ludicrously dismissed the crime as the work of an imitator. At Stride's inquest he claimed that her killer possessed, 'a knowledge of where to cut the throat', a remark which does not require any comment.

Overall, Phillips seems to have been a dog in the manger, highly opinionated, fond of spreading himself and never likely to rethink a position once it had formed in his mind. He was most certainly wrong about the time of Annie Chapman's murder and brushed aside Blackwell's theory of how Liz Stride had been murdered in favour of his own mish mash, delineated by Begg, Fido and Skinner as follows:-

> '*It is impossible to work out what kind of assault Phillips envisaged... This is all geometrically impossible, and there is either misreporting or muddled thinking involved.*'[1]

Phillips final sortie into the ripper murders came at Mary Kelly's inquest where he gave evidence about the cause of death. Presumably he held fast to his opinion about the ripper's expertise despite Doctor Bond's assessment of it which was nil. Bond also reviewed the other autopsy findings in a special report for Anderson. His conclusions are given verbatim in Chapter Seven, but summarised they were that the ripper possessed no surgical or anatomical knowledge

---

1   The Jack the Ripper A to Z p352 (first edition)

*   Quoted from A Summary in 'The Lancet'

of any kind.

Excluding Phillips, and I think we are justified in doing so, it all boils down to this. Killeen, Llewellyn and Brown awarded the ripper varying degrees of anatomical ability but caveats can be inserted into each of their assessments. Bond, Sequeira and Saunders unequivocally found none. They were right. The man who was Jack the ripper had no medical training and no known knowledge of anatomy. He was not a Butcher and he was not a Slaughterman.

His modus operandi was a simple one. In the case of Annie Chapman there was positive evidence of strangulation; in those of Elizabeth Stride[1], Catharine Eddowes and Mary Kelly[2], indications of strangulation[3]. Not so with Martha Tabram and Mary Ann Nichols although the signs probably went undetected. Reviewing the autopsy reports on the victims two of the post war giants of forensic pathology, the late Professor Francis Camps and Professor James Cameron both reached the firm conclusion that the ripper first strangled his victims, and then cut their throats and mutilated them.[4] This dovetails with his final victim who was first strangled and then mutilated.[5]

We can therefore positively answer a number of pertinent questions about the ripper. His crimes were sexual but he also robbed his victims; he had a working knowledge of the East End and lived within easy distance of his crimes, but not in the immediate locale. He was right handed, had no medical or anatomical expertise and strangled his victims before using his knife.

In the final chapter of this book I will show how each of these facts fit Jack the ripper like a glove.

✳✳✳✳✳

The Ripper's reign of terror had ended: Ripperology, the study of his murders, was about to begin. In the Seventeenth Century any old Lady living alone in a rural area with a Black Cat for company was in danger of being burnt as a witch. Ripperology, which forms the next part of this Book, is a more sophisticated version of witch burning, a game of mock trials without any rules of evidence ending in character assassination as a substitute for the victim's execution.

We turn now to this dark Chapter of Criminology.

---

1   See Appendix Three
2   The photograph shows her left fist clenched which points to strangulation.
3   Whether into unconsciousness or death is unclear.
4   Although their surveys probably did not include Tabram.
5   See Chapter Twelve

Part Two

Bringing On The

Empty Horses:

The Story of Ripperology

PROLOGUE

In 1984 Jonathan Goodman, who is one of Britain's most distinguished crime historians, decided to poke fun at ripperology. He invented one, Peter J Harpick, a non-existent character (the name is an anagram of Jack the ripper) and provided him with a spoof biography. He was astonished to find that Harpick was taken seriously, over a dozen people writing to him for more details. Later, in 'Masterpieces of Murder' (1992) Goodman accurately summed up a century of ripperology.

> *'the simple trick is to put forward a few biographical truths that do not conflict with the notion that the candidate fills the bill, add some assumptions in the guise of truths and omit — or think up a way of discounting — proof that the theory is nutty.'*[1]

Welcome to the three ringed circus called Ripperology.

1   Masterpieces of Murder p300

Chapter Seven: The Theorists Take Over

The police closed their files on Jack the ripper in 1892. Precisely why we do not know, but we can make educated guesses. One is that the murders had obviously stopped. The last semblance of a ripper murder was Frances Coles in February 1891 and few police officers were disposed to think of Frances as a ripper victim. Another is that Anderson and Swanson both thought that the killer was safely caged in an asylum, a belief which will be examined later. So the police rested. But not the Armchair Detectives. The crimes which had held all London in terror were officially unsolved and therefore fair game for crime buffs, journalists, cranks and hoaxers. Ripperology had begun.

The study of the Jack the ripper murders seems at times to be a bottomless pit, a never ending round of theorizing and counter theorizing, generally without a scrap of evidence. The nadir was reached in the 1970's and that will be examined in the next chapter. But its seeds were sown many years earlier by writers, many with the best of intentions, who piled speculation upon speculation whilst reality walked off into the mists. Yet the truth about the ripper murders is simple. Several unhappy women, whom Society should have treated much better than it did, were callously murdered by a vicious brute to satisfy obscene sexual cravings. It is this simplicity which has been lost over the last century as the theories became ever more bizarre and outlandish. Jack the ripper was a member of the Royal Family, a top Politician, an eminent Doctor, a Cambridge Don or a coven of witch-like freemasons. In fact he was none of these things: he was a depraved nonentity. Nor could he have been anything else. Achievers do not become sex killers. It has never happened in history. The same dark forces may well up inside them but success is a countering balance. It is the frustrated, the nobody, who gives way and kills. This was Jack the ripper, a frustrated nobody who worshipped sex at dark satanic mills. But before proceeding to unmask him it is necessary to get rid of the clutter which has surrounded the case for the past hundred years and show why and how it has obscured the search for such a simple truth.

Abberline once remarked, and with more than a touch of weariness:

'Theories! We were almost lost in theories; there were so many of them.'[*]

One of the earliest emanated from a crank named Edward Larkins who pestered the authorities with a blatantly absurd idea that the killer was not one but four Portuguese sailors who each had a turn in being the ripper. As soon as it was proved that Seaman X could not have done a particular murder Larkins

---

[*] Cassells Saturday Journal May 22nd 1892

rummaged through his mad hatter's box of names until he found one who was available for it! The fact that he was an obvious nutcase did not deter some people from taking Larkins seriously and he was still at it as late as 1893 when the long suffering Sir Robert Anderson described him as 'a troublesome busybody', a considerable understatement.

Larkins however pales into insignificance beside the number of Landladies 'Jack' lodged with or the legions of people claiming family ties with him. Typical of the latter is the story told by a Mr George Edwards to 'Reynolds News' in 1959. The ripper, said Edwards, was his cousin Frank, an Accountant, who had turned up at Edwards' Northgate home with a razor and a bloodstained collar a few hours after one of the murders. The Jack the ripper murders abound with dotty stories like this. It would be time wasting to analyse them all. We need only concentrate on those which have received serious attention.

Surprisingly, the first important study of the ripper did not appear until forty years after the murders. This was Leonard Matters' 'The Mystery of Jack the Ripper' (1929). Matters, an Australian born journalist and Labour M.P. (he represented Kennington from 1921-31), has rather sadly been reviled as a pedlar of fiction. It is true that his work was more "factional" than serious history but his solution was by no means absurd and he enjoys the distinction of being the only writer to have actually visited Miller's Court[*]. The Ripper, said Matters, was a distinguished surgeon. He never gave him a name except for the pseudonym 'Dr Stanley'. Stanley's son had died after contracting syphilis from Mary Kelly in 1886 when she was allegedly a West End neophyte. Insane with grief, Stanley set out to hunt her down, killing the other victims after he had taxed them for information about her. Following Mary's murder he decamped to Buenos Aires, confessing to the crimes on his death bed. The problem here is not that the scenario itself is implausible but the total absence of any kind of supporting evidence for it. There are also facts which refute it. Nobody has ever been able to trace anyone who might have been Dr Stanley, syphilis takes a lot longer to kill than two years, and Mary Kelly — who was almost certainly living in the East End by 1886 — was not suffering from any form of venereal disease.

Matters was followed into the arena by Edwin Woodhall with 'Jack the Ripper or When London walked in Terror' (1935). It is not definitely established but Woodhall, an ex-policeman, may have been the Edwin Woodhall who tried to catch Percy Toplis the famous 'monacled mutineer' ultimately shot to death by police in Penrith.

Woodhall's book on the ripper was distinguished by only one thing; he advanced the hitherto overlooked possibility that the killer may have been a woman. Unfortunately, his potential suspect, a dressmaker named Olga Tchkersoff, does not seem to have existed, or at least no record of her has ever been found.

---

[*]   It was demolished in 1933

Four years later a journalist named William Stewart picked up Woodhall's baton. Stewart's book 'Jack the Ripper: A New Theory' postulates that the murderer could have been a revenge seeking midwife. There was no definite suspect although Stewart does mention Mary Ann Pearcey who was hanged in 1890 for the murders of her lover's wife and child. The case was one of pathological jealousy which spilled over into horrendous tragedy and there is absolutely no reason to think that Pearcey was already a serial killer. Stewart's overall theory was serviceable but yet again there is just nothing whatsoever to substantiate it. This is the age old problem with such ideas. It is possible to go on and on and on into infinity — and ultimately absurdity — with this kind of theorizing. And a little vicious circle starts to form. The less evidence advanced in support of such claims so the more difficult it is to subject them to critical analysis and logic then begins to be stood on its head. Instead of putting forward evidence the theorist starts to demand proof that his ideas are wrong in the first place. By this yardstick it is possible to pluck any solution out of the air and say disprove it. Ripperphiles tend to become so caught up in their beliefs that they become classic exponents of this sort of illusory reasoning. The supreme example is the case advanced against the Duke of Clarence (which is examined in the next chapter). No evidence is offered; we are asked instead to disprove it. Even when that disproof is put forward — in the shape of Court circulars demonstrating Alibis for Clarence — his adherents simply fold their arms and claim that the circulars have been faked! Another, albeit extreme example, is the 'case' against the Artist Frank Miles. No evidence has ever been produced to associate Miles with the murders. On the contrary, he was in a mental home throughout 1888. But when this seemingly insurmountable obstacle was put in their way the Milesians offered the mind boggling explanation that a premature report of his death was cover up for his escape! Clearly a case of the Old Sandhurst maxim — my centre is broken and both flanks turned so I'll counter-attack!

We have had so far a mad surgeon, a ghostly dressmaker and an avenging midwife and already it can be seen that we are moving farther and farther away from the graviman of the case. Reality is beginning to become suspended. Unhappily, the next 'suspect' takes us even further into the realms of fantasy. I say 'unhappily' because Donald McCormick's 'The Identity of Jack the Ripper' (1959) was the first book I ever read on the subject and I retain a certain affection for it. McCormick has received a rough ride from Ripperphiles over the years. Whether they have been altogether fair to him is arguable but I am afraid that his rather convoluted solution does rest on scotch mist. Having said that he did, unlike previous writers, wholeheartedly commit himself to a named suspect, one Vassily Konavalov; alias Alexei Pedachenko and Andrey Luiskovo, a homicidally bent doctor from Tver in Russia. In broad outline McCormick's thesis goes as follows. Konavalov killed a prostitute in the Montmartre district of Paris in 1886 and skipped across the Channel to Britain where he adopted the Pedachenko alias and committed the ripper murders before returning home to Russia in the guise of Luiskovo. Here he was caught murdering a woman in St Petersburg and was confined to an asylum for the rest of his life. Sounds uncomplicated but now comes the hard part, the evidence, and here it gets very, very messy indeed.

There is no accessible documentary evidence that Konavalov ever existed. The only "proofs" come from two missing documents. One is a mysterious bulletin allegedly issued by the Ochrana — the czarist secret police — in 1909 referring to Konavalov/Pedachenko/Luiskovo and the murders of a woman in Paris in 1881, five women in the East quarter of London in 1888 and a woman in Petrograd (sic) in 1891. A lithograph of this document was shown to McCormick by Prince Sergei Belloselski, a white Russian emigre. It has never been seen since and all attempts to trace it have failed. And there is a very disturbing point about it. In 1909 the name Petrograd did not exist: the city was still called St Petersburg. The other missing document is, yes — you've guessed it, Dr Thomas Dutton's* 'Chronicles of Crime', a handwritten manuscript on crimes and criminals compiled over many years. Only four people are known to have see the Chronicles, Dutton, a Miss Hermione Dudley, to whom he eventually gave them, her father and McCormick. Like Prince Belloselski the first three were dead when McCormick came to write his book. The Chronicles, as described by McCormick, name Konavalov as the murderer. But do they?. Here is what Miss Dudley told the 'Sunday Chronicle' in 1935:

> *'...he (Dutton) knew the identity of Jack the Ripper. He described him as a middle aged doctor, a man who had been embittered by the death of his son. The latter had suffered cruelly at the hands of a woman of the streets and the father believed this to be the cause of his brilliant son's death'*

It is crystal clear that Dutton was referring here to Leonard Matters' fictitious Dr Stanley. That being the case then Dutton was simply purveying things which he had read and not writing from first hand knowledge. His veracity is not helped by his claims to have photographed the Goulston Street writing and assisted at the Post Mortems of the ripper victims. There is no record at all of him having done either.

Donald McCormick's answer to the 'Sunday Chronicle' article was to claim that Miss Dudley had read Leonard Matters' book and confused it with Dutton's Chronicles which, according to his notes, ran as follows:

> *'I have learned from a French Doctor of a Russian Junior Surgeon... he was suspected of having killed and mutilated a grisette in Montmartre, but he left Paris before he could be arrested... This Surgeon, whose name*

---

*   See Chapters Four and Five

was Konavalov, was said to have had a violent hatred of prostitutes due to a relative of his having suffered cruelly from contact with a woman of the streets. The description of Konavalov exactly fits that of Peda-chenko and the final police assessment of what the ripper looked like.'[1]

But what I find worrying is the sentence "having suffered cruelly from contact with a woman of the streets": which duplicates the 'Sunday Chronicles' sentence. If Miss Dudley was not quoting from the same material that McCormick saw then why are these two sentences exactly the same? And if she was quoting from the 'Chronicles', and not just memory, then how could she have been so wrong? Furthermore Konavalov's motive does sound suspiciously like a re-run of Dr Stanley's.

According to the notes which McCormick took, Konavalov alias Peda-chenko worked in London for a hairdresser named Delhaye in Westmoreland Road, Walworth and also helped out at a clinic there, St Saviour's. Here he assisted a Dr John Williams. Allegedly Martha Tabram, Polly Nichols, Annie Chapman and Mary Kelly all attended the clinic. McCormick established that a William Delhaye did have a barber's shop in Westmoreland Road and Dr Williams was attached to St Saviour's Infirmary in the same road. However, their mere existence proves nothing and there is no trace of any Konavalov or Pedachenko working for them; or of Kelly & Co attending the infirmary. Why they should have travelled halfway across London to Walworth is inexplicable.

This is by no means the entirety of a highly complex little knot. Rasputin makes an appearance, William Le Queux, — writer, journalist and liar of gargantuan proportions, an insane religious sect called the chlysty and two nefarious individuals named Levitski and Winberg who assisted Konavalov in his murderous activities —activities orchestrated by the Ochrana in order to discredit the British Police and create a backlash against emigre Russian socialists! Now in fairness to Donald McCormick he does his best to distance himself from these lunatic fringes and it is unfair to judge his work by them. But he seizes eagerly on the fact that the Police were looking for an allegedly insane Russian Doctor, Michael Ostrog, in 1888. Perhaps Ostrog was another alias for Konavalov? Regrettably no: Ostrog was committing crimes in Britain when Konavalov (if he existed) was just six years old and in 1888 he had been in Britain for at least a quarter of a century.

Another named suspect who pops up in 'The Identity of Jack the Ripper' is Severin Klosowski, alias George Chapman. Based yet again on the Dutton Chronicles, McCormick speculates that Konavalov could have been a doppel-ganger for Klosowski. Where Dutton's facts on Klosowski are checkable they

1   The Identity of Jack the Ripper p235

have been shown to be wrong. But the point brings us neatly on to Klosowski's candidacy as the ripper.

Severin Klosowski was born in Nagornak, Poland in 1865. Trained as a junior surgeon, he arrived in Britain in 1887 and for the next three years worked as a hairdresser in Whitechapel before emigrating to America in 1890. He returned the following year and between 1895 and 1901 bigamously married three women (he already had a wife and two children) each of whom he murdered with antimony. He was hanged in 1903. Now this is hardly Jack the ripper country but following his trial Abberline surprisingly nominated him as the ripper. He was wrong and for two major psychological reasons. First, Klosowski would not have stopped killing for several years and secondly, he would not have abandoned murder and mutilation with the knife for the much tamer mode of killing by poisoning. Abberline's decision to plump for Klosowski was a curious one. Begg, Fido and Skinner have cautiously suggested that the Inspector might have been confusing him with a contemporary Police suspect named Aaron Kosminski*. Both were Poles, the same age, worked as hairdressers, had similar names, and lived briefly in Greenfield Street, Whitechapel. However, there are also important differences between the two men. Klosowski was Roman Catholic, married and lived in Greenfield Street until Whitsun 1890. Kosminski was Jewish, a Bachelor, had ceased to work before Klosowski even arrived in Britain and only took up residence in Greenfield Street six weeks after Klosowski had emigrated. Moreover, as Abberline makes clear, he did not come to suspect Klosowski until after his trial opened. All in all it seems to me extremely unlikely that there was any confusion between the two men. The case against Klosowski falls on it own demerits.

A sicker and more loathsome creature than Dr Thomas Neil Cream can rarely have existed. In 1891–92 Cream followed in the Ripper's wake by murdering four young South London prostitutes. They died in unspeakable agony from strychnine poisoning. Earlier Cream had murdered a man in Chicago and there can be little doubt that the mysterious deaths of three other women can be laid at his door. He owed his capture to the fact that he was an exhibitionist of insane dimensions who constantly drew attention to himself by writing letters about the murders and making demonstrably false accusations against others. Convicted and sentenced to hang he reportedly said "I am Jack the…" just as the trapdoor opened. Allegedly he also claimed to be the ripper whilst in the death cell. He was not for the simple reason that he was in Joliet Prison, Chicago (for murder) from 1880 until 1891. There were also vital psychological differences between the two killers: Cream was a poisoner, not a ripper and had no interest in being present at his victims' deaths. He was also an exhibitionist who craved attention, Jack the ripper the complete opposite. Here the matter should

---

* See Chapter Ten

have ended. Sadly it did not. In another example of Ripperology at its worst Cream was argued back into the lists by Derek Davis, a graphologist, and Donald Bell, a Canadian Journalist. Both should have known better. Davis argued that Cream had written both the "from hell" letter and its follow up signed "Jack the Ripper" — to Dr Openshaw*. In fact the handwriting in both letters is markedly different and each is light years away from Cream's handwriting. Davis's answer to this was that Cream had separately disguised his handwriting on both occasions! But why?. He loved publicity and made no attempt to disguise his handwriting during his South London murder spree. And why should he write in a separately disguised hand to Dr Openshaw when he was trying to prove that he had sent the kidney?

Bell's article appeared at the same time as Davis's. Its centrepiece is a claim that the man seen with Mary Kelly by George Hutchinson resembled Cream in appearance and, like him, wore a horseshoe tie pin. Great store is also set by a gold watch and chain with stone and seal worn by Cream, Bell asserting that Hutchinson's man wore a similar watch and chain. Not so. Hutchinson made no mention of a seal in his statement to the police**. As for the horseshoe pin, Bell relies upon a photograph taken of Cream whilst he was at University between 1872 and '76, at least twelve years before the ripper murders! For good measure Hutchinson described the man he saw as being of Jewish appearance. That does not match Cream. But the pièce de resistance is still to come. How could Cream be in two places, Joliet and Whitechapel, at the same time? Very simply, according to Bell. He bribed his way out of prison. But then how does this square with Cream's actual release date of June 12th 1891? Well it doesn't so Bell retreated to the Ripperphile's favourite fall back position, the cover up, citing as 'evidence' the fact that Cream's release received only minimal publicity. How this can possibly be evidence of a cover up is incomprehensible. For the record, there exists affidavits from Cream's uncle and sister-in-law and a letter written by Cream himself showing that he was in Joliet during the ripper murders. He arrived in England on October 1st 1891 and began his murder campaign two weeks later. These are facts, not fantasies. All that Davis and Bell's posturings produced was yet another round of wearying, myopic argument whilst the truth slipped further and further away. Worse, much worse, was still to come.

The next full length book on the ripper following McCormick's was Robin Odell's 'Jack the Ripper in Fact and Fiction' (1965). Odell is a Crime Historian of merit and his work has justifiably been well praised. Odell attempted to take the case back to its origins in Whitechapel, but regrettably he could not resist the temptation to spread himself and theorise. As one might expect from a quality analyst his solution is coherent and cogent but it suffers from the usual defect; there is nothing to underpin it. The ripper, thought Odell, could well have been

---

* See Chapter Five
** A seal was only added later in a Newspaper interview

a shochet, a Jewish Slaughterman and minor Priest used to killing and cutting up animals. This occupation would have provided him with the technique to kill without getting blood on him and a high degree of anatomical knowledge. Shochets needed to be well versed in Talmudic Law which forbade contact with "unclean" women and prescribed the death sentence for harlots. Should such a man become unbalanced then he might well feel that he had a messianic duty to rid the streets of prostitutes.

Odell argues his points well but he was not the first to make this journey of exploration. The Metropolitan Police had carried out extensive inquiries amongst slaughterman in 1888[*] and the City Police had queried whether the special knife used by a shochet could have been the murder weapon. The answer was no. Odell's hypothesis was also resolutely dismissed by Dr Thomas Bond who carried out the Post Mortem on Mary Kelly. In his general report to Sir Robert Anderson about the East End murders Bond noted:

> *'In each case the mutilation was inflicted by a person who had no scientific nor anatomical knowledge. In my opinion he does not even possess the technical knowledge of a butcher or horse slaughterer or any person accustomed to cut up dead animals'*

The main objection to Odell's theory however is that at the end of the day it is just that, another theory, perhaps more credible than most but for all that just a theory. He went nowhere where the police had not already gone, found no suspect and produced no hard evidence. Without being hyper critical it was yet another of the seemingly endless, time consuming notions which for over a hundred years allowed the ripper to remain unmasked.

The last two solutions which we shall look at in this Chapter are of more recent origin. The first focuses upon Mr Melvin Harris's[**] suspect, Roslyn D'Onston or to give him his proper name Robert Donston Stephenson. Of upper middle class origin (his father was a Yorkshire Mill owner) Stephenson was born in 1841. Much of his life is shrouded in mystery. He may have studied medicine in Munich and Paris but we have only his own word to go on and this is hardly reliable. His greatest, perhaps his only talent, lay in creating a fantasy world about himself. Amongst his claims; he had mined for gold in California, conducted experiments with Doppelgangers, was connected with the African slave trade and witnessed devil worship in Cameroun, quested for the Indian rope trick, studied magic in Paris and took part in 42 battles as a Surgeon Major under Garibaldi. And all this apparently by the age of 22 when he settled down to a humdrum life as a Customs Official in Hull! Like his diplomas in medicine, all of these romantic tales of adventure and daring do were strictly that — romances. If we look at his Italian exploits then we find that the last full stage of the Italian wars of

---

[*]   See Chapter Three
[*]   Jack the Ripper The Bloody Truth (1987)

independence opened in 1859 — when Stephenson was only 18 — and ended in 1861. Garibaldi subsequently led two brief corollary campaigns but came out of retirement to do so. The first was in 1862, when, by his own account, Stephenson was engrossed in magical studies in France, and the second in 1867 when he was day dreaming in Hull. That he found space in this most feverishly cluttered of imaginations for gold mining, slavery, devil worship, rope tricks and doppelgangers is quite a feat by itself. As I shall show, Stephenson was able to take in normally alert people with his stories but basically he was an attention seeker, a man saying — "please look at me, I'm really an interesting person; please sit up and take notice of me." The reality is that he was insignificant, both mentally and physically. Like most fantasists he was also a heavy drinker.

Towards the end of the 1860's Stephenson threw up his job and moved to London. The next twenty years are virtually a blank but he seems to have become obsessed with magic and the occult, a classic symptom of this sort of character. Another is the mythical girl friend and the romance that ended in tragedy, in Stephenson's case a prostitute whom (he said) committed suicide over him. He later claimed to have heard her ghostly footsteps on Westminster Bridge.

How he lived is largely unknown, but it seems that he was a freelance journalist of sorts. In June 1887 a Robert Stephenson appeared at Thames Magistrates Court charged with assault but to be fair the name is not uncommon. He was by this time calling himself "Dr Roslyn D'Onston", but still using Stephenson when it suited him[*].

And so on to the year 1888 in which Stephenson became the one thing he was eminently suited to be:— a ripper theorist! On December 1st 'The Pall Mall Gazette' published 'Who is the Whitechapel Demon (By one who thinks he knows)', written by Stephenson. The bare bones of it are that the ripper was a black magician (who else) seeking to achieve "evocation" (whatever that may mean) through: 'means of the most appalling crimes of which murder and mutilation of the dead are the *least* (my italics) heinous. The murderer — sorry magician — was obliged to obtain the skin of a suicide, nails from a murderer's gallows, candles made from human fat and a preparation made up from a certain portion of the body of a prostitute. It was also necessary for his murders to take on the form of a Cross which the murder sites (according to Stephenson) did.

There are of course people, often mentally unstable, who take this sort of garbage seriously. Stephenson was undoubtedly one of them. As a student of magic I suppose that we should therefore expect him to argue that black is white and of course he does. In order to form his cross Mary Kelly has to be discarded as a ripper victim! Where our black magician got his other substances from is unexplained. Presumably he was an ex-mortuary attendant now working as a prison officer and moonlighting as a candlemaker.

---

[*]   A Robert Stephenson also appeared in Court on October 30th 1888 charged with indecent assault

Stephenson's next sally provides us with one of the lighter moments of the Whitechapel murders. Every great man needs his Boswell or Dr Watson, including mythomaniacs. No matter how absurd the stories you can always find somebody to believe in them. Stephenson now found such a sidekick in George Marsh who lived — appropriately enough — in Pratt Street, Camden. Together this intrepid duo set out to play hunt the ripper. There are not many moments of humour in the East End murders but the image of Stephenson — Whitechapel Don Quixote — and his dim witted companion trying to catch a serial killer is hilarious. Both men subsequently ended up at Scotland Yard, Marsh on December 24th and Stephenson on the 26th, where they made statements to an Inspector named Roots. Marsh had apparently concluded that Stephenson himself was the ripper whilst Stephenson entertained the gravest possible doubts about a Doctor named Davies at the London Hospital. According to Stephenson, whilst he (Stephenson) was a patient in the Hospital, Davies had given an over-enthusiastic demonstration of how he thought the murderer killed his victims. Along with his statement Stephenson also submitted the following document:

> '24th December 88 — I hereby agree to pay to Dr R D'O Stephenson *(also known as "Sudden Death") one half of any or all rewards or monies received by me on account of the conviction of Dr Davies for wilful murder (signed) Roslyn D'O. Stephenson MD, 29 Castle Street, WC, St Martin's Lane'.*

"Sudden Death" was apparently agreeing to pay half of his reward money to himself! Doubtless this had been penned during one of his mammoth drinking sessions.

Roots put Stephenson and Marsh's Statements up to his superiors along with his own observations. He had known Stephenson for twenty years and portrayed him as a borderline alcoholic who had recently stood (genuinely) for the Secretaryship of an Orphanage. He also repeated the fictions which Stephenson had woven around himself which proves that you can fool some people all of the time. Swanson's reaction to the whole ridiculous business is unknown but the Police do not seem to have wasted time investigating either Stephenson or Dr Davies.

The story of Robert Stephenson does not end here. Several other players now join the cast. The most significant is Baroness Vittoria Cremers, a member of the Theosophy Society. At around the same time that "Sudden Death" was searching for the ripper at the bottom of a glass, Cremers was forming a relationship with a young woman named Mabel Collins, a fellow Theosophist. During the course of 1889 their friendship grew very close indeed. At the end of the year Cremers went to America for several months leaving Collins to her own devices. When she returned Mabel had a new relationship, with a man whom she described as a "great magician who has wonderful magical secrets". The great magician had also been a cavalry captain, had known the original of

Ayesha, heroine of Rider Haggard's famous novel "She", and had once vanquished a female witch Doctor in a confrontation of magical powers. "Sudden Death" had found a new dupe.

Stephenson, Collins and Cremers set up home together and started a cosmetics business. After a while Collins became disenchanted with Stephenson. According to Cremers, Mabel began to fear him, suspecting that he was Jack the ripper. This was allegedly based on something he had shown her. Intrigued, Cremers went into Stephenson's room whilst he was out and opened up a tin box. In it she found several black ties, knotted and stiff. At the back of each tie there was a congealed stain. Later on, Stephenson himself told Cremers his Dr Davies story adding a suitable embellishment; — Davies had actually confessed to him that he was the ripper. He also intertwined Davies with his 'Pall Mall Gazette' article claiming that the murder sites had been deliberately chosen with a special purpose in mind. The Doctor, said Stephenson, had tucked the victims' missing organs between his shirt and tie.

At this point both Cremers and Collins effectively bow out of the story and are replaced by Betty May and Aleister Crowley, the infamous satanist. May, a "disciple" of Crowley's, allegedly found the stained ties in his home and asked him about them. Crowley repeated to her Vittoria Cremers' story[*] with some embroidery of his own which need not concern us. Later, he also recounted it to a Journalist named Bernard O'Donnell who interviewed Cremers herself. O'Donnell in turn confided the whole story to an unpublished manuscript on the murders. Collins, Crowley and O'Donnell believed that Robert Donston Stephenson, alias Roslyn D'Onston, was Jack the ripper, a belief shared by Melvin Harris who published it as his solution to the crimes in 'Jack the Ripper: The Bloody Truth'.

Melvin Harris is a great debunker of myths and a highly entertaining writer. For the most past 'The Bloody Truth' is first rate. It is sad therefore that he allowed himself to be taken for a ride by Stephenson. Not that he was alone in this; a number of intelligent people took Stephenson's stories at face value including W.T. Stead, the Editor of the 'Pall Mall Gazette', who also seems to have believed at one time that Stephenson might be the ripper.

Obviously then Stephenson was by no means an implausible man, at least not on the surface. Provided no one bothered to scrutinise his Walter Mitty tales (The California Gold Rush for example took place when he was a child of eight), then he could keep up his pretences. He appeared rational, came from a respectable family and was well educated. Most important of all — and this is particularly relevant to the case against him being the ripper — he was not a crook or a con man. His yarns were not spun for gain but for prestige.

The evidence for Stephenson as Jack the ripper is thin to the point of

---

[*]   Cremers was at one time his business manager.

transparency. It is based almost exclusively on Vittoria Cremers' story. And Cremers did not like Stephenson. She was a very tough cookie indeed who was not fooled for a moment by his stories. Above all she wanted Mabel Collins back and was prepared to wait, lynx eyed, for her chance. She knew it would come and it did. Stephenson himself provided it with his story of knowing the ripper. Mabel's affections were already on the wane. Now if she could be persuaded that her lover might himself be the ripper...! Without doubt the little anecdote which Stephenson concocted about the organs concealed under the ties gave Vittoria the opportunity she was looking for. All she needed were a few men's ties, apparently stained with blood but no doubt in reality some form of cosmetic — possibly lacquer — and the impressionable Mabel was convinced. End of romance, end of story.

Apart from Cremers there is really nothing to associate Stephenson with the crimes. If we examine his 'Pall Mall Gazette' article then we find that it is factually unsound. The six murder sites which he nominated do not form a cross. But because of them he was forced to include Emma Smith as a victim and exclude Mary Kelly which is absurd. Melvin Harris attempts to get out of this particular bind by arguing that Stephenson was being very clever, his 'Gazette' article and accusations against Dr Davies were a cunning ploy to draw attention away from himself by posing as a harmless crank. In fact he was drawing attention to himself in the first place, a highly dangerous and unnecessary piece of strategy. It hanged Dr Cream and in Stephenson's case fueled Marsh and Stead's suspicions. But for the fact that he did not fit the man Swanson and Abberline were looking for then Stephenson might have found himself under serious investigation. It is a pity that he did not because then he would have been entirely cleared.

Jack the ripper did not litter Whitechapel with corpses as part of any black magic ritual; he was a sexual killer. If we weigh Stephenson in the balance against the psychological profile of this type of murderer then we find that the scales almost go crashing to the floor in favour of his innocence. Almost. He has two traits redolent of a sex murderer. One is his heavy drinking; the other, a point made very weightily by Melvin Harris, his failure in life, the frustration of a man who wants success, has not the talent to achieve it but believes he deserves it. There can be little doubt that Stephenson was just such a man.

However, by themselves these points are meaningless. They can only be made to count if they are part of a bigger picture, linking together tangible proofs of guilt. Against them are a formidable array of counterpoints. The most obvious is that Jack the ripper would not have simply stopped killing. Nor does Stephenson's age fit. He was 47 in 1888, well above the age at which sexual murderers normally erupt. The witnesses also described a much younger man.

The ripper was a man of violence and violent fantasies. Stephenson had no known history of violence, or for that matter of sexual aberration. The bogus roles which he created for himself were not violent in nature. In particular, he claimed to have studied medicine and then joined Garibaldi's Army as a Surgeon. This is highly illuminating because the fantasies here are of saving life, not taking it. The self image which created those fantasies was not one of evil. Stephenson is always on the side of the Angels. In the Italian war he chooses the heroic side fighting for freedom, one which was also supported politically (and very nearly militarily) by his own country. In his encounter with the Witch Doctor he is the good guy triumphing over wickedness. Those fantasies, and his real life candidacy for the orphanage secretaryship, tell us a great deal about Robert Stephenson and the way he desperately wanted to see himself and be seen by others. He yearned to be a hero. This was decidedly not the self image of a maniac who butchers woman in the streets, nor would that self image have permitted him to do so. On the other hand it is that of a man who fantasises about catching him.

Melvin Harris unfortunately became so trapped by his white is black argument that he lost sight of the essential truth about Stephenson. He was not a black magician but a white magician. Far from being an elaborate ruse to hoodwink the police, Stephenson's "Gazette" article is another example of his good versus evil psyche at work. As he makes clear black magic is an abomination:

> *'Black magic employs the agencies of evil spirits and demons, instead of the beneficent spirits directed by the adepts of la haute magic'*[*]

Further evidence of this can be found in the one positive act of Stephenson's life, his book 'The Patristic Gospels' published in 1904. It is a deeply religious work assessing the Gospels. This apparent lurch to the other extreme leaves the Stephensonites floundering. Melvin Harris tries hard to explain the conversion but doesn't succeed for the simple reason that there was no conversion. This had been Stephenson's character all along. He was sad and rather pathetic but at heart a man who was guided by good, not evil. Like David Copperfield he wanted to be the hero of his own life: unhappily, his shortcomings led him to become the victim of what may well be the ultimate in ripperology — one theorist accusing another.

The final ripper candidate of this chapter was established in 1987 by Martin Fido. Fido's book 'The Crimes, Detection and Death of Jack the Ripper' is a very able piece of work. His suspect is one, David Cohen or Aaron Davis Cohen, a jew of foreign extraction. Cohen was arrested by the police on December 6th 1888, in an East End brothel. Exactly what led to his arrest is unclear but piecing together the various fragments of the story it seems that one of the prostitutes, Ellen Hickey, started a fight with a client, an N. Cohen. The police arrived and arrested Hickey, Gertrude Smith, who kept the Brothel, another prostitute named

[*]   Pall Mall Gazette December 1st 1888

Jones and David Cohen.

All four appeared at Thames Magistrates Court the following day and Cohen was sent for observation to the Whitechapel Workhouse Infirmary where it was found that he was violent and demented. He gave no next of kin and two weeks later was transferred to Colney Hatch Lunatic Asylum where he was certified insane. He proved to be an incorrigible patient, repeating his behaviour in the Workhouse and needing to be force fed. On December 28th he was separated from the other patients because he was a danger to them. He remained at the Asylum until October 20th, 1889 when he died of mania and pulmonary phthisis.

Melvin Fido's thesis about Cohen was originally a rather complex one. His research unearthed a Nathan Kaminsky who had been treated for syphilis at the Whitechapel Infirmary between March and May, 1888. After that Kaminsky seems to have disappeared from the face of the earth. Fido reasoned that Kaminsky was in fact Leather Apron, and in turn Jack the ripper, and that he either changed his name to David Cohen to avoid detection or that it was a badly articulated version of Kaminsky given by him to the Asylum Authorities. Fido goes on to propose that the police got themselves into a muddle and thought, erroneously, that Nathan Kaminsky and the police suspect Aaron Kosminski were one and the same person, a rather refined version of the Klosowski-Kosminski argument.

The death knell to the latter part of Fido's theory was sounded in 1987 when it was established beyond any doubt that Aaron Kosminski was the police suspect. This has led Begg and Skinner to state (Fido presumably dissenting):

> *'The general opinion would be that the 'Cohen' theory fell as soon as the Swanson Marginalia unequivocably identified Anderson's suspect as Kosminski'* [1]

That is altogether too sweeping. Fido was wrong in thinking that the police had confused the two men but David Cohen, either as an alias for Nathan Kaminsky or strictly on his own, does not automatically cease to be a viable suspect because of it. Consider the facts. He was violently insane, apparently sought the company of prostitutes, was at large in the East End and the murders ceased with his incarceration. Ironically, although the police never seem to have considered Cohen as a suspect, he was a much more likely candidate for the ripper than Aaron Kosminski.

One has to look much more closely at Cohen than the confusion with Kosminski to see the cracks. The facts surrounding his arrest have not been

---

1   The Jack the Ripper A to Z p217 (first edition)

ascertained but he seems to have behaved in some sort of deranged way in the Brothel. He was not the N. Cohen who had the fight with Ellen Hickey but it is possible that they were relatives and went there together. If the trouble arose from David Cohen's behaviour then this could explain the fight and David's reluctance to give his next of kin. But this, and his subsequent behaviour, brands David Cohen as an obvious lunatic, not the sort of man who was Jack the ripper. A second point is that, according to the Whitechapel Infirmary, Cohen may at one time have attempted suicide. Contrary to popular belief, suicide is not a trait common amongst pathological sex murderers.

David Cohen was not Jack the ripper for the simple reason that the ripper was somebody else. Cohen was however a realistic suspect and for this reason Martin Fido deserves a good deal of praise. Unlike the flying pig candidates forever being catapulted into the air by obsessed and semi-obsessed ripperphiles, Cohen had wings, wings given to him by meticulous research. Leaving aside the Police suspects, he was the first genuine candidate in almost a century of Ripperology. The others simply wasted everybody's time and allowed one of the most odious men in history to laugh at us from his grave.

But the theorists we have met in this chapter were merely pot boilers, warm up comedians for the real masters of myth and inanity, the friends of the ripper society (albeit unintentionally). These we are about to meet. Perhaps they captured the public mood. The decade of the sixties which had opened so brightly petered out amidst general disillusionment and gave way to the anarchic gloom of the seventies. Possibly then the ripper theories of this period were, in their own tiny way, a symptom of our dissatisfaction with our lives and with institutions which we no longer respected or trusted. Whatever the underlying causes, the seventies did untold harm to the search for Jack the ripper and its effects are still being felt today. The sorry saga opens in November 1970.

Chapter Eight: The Stowell Debacle

'Since every Jack became a Gentleman,
There's many a Gentle Person made a Jack'
(Richard III Act 1 Scene 3)

Thomas Stowell was a harmless old man with a very dangerous bee in his bonnet. A Doctor of some distinction who specialised in Industrial Medicine, Stowell spent the last years of his life working on a preposterous theory that Jack the ripper was none other than Prince Albert Victor, Duke of Clarence and Avondale, Grandson to Queen Victoria and the heir presumptive to the throne!

The British, it is said, are a nation of eccentrics. Eccentricity and the ripper murders make a heady brew. Mix them up with another great British obsession, the Royal Family and the pot starts to boil over. Throw in conspiracy and cover up, the odd charlatan and everybody's love of a good scandal and the whole mess positively explodes into a bacchanalian orgy of mythomania and fantasy.

Stowell first aired his theory over lunch with writer Colin Wilson in 1960. Wilson had just published a series of articles on the ripper murders in the 'Evening Standard'. He correctly attached little credence to Stowell's rambling yarn, but ten years later the Doctor found a more receptive audience in the shape of Nigel Morland, Editor of 'The Criminologist'. Morland published Stowell's claims in the November, 1970 edition of the magazine. Briefly, they were as follows.

Prince Albert, who liked to be known as Eddy, had contracted syphilis on a world cruise in 1880. The Prince was a keen huntsman who was sexually aroused by watching deer being cut up; the process also taught him something of anatomy. By 1888 his syphilis had reached its tertiary stage and fused with his latent sexual sadism to send him running amok in the streets of Whitechapel, killing and disembowelling prostitutes. The Royal Family were aware of these human hunting expeditions and placed Eddy under the care of Sir William Gull, Physician in ordinary to the Queen. They had a fright when a medium named Robert Lees turned up at Gull's West End residence with a police officer but Gull covered up for the Prince with a story that he, Gull, suffered from memory lapses and had once found blood on his shirt. Eddy appeared to respond to treatment, the murders ceased and in 1889 he embarked on a five month cruise. However, he suffered a relapse, was brought home and died three years later of general paralysis of the insane, a condition induced by syphilis. A grieving nation was told that he had succumbed to influenza.

The 'Criminologist' article caused a world wide sensation. Unhappily, it also killed it author. Stowell realised too late the enormity of what he had done. Throughout the article he had referred to Eddy only by the letter 'S' and now he sought to deny that the Prince was his suspect. He died eight days after the

'Criminologist' was published. Behind him he left a legacy which he would not have wanted and could not have imagined even in his worst nightmares. Ripperology was about to take off into the outer regions of the bizarre and the fantastic.

A reasoned analysis of Stowell's claims shows them to be the innocuous musings of an old man with too much time on his hands. Prince Eddy was not Jack the ripper and had no connection with the murders other than to recoil from them in horror along with the rest of Society. Modern day research suggests that he was a closet homosexual, but there is absolutely nothing about him that paints a portrait of a sadistic sexual killer. And crucially he had alibis. Eddy's movements during the Autumn of 1888 are well documented. On August 31st and September 8th he was in Yorkshire, September 30th Abergeldie, Scotland where he lunched with the Queen, and November 9th, Sandringham.

Stowell produced no semblance of a fact to back up his allegations. He was friendly with Sir William Gull's son in law, Theodore Acland, and claimed to have been told certain things by Gull's daughter, Caroline. One was the story of the medium and the policeman calling at the house; another was an entry in her Father's diary which she had seen stating: "informed (blank) that his son was dying of syphilis of the brain". Stowell also claimed that there were whispers that Sir William himself was the ripper. He wrote:

> '...it was not unnatural for the rumour mongers to pick on a most illustrious member of my profession of the time — Sir William Gull'.

In fact nobody had ever picked on Sir William Gull until Stowell dragged his name into the case in 1970. The diary entry, if it existed, provides no clue as to who Sir William was referring to. As for the medium Robert Lees, the time has come to lay this particular hoax to rest.

Anybody who has seen Thames Television's mini series 'Jack the Ripper' (1988) and the earlier film 'Murder By Decree' (1979) can be forgiven for thinking that Robert Lees played a major role in the ripper investigation. In fact his involvement in the case was entirely fictitious. Lees, who also claimed without a shred of proof to be Queen Victoria's medium, was a self aggrandising publicity seeker who claimed to have tracked the ripper down to a West End mansion where he was questioned by Lees and a Police Officer. Afterwards the man, an eminent physician, was removed to an asylum. It was a variant on this story which Stowell said he had heard from Caroline Acland. In fact it never happened. It was a figment of Lees' imagination designed to enhance his reputation as a clairvoyant. Lees did approach the police during the murders. On October 2nd and 3rd 1888 he made a nuisance of himself with the City Police who sent him off with a flea in his ear. He found Scotland Yard a little more diplomatic on the 4th but the end result was the same. Both police forces gave him what is colloquially termed as the bum's rush. There was no visit to a West End mansion and no deranged physician bundled off to a madhouse. Lees began to circulate the story some years after the murders. On his death in 1931 a lurid and quite ludicrous version appeared in the 'Daily Express'. Latter day research[*] suggests that it was concocted by one of the newspaper's crime reporters. I have no doubt that it was this story which fueled Thomas Stowell's over-ripe imagination.

Stowell was dead but the floodgates were open. First through them was Michael Harrison in 1972 with a full length biography of Prince Eddy. Central to the book were Stowell's claims and Harrison's own investigation of the ripper murders. A prolific writer on Victorian England, Harrison is not a crime historian, a handicap all too readily apparent from his book.

Had Michael Harrison simply stuck to demolishing Stowell's fictions then 'Clarence: The Life of H.R.H. The Duke of Clarence and Avondale' would have been a useful piece of work. Unfortunately he didn't. Instead he followed Stowell into the realms of the absurd;— surpassed him in fact. According to Harrison Eddy was not really the suspect; Stowell had simply convinced himself that he was. Unintentionally, the Prince was a sort of stalking horse for the real killer! But let Mr Harrison explain it in his own words:

> *'Clearly, then, Stowell is **not** talking of Eddy, though Stowell wishes us to think that he is'*[1]

But Harrison was operating from two false premises. One was that he took Stowell's nonsenses seriously. The other was that he was misled by Stowell's references to his suspect as 'S'. Had he been more diligent then he would have discovered that this was due to Nigel Morland who thought that the usual 'X' was boring. Stowell then substituted 'S' because it was the first letter of his own surname! There was no other reason.

'S however sent Michael Harrison off on a wild goose chase. Eventually he came up with Eddy's Cambridge Tutor and close personal friend, James Kenneth Stephen. His motive is once again best told in his on words:

> *'...I couldn't leave the reader high and dry, so what I did was find somebody I thought was a likely candidate'*[2]

Branding a man as a hideous sexual pervert is not a sort of game. Nor is James Stephen a likely candidate. In fact he is not a candidate at all, except for the entertainment of Mr Harrison's readers. There is not a glimmer of evidence against him. The only difference between James Kenneth Stephen and Peter J Harpick is that Stephen actually existed.

After Cannae Hannibal's second in command repeated to him the age old wisdom that nobody is born with all the gifts. For a while James Stephen looked

---

1   'Clarence' p152
2   Interview with the BBC August 17th, 1972

*   See Melvin Harris' 'Jack the Ripper: the Bloody Truth'

as though he might confound this truism. Scion of a wealthy and influential family, Stephen was a Cambridge Don at 26, a Barrister and a halfway decent poet with two books of published verse to his name. Inordinately handsome with a magnetic personality to match his looks, a brilliant classical scholar and a scintillating orator, Stephen appeared to have it all. And maybe he did until the age of 27 when fate quite literally struck him a cruel blow. He was hit on the head by a windmill vane and never properly recovered dying in a mental home six years later.

Harrison's theory, for what it is worth, is that Stephen and Eddy formed a strong emotional, possibly homosexual, attachment at Cambridge. Afterwards they went their separate ways but Stephen pined for his friend. Following his accident he became insanely jealous of Eddy's friendships with other men. However it was the Prince's relationship with a woman, real or symbolic, which tipped Stephen over the edge and he then embarked on turning Whitechapel into a slaughterhouse. His identity as the ripper became known but was covered up because of his relationship with Eddy. He was treated by Sir William Gull and watched carefully. In 1891 Eddy was betrothed to Princess Mary of Tech and fearing a new homicidal outburst Stephen's family finally had him incarcerated. After the Prince's death in 1892 he lost all will to live and effectively committed suicide by starving himself to death.

By way of "evidence" Harrison offers the following: (1) Stephen's friendship with the Prince (2) a strain of misogyny which runs throughout his poems (3) Stephen's accident and a skein of mental illness which affected his family in general (4) he was treated by Gull (5) the murders (of which Harrison claims there were 11) took place during University vacations or half term holidays (6) they were symbolically linked with 10 Royal or classical occasions (7) the 'Jack the ripper' poems are similar in style to Stephen's verses and both men formed the letter 'K' in the same way (8) Stephen had given one of his poems the heading "Air: Kaphoozelum". The actual poem itself was innocuous but the heading "Kaphoozelum" was derived from an unpleasant piece of doggerel about the murders of ten prostitutes in Jerusalem. Harrison reasoned (for want of a better word) that Stephen, as Jack the ripper, was imitating 'Kaphoozelum'! (9) Stephen's father and cousin went to pieces following the murders (10) Stephen had once skewered a loaf of bread with a swordstick, a definite Freudian link according to Mr Harrison!

Anybody who has to rely on spearing a piece of bread as proof of being Jack the ripper is clearly in deep trouble. And unhappily for Michael Harrison it gets worse. With the possible exception of the "from Hell" letter no serious commentator believes that the "Jack the ripper" correspondence emanated from the killer. Moreover, the similarity of style and the letter 'K' claimed by Harrison exists only in his eyes. But it is with the murders themselves that he really falls flat on his face.

Harrison lists eleven victims, Smith, Tabram, Nichols, Chapman, Stride, Eddowes, Kelly, Annie Farmer, Mylett, McKenzie and Coles. Without any shadow of a doubt Emma Smith was not a ripper victim. Nor were Alice McKenzie and Frances Coles and no criminologist or crime historian believes they were. Rose Mylett has hitherto been discarded; it is plausible that she was killed by the ripper but it will never be possible to say so definitely. Tabram, in my opinion, was. But as for Annie Farmer she was not a victim; she was not even murdered. Annie was a prostitute who suffered a minor throat injury whilst bilking a client in November, 1888. The police believed she had inflicted it on herself.

But the number of occasions on which the ripper killed was important to Michael Harrison. He was convinced that 'ten' was significant to his theory. This was crucial to his belief that Stephen was acting out 'Kaphoozelum'. Even so, in order to try to squeeze the square peg of his ideas into the round hole of reality he not only included a murder which never happened but was forced to count the double event of Stride and Eddowes' murders as one! There is really no need to go any further, but the plain fact is that none of Harrison's "tens" amount to anything coherent anyway. His royal and classical occasions are strictly a hybrid collection without any evidentary value[*] and the only connection with 'Kaphoozelum' is that Stephen once chose the name as the air for one of his own works.

There is nothing else. That the murders fell during University vacations or half term holidays would only be relevant if there was some genuine reason to associate Stephen with them, but there isn't. Stephen's father Sir James Fitzjames Stephen, a High Court Judge, suffered a nervous breakdown whilst conducting a trial in 1889 but his problems had actually begun four years earlier. Sir Leslie Stephen, cousin to James Kenneth, also had a breakdown in 1889 but this, and Sir James illness, are amply explained by the family history which was one of such occurrences. James Stephen was undoubtedly a close friend of Prince Eddy's and he seems to have disliked women but once again these factors would only be important if they were part of a solid block of evidence against him.

By themselves — and they are all that is left in the rag bag of Mr Harrison's peregrinations — they are nothing. On the other hand some facts to confound them. James Stephen exhibited no signs of violent tendencies during his tragic decline, he fitted none of the descriptions of the ripper and possessed no known knowledge of the East End of London. And he was certainly not Sir William Gull's ever elusive patient dying from syphilis.

If this sounds harsh towards Michael Harrison it is because it is harsh. Theorizing on false premises and without hard evidence about a suspect plucked from peaceful obscurity to keep audiences happy is simply not good enough. But to soften it a little, Harrison was seduced by the controversy surrounding

---

[*]   He gets three of the dates wrong anyway

Stowell's idiosyncrasies. He, Harrison, set out with a decent objective and allowed himself to be carried away. Others were to produce far worse without his basic integrity.

The Stowell bandwagon rumbled on. Amidst the crevices which it left were two outstanding works on the ripper; Donald Rumbelow's 'The Complete Jack-the-Ripper' and Richard Whittington-Egan's 'Casebook on Jack-the-Ripper',[*] also a meritorious assessment of the case against one of the genuine Police suspects, Montague Druitt, in Dan Farson's 'Jack-the-Ripper'. But these were books given to the serious study of the crimes and, for the moment, that had departed to the periphery of ripperology. The inmates had taken over the Asylum.

Whether Frank Spierings 'Prince Jack' is a serious analysis of the murders is entirely a matter for his readers to judge and I am not one of them. An American ex-private detective, he and his work were much praised by Nigel Morland. Unfortunately, the book was never published in Britain and my attempt to get a copy from his US Publisher in 1989 ended in failure. Spiering took the Prince Eddy and James Kenneth Stephen theories one step further and amalgamated them. Prince Eddy was the ripper supported and encouraged by Stephen who wrote the letters and poems. Lurking in the background was Sir William Gull, who treated them both[**]. Spiering claims that his case is supported by Gull's private notes which he saw in the New York Academy of Medicine. Amongst them, a document stating that he, Gull, had informed the Prince of Wales that Eddy was dying from syphilis of the brain. Regrettably nobody else has ever seen these notes and the Academy cannot trace them. Without them the theory is strictly on a par with Edward Larkins' Portuguese seamen and serious comment is impossible.

Spiering's book was published in 1978. It failed to generate a great deal of interest, not because the Public had grown tired of royal rippers, but because Spiering had been ferociously upstaged two years earlier. It is now time for the entry of Thomas Stowell's ultimate creation, his alter ego writ large, his Frankenstein Monster. Ladies and Gentlemen, please put your hands together for Stephen Knight and the Masons!

The saddest part of the whole story is that Knight was such a talented writer. He had a powerful and evocative style of prose, the ability to hold his readers in the palm of his hand and do what he wanted with them. Such art is dangerous; it bears a heavy responsibility for integrity. Used wrongly it seduces the unwary and makes lies truth. Unhappily, Stephen Knight chose to prostitute his gift. 'Jack-the-Ripper: The Final Solution' was a worldwide bestseller and an abomination. In part it relied upon history's most infamous faked book, 'The Protocols of the Elders of Zion', a grotesque forgery which carried within itself the seeds of a far more appalling final solution. Knight's work fortunately has no similar

---

[*]   Neither offered solutions.
[**] For a more detailed account see Melvin Harris' 'Jack the Ripper: The Bloody Truth'

potential for tragedy but in linking itself with the 'Protocols' it is contaminated by them.

The story begins in the early seventies when the BBC was planning a major series on the Jack the ripper murders. During the course of their research Paul Bonner, the Producer, and Elwyn Jones, one of the scriptwriters, had lunch with a senior police officer from Scotland Yard who put them on to one, Joseph Sickert, an artist and picture restorer living in Kentish Town. Sickert was at length persuaded to appear on camera and tell a story which was sensational even by the bizarre standards of the ripper murders. Within a few weeks of his television appearance Sickert was contacted by a young journalist named Stephen Knight who proposed a book on Sickert's revelations. Knight fleshed the story out and in June, 1976 his 'Jack the Ripper: The Final Solution' was published. The result was an even greater furore than Sickert had caused originally.

According to Joseph Sickert he is the Son of Walter Sickert, the famous painter, and the grandson of none other than our old friend his grace The Duke of Clarence and Avondale, Prince Eddy! In 1884 Eddy's mother, Princess Alix, became concerned about his development. Of Danish origin, Alix turned to the painter Walter Sickert who was himself partly Danish and whose father and grandfather had been artists to the Royal Court of Denmark. In effect Alix farmed Eddy out to Sickert in order to broaden his horizons.

Sickert had a studio in the heart of London's West End, at No 15, Cleveland Street. Here Eddy visited him during University vacations posing as his brother. Across the road from No 15 was a Tobacconist shop and in it worked a young woman named Annie Elizabeth Crook who also lived in Cleveland Street in a basement flat at No 6. Annie was friendly with another young woman who like her worked in the shop. This was none other than Mary Kelly! Exactly where Mary was supposedly living is unclear but she had links with a nearby Roman Catholic Convent at Harewood Place. Eddy was attracted to Annie Crook and the pair became lovers.

Sometime around July, 1884, Annie became pregnant and in April, 1885 she gave birth to a little girl, Alice Margaret, at Marylebone workhouse. Three years later, in 1888, Eddy and Annie were married at St Saviour's Private Chapel, Sickert and Mary Kelly being the witnesses.

Although the marriage was a closely guarded secret it somehow became known to the Government and the royal household. They were horrified. Not only was Annie Crook a common shop girl but she was also a Catholic. The Monarchy was deeply unpopular, anti-Catholic feeling was rife and the country was going through a bleak period of recession. The spectre of revolution hung in the air haunting the minds of the upper classes. Should it become common knowledge that the heir presumptive to the throne had married a commoner and Catholic and fathered a child by her then it might provide the spark needed for the overthrow of the monarchy swiftly followed by the rest of the aristocracy.

The Government decided it had to act and it did so ruthlessly. On the orders of the Prime Minister, Lord Salisbury, a raid took place on Cleveland Street. Eddy and Annie were both dragged off in separate carriages, he to the palace, she first to Guy's Hospital and then later to another hospital in the Fulham Road. Here she was certified insane at the instigation of Sir William Gull who also performed some sort of operation on her, presumably a frontal lobotomy. She was later released but the operation had rendered her a shambling derelict who drifted in and out of asylums until she died in the Fulham Hospital in 1921. She and Eddy never saw each other again.

There remained Sickert, Alice Margaret and Mary Kelly. On October 1st, 1888, the day after the murders of Liz Stride and Cathy Eddowes, an attempt was made to run the child down in a coach driven by John Netley, a freelance coach driver who had driven Eddy on his excursions to Cleveland Street. She was taken to St Bartholomews Hospital where she recovered. Sickert took the little girl under his wing but in February, 1892 Netley tried again, this time in Drury Lane. He was pursued by a crowd to Westminster Bridge where he killed himself by jumping into the Thames. Following this incident Sickert took the little girl to Dieppe. On one occasion Lord Salisbury visited his studio there and wordlessly paid Sickert £500 for a canvas he was finishing without even looking at it. When Alice grew up she married a boxer named Gorman who proved to be impotent and she turned to Sickert instead. By him she had two sons, one of whom, Charles, disappeared at the age of two. The other son was Joseph.

Mary Kelly meanwhile had fled to the East End, to a Sister Convent of the Harewood Place Nunnery, located in Dorset Street. After a while she moved to Miller's Court, fifty yards away, and fell in with a group of drunken prostitutes to whom she confided the story of the Royal marriage and the child. Those women were Polly Nichols, Annie Chapman and Liz Stride. Eventually, the four women tried to blackmail the Government. Salisbury turned to his fellow Freemasons for help leaving it up to them as to how they resolved the problem. The upshot was that Sir William Gull was charged with the task. Accompanied by John Netley and a third man, Gull tracked the four women down and slew them into silence. Cathy Eddowes was murdered in error because she sometimes used the name Mary Kelly[*]! Nichols, Chapman and Eddowes were all lured into Netley's coach where Gull killed them, afterwards dumping the bodies where they were found. Liz stride refused to get into the coach and was pursued and murdered by John Netley and the third man. Mary Kelly was jointly murdered by Gull and Netley. Nichols, Chapman, Eddowes and Kelly were all slain in accordance with masonic ritual by having their bodies torn asunder and their entrails draped over their left shoulders. This was also meant as a sign to his fellow masons that Gull was on the job. After it was over Gull became

---

[*]   She did in fact give this name to the Police on September 29th

dangerously insane and was carted off to an asylum where he was known as "Thomas Mason". Officially it was announced that he had died of natural causes, a pauper being buried in has place. He finally died in 1896 and was secretly interred in the same grave. John Netley returned to his obscure life as a coachman. The third man was a famous painter who later made veiled references to the truth about the murders in his pictures. His name? — Walter Sickert!

This then was the mind boggling story which was fed to a global audience in the long, hot summer of 1976. As a rather harrowing entertainment it is quite superb and has since spawned an enjoyable Sherlock Holmes v Jack the ripper film, 'Murder By Decree'. As a factual inquiry into the deaths of five tragic women in Victorian England it is an insult to their memories. And for Gull, Netley, Salisbury, Walter Sickert and Sir Charles Warren — accused by Knight of engineering a cover up to protect his masonic brethren — it was an obscene piece of character assassination.

To begin with it is not really one story but two. There are marked differences between the version which Joseph Sickert gave to the BBC in 1973 and that which appeared in Knight's book three years later.

Nobody has satisfactorily explained why Sickert only produced his tale in 1973, *after* Thomas Stowell had dragged Eddy and Sir William Gull into the fray. He claims to have heard it from Walter Sickert as long ago as 1939 when he was fourteen. In the BBC version he made no mention of Masons, Masonic rituals, coaches, blackmail attempts, Netley's attempted murder of Alice Crook in 1888 or a third murderer. These came later. And there is an absolute contradiction between the reasons given for the murders of the first four victims. In the BBC version they were slain to make it appear that Mary Kelly's murder was the last in a series of random killings. In 'the final solution' the victims were killed to snuff out a blackmail plot.

Joseph Sickert himself seems to be much given to making outlandish claims. His assertions of being Walter Sickert's son have failed to convince any authority on the painter's life and works particularly as the allegedly impotent William Gorman fathered four other children with Alice Margaret. Another of Joseph's startling statements is that Peter Sutcliffe, the Yorkshire ripper, once drove his car at him. People seem to make a habit of trying to run down Joseph Sickert and his family. Disturbingly, on June 18th, 1978 he recanted virtually the whole of his ripper story in the 'Sunday Times', admitting that it was a hoax. Only the paterfamilias with Prince Eddy survived.

However the retraction itself has subsequently been retracted and Sickert now has a document which he claims entitles him to share the profits of 'The Final Solution'. Moreover, this latest u turn opened the way for yet another foray into the Whitechapel murders, a book entitled 'The Ripper and the Royals' written by Joseph's friend Melvyn Fairclough. More of 'The Ripper and the Royals' later. For the moment let us stay with Mr Knight and his work.

Knight has received a surprisingly easy ride from more honest crime historians, probably because he is now dead. But he was quite prepared to indulge in character assassination of the most repulsive nature imaginable at the expense of men no longer able to defend themselves and he must reap what he sowed. He was himself quite brutal in branding other ripperphiles as liars when in fact they were guilty of no worse than simple error or faulty research. He wrote:

> *'It is a sombre reflection that in the case of Jack the Ripper several so called historians have betrayed their responsibility and set down in print their own invented details and baseless speculation as definite fact... Their dishonesty has done more to hinder the search for truth than all the hundreds of honestly concocted fables that have spilled from almost every front parlour and public bar in the East End.'*[1]

As I shall demonstrate, people who live in glass houses should not throw stones.

Knight's opening claim is the link between the Sickerts and the Danish Royal Family. According to Dr Wendy Baron, a leading expert on Walter Sickert and his work:

> *'There is no known connection between Sickert and Princess Alexandra. There is no evidence of any remotely intimate relationship between the Sickert family and the Danish Royal Family'.*[2]

For good measure Princess Alix was probably the last person to have thought the World of Art a suitable place for her son. When Eddy's first tutor, Canon John Neale Dalton, attempted to stimulate his interest in French by getting him to read Dumas, his initiative brought a very sharp reproof from Alix:

> *'Though I have no doubt that Dumas' novels are very interesting still I cannot help thinking that Novels, are not useful reading and do the boys no good'.*[3]

Knight ignored Dr Baron's assessment and the Princess's letter to Canon Dalton — even though it is quoted in Harrison's biography of Clarence — and the scene now moves on to Sickert's studio in Cleveland Street. Or rather it doesn't because Sickert never had a studio there. No 15 was in fact pulled down in 1886 and rebuilt the following year as a Nurses Institute. Sickert did eventually set up a studio in the area but in adjacent Fitzroy Street and not until 1922! Annie Elizabeth Crook did exist and she was Joseph Sickert's Grand-

1   Jack the Ripper: The Final Solution p47
2   The Ripper Legacy p49
3   'Clarence' p69

mother, giving birth to Alice Margaret on April 18th, 1885 at Marylebone Workhouse. Annie is described on the birth certificate as a confectionery assistant of Cleveland Street, Fitzroy Square. The name and occupation of the father are left blank. So far so good. But according to Knight, Annie Crook also lived in Cleveland Street, at No 6, and it was from this address that she was abducted in 1888.

Happily not. No 6 was demolished in 1887, rebuilt as part of an apartment block and renamed Cleveland Residences. The inaugural tenant of No 6, Cleveland Residences was an *Elizabeth Cook* who lived there from April, 1888 to 1893, when she died age 73. As for Eddy being the father of Alice Margaret, the child would have been conceived in late July or early August 1884. From June 18th to August 18th, 1884, Eddy was in Heidelberg.

Three years later, says Knight, the couple were married at St Saviour's Private Chapel. Absolutely no trace of such a marriage at anywhere called St Saviour's has ever been found*. However, this apparently non-existent wedding gave the government apoplexy and sent a shudder through the Royal Family, mainly because Annie Crook was a Catholic. Again no. The records of Marylebone Workhouse (a strange place for even an illegitimate Royal baby to be born) show that she was Church of England as were her parents and sister.

Annie's fate following her abduction is a particularly tragic and poignant part of the story. Fortunately, most of it is pure fiction, as is Knight's account of Alice Margaret living with Sickert, first in London and then in Dieppe. The records indicate that Alice was living with her mother up to at least 1906. For part of that time they lived at 9, Pitt Street and later 5, Pancras Street, where Annie was employed by Crosse & Blackwell. On one occasion she served a prison sentence during which Alice was sent to a holiday camp. The records also indicate that from 1906 to 1913 Annie's mother was living with her. She did die in a Fulham lunacy ward but the evidence is that she only became insane at the end of a hard and depressingly impoverished life. The institution in which she died was in fact a workhouse infirmary and not a private hospital as Knight implies.

There was a John Netley and he was a coachman. Allegedly, Netley was not only an integral part of the Jack the ripper murder team but also twice attempted to kill Alice Margaret. On the first occasion she had been crossing Fleet Street with a relative when Netley's coach ran her over. Knight found that such an accident had occurred and triumphantly quoted the Press report of it. Indeed it did but the victim was not Alice Crook aged three, but one Lizzie Madewell, age nine.

On the second occasion, in February, 1892, Netley was alleged to have tried to knock her down in Drury Lane, crashing his coach into the bargain,

---

* Melvyn Harris makes the interesting point that Donald McCormick had previously raised St Saviours (Clinic) in 'the Identity of Jack the Ripper'

whereupon he jumped down and ran away pursued by an angry crowd. On reaching Westminster Bridge he threw himself into the Thames and was drowned. No record of the accident has ever been located, John Netley did not die until 1903 and Westminster Bridge is a long way from Drury Lane. There was an attempted suicide at Westminster Bridge on February 7th, 1892 but the man's name was Nickley. It was a deliberate act. Nickley took off his boots and coat and placed them under a seat before jumping into the water*.

Exactly how John Netley, the coachman, comes to be included in this garish story can only be guessed at but according to Keith Skinner and Martin Howells, Authors of 'The Ripper Legacy', Joseph Sickert has a photograph of Netley of a personal nature. This has led them to speculate that he might be Alice Margaret's real father and Joseph's Grandfather**.

The final part of the story centres of course around Mary Kelly. The Harewood Convent did have links with the Providence Row Convent in Crispin Street, next to Dorset Street, and there is a hand me down story amongst the Nuns at Providence Row that Kelly stayed there at one time. Possibly; the convent was also a night refuge and there is no reason why Mary should not have used it. But she arrived in the East End well before 1888, probably as early as 1885. It is plausible that she was friendly with Annie Chapman and Liz Stride. They were all occasional prostitutes, lived in close proximity to each other and may have used the same pubs. Polly Nichols however is much more problematic for the simple reason that she only arrived in Spitalfields on August 2nd, less than a month before her murder. And if these three women were, specifically, Mary's blackmail team then it is inconceivable that she would not have realised that they were all being silenced one by one, in which case she would surely have either raised the alarm or fled the East End.

Knight's tale of coaches and ritual murders is what reviewers of pulp fiction used to call "a rattling good yarn". And fiction is what it is. From start to finish. Ironically he almost stumbled on the truth by accident because Jack the ripper did drive a pony and cart. A coach, however, would have stood out like a sore thumb in Whitechapel, rather like Peter Sutcliffe touring the red light areas of Leeds and Bradford in a Rolls Royce or a Limousine.

How Freemasonry and its rituals came to be interwoven in this saga is an interesting topic in itself. Joseph Sickert made no mention of it when he appeared the BBC's 'Jack the Ripper' series. However, the subject had been aired separately in an earlier episode. How it so came we do not know. But, the BBC team were in contact with Scotland Yard and there is a suspicion that in the early seventies a power struggle was going on at the Yard between Masons and non-Masons. It would be wrong to speculate further without evidence but the story which went out over the airwaves to millions of viewers can only have

---

*   Melvyn Fairclough 'The Ripper and the Royals', claims this was a faked suicide
       bid by Netley to escape Inspector Abberline's attentions!

**   A photograph purporting to be Netley appears in 'The Ripper and the Royals'

been acutely embarrassing to Freemasonry. At this point I feel obliged to make it clear that I am not a Mason, nor have I ever been. But the order has received a very raw deal over the ripper murders and it is time to put this right.

The BBC's account harks back to the days of Solomon and may be entirely mythical. That however is immaterial. The story runs as follows.

Solomon's temple was being built by the masonic Grand Master, Hiram Abiff. A cabal of 15 Apprentice Masons conspired to extract Abiff's secrets from him, resolving to kill him if he withheld them. At the last moment twelve of the Cabal got cold feet and relayed the plot to Solomon. It was too late to save Abiff who was murdered by the remaining three, Jubela, Jubelo and Jubelem, Jubelem striking the fatal blow. The trio of assassins were brought before Solomon who had them executed in the following ways:

> Jubela; his throat cut and tongue torn out and buried on the sea shore where the sea would wash over his grave twice daily.

> Jubelo; his left breast torn open and his heart and vitals plucked out and thrown over his left shoulder.

> Jubelem; his body severed in two at the middle and divided to the north and south with his bowels being burnt in the centre.

The BBC team, making their own half baked contribution to seventies ripperology, speculated, or rather fantasised, that the ripper murders could have been part of some dark Masonic plot. They theorized that the murders of Annie Chapman and Cathy Eddowes resembled the ritual executions of Jubela, Jubelo and Jubelem and that the message scrawled on the wall in Goulston Street referred to the Masons and not the Jews. Here, the key word Was "juwes", not a mis-spelling for 'Jews' but a reference to Jubela & Co. Allegedly Warren, as a high ranking Freemason, had the message rubbed out for that reason.

Whether Scriptwriters Elwyn Jones and John Lloyd had their tongues in their cheeks when they penned this nonsense is unknown. Stephen Knight most certainly did not. It was too good an opportunity to miss and he made the most of it. When 'The Final Solution' was published the BBC's quirky theorizing had been turned into established fact. The Masonic connection has been dismissed by most subsequent writers but none has examined it in precise detail. I shall do so because it gives the clearest possible example of the way in which Knight sought to mislead everybody, his manipulation of the facts, opportunism and sheer deviousness. We begin with his description of the murder of Hiram Abiff.

> *'Having murdered Hiram the apprentices fled, but they were discovered... and they were themselves murdered, by the breast being torn open and the heart and vitals taken out and thrown over the left shoulder'.[1]*

---

1   Jack the Ripper, The Final Solution p168

Jubela, Jubelo and Jubelem were not in fact murdered. They were legally put to death by Solomon's Command, a point which Knight slyly omits because this was all part of his polemic against freemasonry and portraying legal execution as murder adds grist to his mill.

But the sleight of hand really gets under way when he compares the executions of the "Juwes" with the Whitechapel murders. No mention whatsoever is made of the ways in which Jubela and Jubelem were slain, only Jubelo. The reader however is left with the clear impression that all three men were killed in the same manner by having their breasts torn open and their hearts and vitals plucked out and thrown over their left shoulders. Even here there is a subtle but crucial difference between Knight's rendition of Jubelo's execution and that which is, or rather was, a part of Masonic ritual.* The word 'left' has been omitted in front of 'breast'. Yet the rest of Knight's description of the execution — reproduced by him in italics — is an exact quote from that given by the BBC**. As we shall see there is a reason for this omission.

The executions of Jubela and Jubelem were fundamentally different from that of Jubelo. This did not suit Knight at all so he discarded them and pretended that all three had died in the same way. No ripper victim had her tongue torn out, was left in or near water (although the Thames was only a short coach ride away), had her body actually severed in half or her bowels burnt. And to reverse the position only Jubela had his throat cut. Disinformation was riding high here.

Equally Cavalier (to put it mildly) is Knight's treatment of the murders themselves. Liz Stride was not mutilated so Knight has her refusing to get into the coach and being pursued and murdered by Gull's accomplices. Polly Nichols on the other hand was mutilated but not in any way which could be ascribed to Masonic ritual so she almost disappears from this part of the scenario, Knight explaining:

'there is no reliable description of the precise form her mutilation took'[1]

And a little further on:

'...she had certainly been "torn open" in true Masonic style'[2]

Both these statements are completely untrue.

The same crafty manipulation is evident with the deaths of Annie Chapman and Cathy Eddowes. It is at this point that Knight's omission of the word 'left'

1   Jack The Ripper: The Final Solution p168
2   Jack The Ripper: The Final Solution p169

*   The executions were dropped from English masonry early in the nineteenth Century.
**   See 'The Ripper File' (pbk edition)

comes into play. Jubelo specifically had his left breast torn open. But this did not dovetail with Chapman's and Eddowes' mutilations so what was specific now became a generality which in turn made the two murders appear more like Jubelo's execution.

Both victims had their intestines thrown over their shoulders but neither had her heart removed. No mention is made of this, no explanation given. Instead Knight hurries on to other details. He repeats the canard that Chapman's brass rings were found at her feet* (a detail which he must have known was wrong because he had examined the police files), claiming that brass was a masonic symbol linked to Hiram Abiff. And Cathy Eddowes facial mutilations become a symbol of a masonic arch! This is mendacity writ large. Major discrepancies are ignored, errors repeated and butchery proselytised in order to circumvent the truth. Even with the intestines Knight was in trouble. Dr Bagster Phillips was not specific as to which shoulder Annie Chapman's intestines had been draped over. Cathy Eddowes was left with most of her intestines thrown over her *right* shoulder. Knight's explanation of this is that the killers were in a hurry. In fact the ripper placed a small part of Cathy's intestines *between her left arm and her body*.

Naturally, Knight ignored this. Well he would wouldn't he.

The problems posed by Chapman's and Eddowes' murders were as nothing beside those of Mary Kelly's. She was the most extensively mutilated of all the victims. Virtually all her organs and her intestines had been removed from her body. But nothing had been placed on either shoulder and her killer had taken her heart away with him. How then was Knight to wangle Mary's death into the masonic fit up? He applied what is best described as the Edgar Wallace solution. Asked how his character would escape from a seemingly impossible situation, Wallace replied— "see next week's issue". That episode opened: 'with one bound — was free!' I use the comparison not to be flippant (there is nothing frivolous about the murder of a young woman), but because this is precisely the tactic which Knight used. He wheeled out a painting by Hogarth, himself a mason, depicting a rather gruesome operation and claimed that it was an exposée of a masonic ritual which the murderer had been following step by step as he butchered Kelly! The comparisons which he lists have nothing to do with the execution of Jubelo (or for that matter any other known form of masonic ritual) but, like Wallace, Knight banks on his readers having by this time forgotten what the original proposition was. For the record Hogarth's painting 'The Reward of Cruelty' was an attack on 18th Century Surgical methods**. The plain fact is that none of the Whitechapel murders had anything to do with so called masonic ritual and when that doctrine is applied the killings actually contradict each other.

Lord Salisbury was not a Freemason. Nor did he pay Walter Sickert £500 for a painting. This was purloined for Knight's collection of lies from a story

---

* See chapters three and four.
** Violence and obscenity were often used in 18th Century lampoons to emphasize the point being made.

recounted by Walter Sickert to his friend Osbert Sitwell. Salisbury had commissioned a portrait from a painter named Vallon for £500. His silence when paying for it was caused by his disgust at its quality. The painting itself still hangs in the family home.

Sir William Gull was 72 when the ripper murders took place, hardly an age when anyone would want to be driven around the streets hacking prostitutes to death. Particularly if they had suffered a stroke the previous year as Gull had. Gull was a distinguished physician who rose from very humble origins to become one of the foremost medical men of his day. Knight begins his book with a quotation from Shakespeare: 'Here comes my noble Gull catcher'. What he actually does is to traduce the reputation of a man far better than he was, load it with false calumny and walk away with a lot of money into the bargain. Do not ask for evidence against Gull. There isn't any. None whatsoever.

The Freemasons have only themselves to blame for the attacks of the Stephen Knights of this world. Any quasi secret society is an open invitation for charges of conspiracy and connivance. However, in order to indict the Masons Knight was forced to rely heavily on the aforementioned 'Protocols of the Elders of Zion' which can justifiably be described as a sort of Nazi handbook for attacking Jews and Masons. Allegedly written by Zionists seeking world domination it was in fact an anti semitic forgery. Its exact origins are a matter of dispute. Some say it originated in France at the time of the Dreyfus affair, others that it emanated from Czarist Russia and was used to incite pogroms there. Later, it helped fuel Hitler's paranoid fantasies. This then was the tome which Stephen Knight employed to link masonry with the ripper murders. Any further comment is superfluous.

The third man was grafted on to the conspiracy between Sickert's television appearance and Knight's finished manuscript. Originally he was supposed to have been no less a person than Sir Robert Anderson! But Knight thought that Anderson was a horse that would not even get out of the starting gate, let alone run and so he turned instead to Walter Sickert. Joseph was kept in the dark about this manoeuvre until the manuscript was finished. After some argument he was persuaded to sign a document agreeing with Knight's conclusions and this appeared as a postscript to the book. Joseph has since repudiated it and continues to do so.

Perhaps the most obvious flaw in the Walter Sickert scenario is the very idea of a young and talented Artist, sensitive, rational and well balanced, stalking the slums and helping to murder and mutilate a number of poor women:— including one whom he knew and liked. The thing is unreal; absurd. It was a piece of breath taking effrontery on Stephen Knight's part. He sought to justify it by claiming that Walter Sickert was obsessed by Jack the ripper and painted clues to the truth into his pictures.

Walter Sickert was certainly interested in the ripper murders. One could well imagine him reading the books and articles on the subject which appeared during his lifetime. He had a ripper yarn of his own; a story about a young veterinary student who occupied a room before him being the killer. The story itself is simply another hoary old landlady tale. Its main interest lies in the fact that the ripper story which he allegedly regaled Joseph with was not the first he had told. But be that as it may, the fact that Walter Sickert was something of a Ripperphile is hardly evidence that he was a ripper himself. Experts on Sickert have also pointed out that he was interested in other crimes as well, particularly the unsolved murder of a prostitute in Camden Town in 1906. A young artist named Robert Wood stood trial for it and was very properly acquitted. Sickert himself later painted a series of pictures about the murder. As for the so called 'references' to the ripper murders which Sickert allegedly put into his works, the kindest comment is that Knight simply allowed his imagination to run riot. Walter Sickert did *not* murder anybody, was *not* part of a conspiracy to murder anybody and knew no more about Jack the ripper than anyone else did.

I have dwelt at length on Stephen Knight's fables not to expose him as a fraud — that has already been done by previous writers — but because of the effect which his falsehoods have had on any serious study of the crimes. 'The Final Solution' was a global bestseller, without any doubt the most popular 'ripper' book of all time. A great many of its readers were new to the subject and became convinced that Knight's book held the answer. Most of them will probably not have read subsequent works exposing it as a fake, or be aware of Joseph Sickert's confession that it was a hoax. Because of this sensible analysis of Jack the ripper and his crimes has suffered. Martin Fido, author of 'The Crimes, Detection and Death of Jack the Ripper' says of Knight:

> '...he holds an honoured place among historians of Jack the Ripper'.[1]

Whilst I agree with Fido that Knight's research did throw up some genuine nuggets, I am afraid that I must demur from his conclusion. Stephen Knight was not an historian of merit. He produced mainly vile character assassination. He damaged the quest for the truth about these murders and set it back many years.

Melvyn Fairclough in 'The Ripper and the Royals' (1991) repeats many of Knight's canards, although in his case it is clear that he has a genuine belief in them. Indeed, his beliefs are quite extraordinary. Joseph Sickert now not only claims descent from the Duke of Clarence and Walter Sickert but also the poet Dryden. His grandmother Annie Crook was not really just a humble shop assistant but was related to James Kenneth Stephen, Lord Salisbury, Lord Arthur Somerset (equerry to the Prince of Wales) and Sir Charles Warren. In Joseph's

---

1   The Crimes, Detection and Death of Jack the Ripper p196

words: 'it was all one big family affair.'[1] There is even an implication that Mary Kelly might be descended from the Kings of Ireland.

But the story is only just beginning. It is inferred that Eddy's younger brother, King George V, was not really sired by Edward VII at all but Grand Duke Nicholas of Russia. If true, then by birth the rightful king of England is in fact Joseph Sickert!

Another mind boggling story — call it a twentieth century update of 'The Prince and the Pauper' — centres around Joseph's elder brother Charles, allegedly also Alice Crook's offspring by Walter Sickert. This story runs that King George V's fifth child, Prince John, died secretly as a baby and was replaced in the Royal household by Charles Sickert who died in 1919 still masquerading as the Prince.

Meanwhile, poor old Eddy had not perished in 1892 but, in the best traditions of 'The Man in The Iron Mask', was shut up in Glamis Castle[*] where he survived until the age of seventy three, frightening children (touch of Hammer horror here), writing poetry, painting pictures and fretted over by Inspector Abberline.

The pièce de resistance is still to come. Edward VIII, the late Duke of Windsor, on discovering that his father was illegitimate, his uncle still alive at Glamis, and the truth behind the ripper murders, resolved never to accept the throne. This, and not his love for Mrs Simpson, were, according to Sickert and Fairclough, the real reasons behind his abdication! And we all thought the ripper crimes were just the tale of a serial killer and his victims!

As for the murders, the same team has saddled up again but with one exclusion, Walter Sickert, and no less than *ten* additions. Prince Eddy, James Stephen and Sir Charles Warren became fully fledged members of the cabal, Lord Arthur Somerset and Lord Euston, soon to be revealed as prominent homosexuals (see the next chapter) appear as invigilators, Sir Robert Anderson is 'in' again, the Duke of Marlborough prelates and two shadowy supporting heavies, John Courtenay and Frederico Albericci (allegedly Gulls's ex-footman) render their services. Missed anybody out? Ah yes. The Capo Di Capo, the supreme honcho, Lord Randolph Churchill, younger brother of Marlborough and father of (wait for it) Sir Winston Churchill. Salisbury again sets them on to silence the royal marriage blackmail scheme, Eddy's brother, the future George V, a hands wringing figure in the background. Not even Winston Churchill remains unsullied, Fairclough theorizing that he might have destroyed papers pointing to his father's guilt when he became Home Secretary in 1910.

Emma Smith is added to the list of the ripper gang's victims (poor Martha

1   'The Ripper and the Royals' Second (pbk) Edition p155

*   Scotland

Tabram must feel very left out) and Mary Kelly escapes the Miller's Court holocaust, a Winifred Coilis being murdered in her place. Afterwards the 'dirty dozen' fall apart. Eddy plans to murder Queen Victoria and is pushed over a cliff by Albericci and Netley. Netley in turn is silenced by Albericci and Stephen is banged up in his lunatic asylum where he too is probably done to death. But not before revealing all to Abberline who records it in a series of diaries, passed to Walter Sickert and handed down to Joseph. One can perhaps be forgiven if this brings to mind Michael Caine's* disgust in the final scene of Thames 'Jack the Ripper'.

Hard evidence may of course exist to substantiate some of these claims (aside from the ripper) but you won't find it in Mr Fairclough's book.

The (hopefully) dying embers of this grotesque saga belong to Jean Fuller and her offering, 'Sickert and the Ripper Crimes' (1990). Mrs Fuller's mother, Violet, was friendly with a woman named Florence Pash, in turn a friend of Walter Sickert's and allegedly, also of Mary Kelly. According to Florence Pash the story of Prince Eddy's illicit affair with Annie Crook is true. Alice Margaret was Eddy's daughter and she did have an affair with Walter Sickert which produced Joseph Sickert. Pash also claimed to have been with Alice Margaret when Netley tried to run her down in 1892. Her account, given to Violet Fuller in 1948, goes on that Kelly was blackmailing Sickert; that Sickert knew the ripper's identity and, echoing Knight, left references to the crimes in some of his paintings. But the crux of the story was that Sickert was able to describe the bodies of the victims as if he had seen them and from this Violet Fuller deduced that he must have viewed them at the murder sites. This in turn led Jean Fuller to hypothesise that Walter Sickert himself was Jack the ripper and committed the crimes to put an end to Kelly's blackmailing activities.

The highest level on which this can be put is chinese whispers. Florence tells Violet who makes assumptions and in turn tells Jean who jumps to conclusions. It has taken a very long time for the story to emerge, which is puzzling, and there is no corroboration of it. Mrs Fuller also repeats the erroneous tale of Salisbury buying the painting from Sickert. As with so many ripper theories it is highly speculative but soft at the core where hard evidence should be.

We end this chapter where we began, with Dr Stowell. A declining old man, once respected, listened to, his opinions sought after, now seeking attention in the twilight of his life. His ripper fantasy stemmed from this (Dutton's too) and no doubt he came to believe in it, a sort of obsessional delusion. Had he presented a medical theory to the 'Lancet' then they would have required supporting data before publishing it. Unhappily the 'criminologist' applied no such criterion. Apparently anybody with a ripper theory could wander in off the street and get it published. The Editor, the late Nigel Morland, was a ripperphile himself and seems to have had a weakness for stories linking the murders to the monarchy.

The latest book on the ripper, 'Murder and Madness: The Secret Life of

---

*   Caine plays Abberline

Jack the Ripper' by David Abrahamsen (1992) returns to Stowell and then builds on Michael Harrison's work to promulgate a theory that Eddy and James Stephen carried out the murders together. Essentially this is Frank Spiering's theory carried forward but with Stephen as prime mover and not just writing the letters.

Dr Abrahamsen depicts Eddy and Stephen as homosexual misogynists, fixated in different ways by their mothers. Abrahamsen is a distinguished American psychiatrist who has interviewed many murderers, including David Berkowitz (see chapter five), and I am not competent to assess his freudian judgements. However they obviously suffer from one major weakness: the data he is using comes from biographical details and not information offered at first hand. In 1988, Dr Murray Cox, a consultant psychotherapist at Broadmoor, had this to say about the ripper and his motivations:

> *'Unless one knows an individual at depth for a prolonged time, knowing his fantasies, his dreams, understanding his inner world from the inside, we're really left with conjecture, inference and really guessing... we don't know.'* [1]

A second point which can fairly be made is that sexual killers traditionally seek victims of their own sexual orientation. Heterosexuals kill women, homosexuals kill men and bi-sexuals both. As far as I am aware there is no known case of a strictly homosexual serial killer murdering women, or vice versa for that matter. For good measure, Dr Abrahamsen's psychological profile of the ripper differs quite substantially from the profile prepared by the F.B.I. serial killer unit.

Which brings us to the hub of the problem. Whilst it is obviously important to know the sort of man you are looking for, psychological evidence, even based on uncontroverted first hand knowledge, cannot be wholly substituted for evidence actually linking the perpetrator with the crimes. This is what Dr Abrahamsen attempts to do. It doesn't work. Without supporting facts he is left blathering about rumours connecting Eddy with the ripper, a theme he returns to over and over again. 'Another name bandied about' (p103) 'Contemporary gossip claimed' (p112), 'what had earlier been talked about' (p165) and 'rumours that were rife' (p181). These rumours never existed. Until Thomas Stowell brought the Prince into the case his name had never been linked or associated with the Whitechapel murders in any way, shape or form. It is surely high time that this whole suppurating mess was now decently laid to rest.

We can now turn away from these assorted Peter J Harpicks and look at the police suspects. Two names emerge prominently. Neither was Jack the ripper but is important to say why they were not and see why the police got it wrong.

---

1   'Timewatch: Shadow of the Ripper' BBC Television July, 1988

Chapter Nine: Monty Druitt's Flying Circus

If there was a league of Jack the ripper suspects then Montague John Druitt would top it. Years of research, hundreds of thousands of words and many gallons of printers ink have gone into branding this mediocre schoolteacher and failed Barrister as history's most notorious serial killer. Sadly, it has all been in vain. Druitt was not Jack the ripper and all attempts to link him with the crimes have failed utterly.

Druitt was born on August 15th, 1857 at Wimborne in Dorset. His father, William, was a prominent local Surgeon. Druitt's mother, Ann, came from a family named Harvey and carried within her genes the seeds of paranoia and melancholia. Both her mother and her sister were committed to asylums, the mother killing herself and the sister attempting suicide. Two of Ann's own children were destined to take their own lives.

Montague at first seemed to be a gifted boy winning a scholarship to Winchester and then a place at Oxford. He also excelled at Sport winning the School Fives Championship at Winchester, a feat he later repeated at University. Cricket was his primary passion, one which stayed with him throughout his life.

The cracks began to appear whilst Montague was at Oxford. He managed only second class honours in classical moderations and slumped to a third in classics, the degree with which he graduated. Nor did he succeed in winning a cricketing blue as he might have hoped. Whether this was simply a case of a bright child who did not really have it at the highest level or hereditary mental illness had begun to set in we do not know.

After leaving Oxford in 1880 Montague took a job as an Assistant Master at a Crammer in Blackheath. He was to remain there for the rest of his short life. His salary would have been in the region of £200 per annum, about £13,000 by today's standards. It was neither an exciting job or a brilliant wage but saddled with such a poor degree Druitt could not have expected better in the teaching profession. Then as now the good jobs are the preserve of those with the best academic qualifications.

In 1882 Montague sought to better himself by studying for the bar. He had shone as a debater at Winchester and may well have imagined that he had a talent for advocacy. If so then he was to be sadly disappointed. Called to the Bar of the Inner Temple as a member of the Western Circuit in 1885 he joined Arthur Jelf's Chambers at 9, King's Bench Walk, but no briefs were to ever come his way. By 1887 he had been reduced to finding work as a special pleader, a sort of technical advisor to other Barristers, normally carried out by law students. As with university his career simply failed to take off. Still, there were consolations. Although he gained nothing from his father's Will when William died in 1885 he had already received a lifetime gift of £500, worth today £30,000, and he may also have received financial support from his mother. He involved himself in a variety of sporting activities, most notably his beloved cricket. By 1888 he had become a member of the M.C.C., played regularly for two clubs and was the Secretary of one, Morden in Blackheath.

The death of William Druitt was not unexpected: he had been in poor health for sometime. But it had a catastrophic effect on Ann Druitt who began a downward spiral into insanity. In July, 1888 she attempted suicide, was certified insane and incarcerated in the Brooke Asylum at Clapton. It was at this point that Montague's life began to unravel dramatically. Had he had a successful, upward looking career to sustain him then he might have coped with it. But instead there stretched before him the vista of drudgery and empty years going down to the grave. No matter how much he immersed himself in sport it could never be a salve for the failure and the deep gloom that was settling over him.

At the end of November Druitt was suddenly dismissed from his teaching job at Blackheath. Exactly why we do not know; all attempts to discover the reason have ended in failure. The consensus is that it was for homosexual behaviour of some sort. Although this cannot be verified it seems the likeliest explanation.

On December 1st Montague set out on what was to be his final journey. He travel led from Blackheath to Charing Cross and there purchased a return ticket to Hammersmith. He was not to make use of the return half. Instead, on that bleak and blustery day, he walked down to the River Thames at Chiswick, put four large stones into each pocket of his top coat and drowned himself. It was a sad end to what had once been a promising life.

The body lay in the Thames for almost a month before being fished out. An inquest was held on January 2nd, 1889 at Chiswick. The only witness of substance was Montague's elder brother, William, a solicitor living at Bournemouth, who produced a suicide note from Montague. The exact text has not survived but the 'Acton, Chiswick and Turnham Green Gazette' summarised it as follows:

> *"Since Friday I felt I was going to be like Mother, and the best thing for me was to die."*

In Montague's pockets had been found the usual personal possessions, two cheques amounting to £66.00, £2.86 in cash, the return ticket and a first class season ticket from Blackheath to London. The verdict, suicide whilst of unsound mind, was a formality.

And there it should have ended. An unhappy and unfulfilled young man had taken his own life. He should have been allowed to rest in obscurity and peace. And he would have done but for the antics of one man. Step forward Sir Melville Leslie Macnaghten.

Macnaghten was born into a distinguished family in 1853. Educated at Eton he did not go on to University but was instead sent to India where he became an overseer at his family's tea plantations. Here he met James Monro who became a close personal friend.

In 1887 Macnaghten returned to England and wandered into the infighting between Warren and Monro. Monro was effectively expanding his power base and had gained reluctant approval from Warren to create a post of Assistant chief Constable for his department. This position Monro offered to Macnaghten. However the appointment was subject to Warren's approval. Initially this was given but the Commissioner then seems to have learnt of Monro and Macnaghten's personal friendship for he withdrew his endorsement on the spurious ground that Macnaghten had once been beaten up by Hindoo's! The reality of course was that he realised that Monro was manoeuvring one of his cronies into a position of power and influence. But, politics aside, it does need to be said that Warren was quite right to object: Macnaghten had no knowledge or experience of police work and was not a man who had demonstrated any outstanding capabilities.

Monro became Commissioner in November, 1888. The following June Macnaghten finally took up his appointment as Assistant Chief Constable. Monro's tenure did not last very long. In 1890 he went the way of his last two predecessors and was forced out of office. Macnaghten survived becoming Chief Constable after the death of Frederick Williamson in 1889. There was however a gap before Macnaghten stepped into the post in 1890 which suggests that there may have been opposition to his promotion. In 1891, without his mentor to protect him, an attempt was made to shunt Macnaghten off into the uniform branch. This may have been office politics; on the other hand it could have been due to limited efficiency. Whatever the reason the move failed and he remained in the Detective division. He might have hoped to become Assistant Commissioner and Head of the C.I.D. when Anderson retired in 1901 but was passed over in favour of Major Edward Henry. Henry himself became Commissioner in 1903 and Macnaghten finally stepped into his shoes. His performance was distinctly lacklustre, the "police review" commenting that his rule did not enhance the proficiency or reputation of the C.I. Department. A career which probably brought more reward than it merited came to an end with his retirement in 1913. He died in 1921.

Macnaghten's importance is that he was effectively the first of the ripperphiles. The murders clearly fascinated him. For many years he kept the gruesome police photographs of the victims in his desk and he gave as one of the two greatest disappointments of his life the fact that he had never had the opportunity of catching the ripper personally. He did however become involved in the case with results which leave much to be desired.

In 1894 Macnaghten was asked to prepare a report for the Home Secretary on a series of sensational newspaper articles which claimed that the ripper was a certified lunatic named Thomas Cutbush. Early in 1891 there was a series of knife attacks on women in Kennington. A man named Colicott was arrested but witnesses failed to identify him and he was released. A few weeks later two more women were attacked in the same district. This time the police arrested Cutbush. Rather embarrassingly he had earlier been detained as a lunatic but had escaped the same day. Equally embarrassingly, the police made no attempt to establish whether Cutbush could have been the ripper. Instead he was quietly packed off to Broadmoor. It was left to the "Sun" newspaper to make the case against him which it did three years later.

The report which Macnaghten produced was destined to become the single most controversial document in the history of ripperology. Now known as "The Macnaghten Memorandum" it has been endlessly debated, discussed and argued about until it has become almost a case within a case, a little cottage industry in its own right. The reality is that it is a thoroughly mediocre, haphazard and badly researched job of work.

There are believed to exist three versions of the Macnaghten Memorandum. One, which first came to light in 1959, is partially typed and partially handwritten. It was in the possession of Sir Melville's daughter, Lady Aberconway. The second is handwritten by Macnaghten and is in the police files which are now in the Public Records Office. The third cannot be traced but was seen by the writer and journalist Philip Loftus in 1950. The first two versions differ slightly, the third is thought to be markedly different but the source for this is Mr Loftus's memory. Without belittling him it would be unsafe to place too much reliance on his recollections of a document seen many years before. We are therefore left with the first two versions. Both name the same three suspects but in one Macnaghten gives his opinion as to which of them he personally favours. The name of that suspect is Montague John Druitt.

Objectively, we should only really examine the memoranda in terms of what Macnaghten says in the Scotland Yard version. This was personally written by him less than six years after the murders and when he had access to the files and the opinions of Anderson and Swanson.

The first part of the Memorandum discusses the Kennington stabbings and the case against Cutbush as the ripper. Macnaghten then goes on to give a potted history of the Whitechapel murders. But it is just about at the halfway point that the document becomes really interesting. Dismissing the possibility of Cutbush being the ripper, Macnaghten writes:

> *"No one ever saw the Whitechapel Murderer: many homicidal maniacs were suspected, but no shadow of proof could be thrown on any one. I may mention the cases of 3 men, any one of whom would have been more likely than Cutbush to have committed this series of murders:-*
>
> *(1) A Mr M J Druitt, said to be a doctor and of good family, who disappeared at the time of the Miller's Court Murder, whose body (which was said to have been upwards of a month in the water) was found in the Thames on 31st December — or about 7 weeks after that murder. He was sexually insane and from private info I have little doubt but that his own family*

believed him to have been the murderer.

(2) Kosminski, a Polish Jew and resident in Whitechapel. This man became insane owing to many years indulgence in solitary vices. He had a great hatred of women, specially of the prostitute class, and had strong homicidal tendencies; he was removed to a lunatic asylum about March 1889. There were many circs connected with this man which made him a strong 'suspect'.

(3) Michael Ostrog, a Russian doctor and a convict, who was subsequently detained in a lunatic asylum as a homicidal maniac. This man's antecedents were of the worst possible type, and his whereabouts at the time of the murders could never be ascertained."

This is the hub of the Memorandum. Afterwards Macnaghten goes on to attack inaccuracies in the 'Sun' and delves into other murders such as Alice McKenzie and Frances Coles. He ends by implying — very strongly — that McKenzie and Coles were both murdered by Thomas Sadler.

In the Aberconway version Macnaghten amplifies his details of the three suspects. Druitt's age is wrongly given as 41, Kosminski is said to have resembled a man seen near Mitre Square by a police constable and more is provided on Ostrog, to wit: (he)'was habitually cruel to women and for a long time was known to have carried about with him surgical knives and other instruments'. Macnaghten also give us his choice of suspect, Druitt, although he adds: 'The truth, will never be known.'

It has been suggested that the Aberconway version is a copy of a first draft of the Scotland Yard Memorandum. This is very possible. Before being put up to the then Commissioner, Sir Edward Bradford, such an important report would have had to have been approved by Anderson who no doubt would have shown it to Swanson for his comments. Anderson would then have corrected some of the mistakes and returned it to the Chief Constable for a rewrite, minus also his personal opinions. Anyone well versed in writing reports for superiors will know that such opinions are often anathema.

Despite this the final Memorandum is littered with errors and statements for which there is no verifiable justification. Druitt is said to have been a doctor which of course he was not. Macnaghten also seems to have been under the impression that he had committed suicide immediately after Mary Kelly's murder. In fact it was three weeks later. Kosminski, the second suspect, was not committed to an asylum in March 1889 but almost two years later in February 1891. Although Kosminski was certainly a lunatic there is no supporting evidence for Macnaghten's claims of homicidal tendencies, or of a great hatred towards women. He had once threatened his sister with a knife and on another occasion picked up a chair against a man but that was all. Ostrog fared no better. He was a recidivist with a long record of theft and swindling but he had no history of violence aside from once threatening a police officer with a gun he had stolen. By no stretch of the imagination could he be described as a homicidal maniac.

One may also question Macnaghten's claim that he was confined in an asylum after 1888. This seems to be an exaggeration of what is actually known about Ostrog which is that he had once unsuccessfully feigned insanity to escape a gaol sentence but later succeeded in getting himself transferred to an asylum. He was released as cured on expiry of his sentence five months later which suggests that he was shamming again.

Just how close a grasp Macnaghten had on his facts can be seen from his remark that 'nobody ever saw the Whitechapel Murderer'. In fact he was definitely seen with Eddowes, Stride and Chapman and probably Kelly also. As for the statement that either Druitt, Kosminski or Ostrog was a more likely suspect than Cutbush this too really does not stand up to examination. Unquestionably, Macnaghten was right in concluding that Cutbush was not the ripper and for the reason which he gave in the report; a man who had killed and mutilated several women would not have recommenced his activities over two years later and been content with just wounding. But a more substantial theoretical case can be fashioned from the facts about Cutbush than from what we know about Macnaghten's trio of suspects.

Thomas Cutbush was in his mid twenties when he attacked two women in Kennington. Whether he also carried out the earlier assaults is problematic. Macnaghten was convinced that Colicott was the guilty party escaping justice because of faulty identification (his words). But anyone familiar with the workings of the police mind knows that they have never arrested the wrong man in their history! Here, Macnaghten was also oblivious to the possibility of Sadler's innocence even though no case existed against him. The Kennington stabbings certainly came to an end with Cutbush's arrest. Forced to do the research which they should have done three years earlier the police came up with some interesting data on Cutbush. He had previously worked in the East End and apparently contracted syphilis in 1888, afterwards suffering from paranoid delusions. He had thrown in his job and taken to studying medicine books and staying out at night, returning home in a muddy condition. His movements could not be accounted for during the murders. Although he was very definitely not the ripper he was actually a more plausible suspect than the men Macnaghten named. Ostrog's crimes were economic: he was a thief and a confidence trickster. The hard evidence against Kosminski is examined in the next chapter but it is fair to say at this point that he was more dangerous to himself than others.

Which leaves us with Macnaghten's favoured suspect, Montague Druitt and the question of why he suspected him.

Macnaghten says that he was sexually insane. Given his penchant for exaggeration we cannot be sure what this means; perhaps simply that Druitt was gay. As for the private information, who provided it and more importantly what was it?

The information could conceivably have come from Walter Boultbee, private secretary to Warren, Monro and Bradford. Boultbee's wife Ellen was the niece of Alfred Mayo who in turn was distantly related to Thomas Druitt, an uncle of Montague's. But by far the likelier possibility is that Macnaghten received it either from his own or Druitt's family. There were links between the two families from India. However, exactly what that information was is a complete mystery. All that we know is that Montague's family suspected him and even here Macnaghten's comments are guarded. He is much more circumspect than with Kosminski and Ostrog whom he very tendentiously portrays as homicidal maniacs even though his conclusions are not supported by the known facts. Macnaghten also admits that there is no actual evidence against Druitt and although he promoted him as a suspect he seems to have been in a minority of one in doing so. Druitt was of no interest to Anderson and Swanson whilst Abberline was openly dismissive. Asked about the drowned doctor theory which by 1903 had been aired in Major Arthur Griffith's 'Mysteries of Police and Crime' Abberline told the 'Pall Mall Gazette'

> *'I know all about that story. But what does it amount to? Simply this. Soon after the last murder the body of a young doctor was found in the Thames, but there is absolutely nothing beyond the fact that he was found at that time to incriminate him'.*

Macnaghten himself was distinctly unwilling to leave whatever materials he had for posterity and crime historians to judge. He destroyed his papers on Druitt before leaving Office!

What we are left with is the suspicion that like so many ripperphiles since Macnaghten wanted a suspect of his own and seized upon a piece of gossip told to him by a relative of Montague's, something no more reliable than the Frank, the mad accountant story.

*****

Since the discovery of the Aberconway version of the Memorandum in 1959 the most strenuous efforts have been made to find some glimmer of evidence against Montague John Druitt. All have been entirely fruitless.

The discovery of the document itself was the work of writer and broadcaster Dan Farson. In 1959 Farson was presenting a weekly television series called 'Farson's Guide to the British'. Its highlight was two programmes on the ripper murders broadcast on the 12th and 19th of November. Farson's research took him to Wales where he was permitted to examine the Aberconway copy. It appeared to be a major breakthrough but unfortunately Farson was placed under very considerable restraints by Lady Aberconway. He could view the Memorandum but not quote from it, nor divulge any of the suspects' names. In the end he had to settle on screen for merely giving Druitt's initials and displaying a copy of his birth certificate with the name blanked out.

No such constraints were placed on Tom Cullen six years later when he published his book 'Autumn of Terror'. Cullen, an American Journalist and Crime Historian domiciled in England, was granted access to the Memorandum and published Druitt's name for the first time. 'Autumn of Terror' is a work of great skill and lucidity which falters at the end because Cullen was unable to find any extraneous evidence to associate Montague with the crimes. In the finish Cullen was reduced to theorizing that Druitt might have done voluntary work in the east end and committed the murders to draw attention to the dreadful social conditions there. Unfortunately "might" is the most commonly used word in the annals of Ripperology. No amount of them will substitute for hard evidence.

Seven years later Dan Farson finally published his own book on the case. Despite considerable media hype the end result was again disappointing. However, Farson did expand on Cullen's work and produced the exciting possibility of a document which might provide the missing link between Druitt and his inclusion in the Macnaghten Memorandum. He also thought that he had found a firm connection between Montague and the East End. A new player now appears on the scene, Montague's cousin Lionel.

Lionel Druitt (1853–1908) was a doctor who emigrated to Australia in 1886 and lived there for the rest of his life. Farson discovered that Lionel had at one time been in general practice in the Minories. It was not much but it did provide a tenuous link between the Druitt family and the East End of London. Moreover Farson's research had thrown up something else about Doctor Lionel Druitt; the possibility that he had once written a pamphlet entitled 'The East End Murderer — I Knew Him'.

Early in 1959 Farson had appealed for information about the 'ripper'. This produced the usual collection of "my granny spoke to him in the street" letters but there were some items which were of interest. One was a letter from an A Knowles who mentioned a document called 'The East End Murderer — I Knew Him' written by Lionel Druitt, Drewett or Drewery in 1890 and privately printed by a man named Fell in Dandenong, Australia, which Knowles claimed to have read. A second letter seemed to provide independent corroboration of Knowles' recollections and the existence of such a document. This was from a Maurice Gould who claimed to have learnt from two separate sources of the existence of such a document. One of Gould's sources, a man named McGarrity had spoken of papers owned by a W.G. Fell of Koo-wee-rup, Australia which proved the ripper's identity. The second, a journalist named MacNamara, had told Gould the same story adding that Fell had obtained the papers from a man called Druitt who had stayed with him.

At the time Farson had not seen the Macnaghten Memorandum and so the letters did not seem particularly relevant. The Knowles letter vanished anyway when somebody stole Farson's file on the murders! The discovery of Macnaghten's papers shed an entirely new light on the matter. The stolen letters and Gould's recollections now assumed massive importance and led Farson to go to

Australia himself. Unfortunately his visit was abortive. The nearest Lionel Druitt had ever come to the Dandenong ranges was the town of Drouin sixty miles away and he had not arrived there until 1903. No W.G. Fell could be traced in the Dandenong ranges or Koo-Wee-Rup. At nearby Lang Lang Farson found a storekeeper named Fell but he proved to have no connection with the Fell who had allegedly printed the pamphlet. A comprehensive search of the Archives in Australia failed to reveal the existence of 'The East End Murderer — I Knew Him'. Ten years later the BBC, researching for their series on Jack the ripper, made the same searches as Farson. Despite the massive resources at their disposal they too drew a complete blank.

Nothing daunted Dan Farson continued to believe in the existence of 'The East End Murderer — I Knew Him' and it provided the cornerstone of his case against Montague Druitt. From it he constructed a workmanlike thesis. As a child Montague might have watched his father perform operations and gleaned some anatomical knowledge from them. During University vacations he could have stayed with his cousin Lionel in the Minories and gotten to know the East End. His own hopes of a good career faded, he was overtaken by the same insanity which had afflicted his mother and became Jack the ripper. After killing his victims he fled to his chambers at King's Bench Walk. Later, overcome by his terrible deeds, he committed suicide. Farson's research revealed that Ann Druitt had died in the Manor House Asylum at Chiswick in 1890 and it seemed logical to assume that he had paid her a final visit there before killing himself nearby. The Family meanwhile had become aware that Montague was the ripper, later relaying this privately to Macnaghten. Lionel Druitt had been in Australia for two years prior to the murders but Farson found out that Montague's younger brother Edward, an Army Officer, had visited Australia in 1889. Here again, logic suggested that Edward had acquainted Lionel with the news after which Lionel wrote 'The East End Murderer — I Knew Him'. Farson did not pretend that there were not weaknesses in his theory but he did his best to explain them. Unfortunately for him the whole thing was a house built on sand.

Lionel Druitt's association with the East End was just fleeting. He practised in the Minories for only a few months from 1879 to 1880. Barristers' Chambers are used to conduct their business from, not as residences. Although Ann Druitt died at the Manor House, Chiswick, she was not transferred there until May, 1890. In December 1888 she was being cared for in Brighton.

Perhaps the weakest point of all was what Farson — and others — have wrongly perceived as the strongest. Sexual murderers do not commit suicide. They feel no pity, no remorse. They are like sharks feeding. The victim is there to be used and discarded. In Dennis Nilsen's chilling phraseology, they are the dirty platter at the end of the feast[*]. The only known case in which a sexual murderer *may* have committed suicide is that of the Thames Nude Killer in the

---

[*] In November 1983 Nielson was sentenced to life imprisonment for the murders of fifteen young men.

mid sixties. A security guard suspected by the police of being the murderer killed himself after which the crimes ceased. But the suicide was not due to remorse. The suspect feared that his arrest was imminent. Montague Druitt's suicide note was very decidedly not that of a man suffering remorse for a string of ghastly murders; — or for that matter a man fearing that he was about to be arrested. It was that of a melancholic. Today we call that illness acute depression. He believed, rightly or wrongly, that he was suffering from the same malady which had struck down his mother. He had also just been sacked from his job.

In terms of documentary evidence the most powerful argument which Farson had was 'The East End Murderer — I Knew Him': — if it existed. Here he was forced to rely on Maurice Gould and his own memory of the contents of the missing Knowles letter. And memories play tricks on us. They embellish and distort things we have seen or heard. Often names and details which we think we have read turn out to be quite different when we go back and check on them.

Farson had attempted to trace the mysterious Mr Knowles but without success. By the mid 1980's two other men were on the same trail, Martin Howells and Keith Skinner researching a book of their own on the ripper. Like Farson they drew a blank with Knowles but they were able to track down Maurice Gould, now an old man. Gould's recollections were hazy but he recalled his conversation with MacNamara. They had discussed Frederick Deeming who was hanged in Melbourne in 1892 for the murder of his Wife. That topic had led on to Jack the ripper and MacNamara had produced two or three handwritten sheets of paper which, Gould thought, had been a confession of some kind. On Dandenong and Druitt or Drewett Gould could no longer remember why they had been important. Nor could he recall whether the name Fell was correct. In point of fact it was. Independent research was to establish that Gould had worked for W.G. Fell and that he was the same Storekeeper whom Farson had interviewed all those years earlier!

What seems clear from all this is that Dan Farson was unintentionally led astray by Maurice Gould's flawed memory of events many years earlier. Essentially Gould and MacNamara were talking about Frederick Deeming and *his* possible candidacy for Jack the ripper! Although Deeming was hanged for the Melbourne Murder he had earlier murdered his first wife and their four children and buried their bodies under the floor in Liverpool. It was said that before his execution he confessed to two alleged ripper murders[*] and for many years Scotland Yard kept his death mask in their black museum as Jack the ripper's death mask. In fact it was widely believed that Deeming was the ripper until it was discovered the he had been in South Africa during 1888. Deeming used aliases during his time in Australia one of the most frequent being Drouin or Drewen! As for the handwritten confession, MacNamara was apparently

---

[*] This was strongly denied by his solicitor.

trying to sell it for £500! Obviously it was a faked version of what Deeming may or may not have said in the death cell.

Here then was the answer to at least one part of the puzzle.

But that of Knowles? Here again independent research, uncovered by Howells and Skinner, helps towards the answer. There *was* a pamphlet of sorts along the lines of 'The East End Murderer: — I Knew Him' and it had appeared in 1890. But it was as a supplement to an Australian Newspaper, the 'St Arnaud Mercury' and had been reprinted from the 'New York World'. The gist of it was that yet another landlady suspected her lodger of being the ripper. It had absolutely nothing to do with Montague Druitt and most certainly did not emanate from Lionel although interestingly enough he had lived in St Arnaud until three months before the story was printed.

The most practical explanation of the Knowles letter is that it was this document he was referring to. Knowles was writing a very long time after seeing it and his memory must be held as distinctly suspect. Perhaps he confused the supplement with Deeming. He may have heard of — or even known — Lionel Druitt and mistook him for Deeming/Drewen/Drouin. But it is more likely that Dan Farson's memory played tricks on him and he unconsciously fused Knowles' letter with Gould's. Whatever the case we can be sure of one thing, 'The East End Murderer — I Knew Him' by Lionel Druitt never existed.

Although their research effectively destroyed the last vestiges of Farson's case against Druitt, Howells and Skinner nevertheless became convinced that Montague was the ripper. Their book, 'The Ripper Legacy' published in 1987, is thoroughly readable and entertaining but its conclusions are more in keeping with a novel than a work of non fiction. Broadly speaking, the Authors theorize that Druitt was a member of a clique of upper class homosexuals including possibly the Duke of Clarence (again). Somehow they found out that Montague was the perpetrator of the ripper murders and murdered him to protect themselves from scandal when he was caught. As an important corollary to this, Druitt bore an uncanny likeness to Eddy and there were fears that suspicion could fall on the Prince because of it.

The first thing which needs to be said is that the theory itself is tenable. A year after the ripper murders the police uncovered a male brothel in Cleveland Street which was being frequented by a number of aristocratic homosexuals including Lord Euston and Lord Arthur Somerset, the Equerry to the Prince of Wales. There was also evidence that Eddy had visited the place. At once a cover up swung into action. Somerset was allowed to flee abroad. Eddy was referred to only as P.A.V. and his involvement kept a closely guarded secret. Euston escaped prosecution by claiming that he had been tricked into going to the brothel. The press was muzzled with the exception of an enthusiastic editor named Ernest Parke who tried to probe deeper. He was sent to prison on a trumped up charge. It is even possible that the affair helped precipitate Monro's fall from grace on the grounds that he initially allowed Scotland Yard to investigate a little too zealously. It was a thoroughly ruthless performance by the British ruling class and adds a great deal of weight to Howells' and Skinner's scenario. Additionally, Montague Druitt did resemble Eddy. But is there any actual evidence to back up Howells' and Skinner's assertions?.

The two authors believe that Druitt was lured to Chiswick, poisoned, and his suicide faked with the connivance of his elder brother William[*]. Why, they ask, should Montague have brought a return ticket from Charing Cross to Hammersmith if he did not expect to return? And if he was not travelling to Chiswick to visit his mother then who was he going to see? It was a long way to go to commit suicide. Howells and Skinner also drew attention to a lie which William Druitt told at the inquest, that Montague had no other relatives aside from himself and their mother. In fact there were three sisters and two younger brothers. What prompted this falsehood?

These are all pertinent questions. They are not however prima facie evidence of murder and conspiracy. Threatening to commit suicide is one thing; doing it is quite another. Obviously Montague did travel to Chiswick to see someone; perhaps a friend, perhaps a lover. Who or why we shall never know. Afterwards the final, irrevocable decision was made. He was after all a manic depressive and as such subject to violent swings of mood. As for William's lie, it was a very minor matter and clearly designed to shield the rest of the family from intrusion.

The major portion of Howells' and Skinner's case lies in trying to show that Druitt could have been a member of Prince Eddy's circle of friends. One does not want to be too harsh on a pair of good writers who did some outstanding research but the fact is that they failed completely. In the end they were reduced to the usual depressing collection of 'coulds' and 'mights' which are the hallmark of theories without substance. And underlying the whole failed exercise is one simple point: — there is still no evidence to prove that Montague John Druitt was Jack the ripper in the first place. Here the Authors were victims of their own success. Sterling research had blown Dan Farson's case out of the water but there was nothing to put in its place. Unhappily, their very strength was also their weakness. No amount of meticulous research could bring the crimes home to Druitt.

Howells and Skinner imagined that they had established a link of sorts between Montague and the East End. Ann Druitt's first Asylum was in Clapton which lies to the North East of Whitechapel. According to the Authors, his route when visiting his mother would have taken him directly through Whitechapel. Moreover, after killing Cathy Eddowes the ripper fled into Goulston Street, 'Northwards towards his (Druitt's) ailing mother' theorize Howells and Skinner. Unfortunately not. By then Ann Druitt was no longer resident at Clapton. She had been transferred to Brighton. Her stay in an Asylum on the periphery of the

---

[*]   The autopsy found no evidence of poison.

East End lasted for only a few short weeks. And that was that. The authors could find nothing else beyond this non sequitor to provide even a ghost of a piece of evidence against Montague.

The case against Montague Druitt does not exist. It never has. All he was was a hapless young man drawn into a nightmare of innuendo because he killed himself at the wrong time after which he posthumously fell foul of Sir Melville Macnaghten's obsession with the murders.

There let it rest.

Chapter Ten: Ripper's Cube: The Riddle Of Aaron Kosminski

The Jack the ripper murders and their aftermath embraced no less than five police Commissioners, two assistant Commissioners and three Senior Scotland Yard Detectives. But anyone expecting a wealth of material from them would be disappointed. They left very little and what the did say was mostly insignificant.

Surprisingly, it was the Commissioners who provided the least. Sir Charles Warren left no detailed views about the killer. According to his Grandson and Biographer, Watkins Williams, Warren believed that the ripper might be the drowned doctor (sic) found in the Thames on December 31st, 1888 (i.e. Druitt), but it is plain that Sir Charles was simply repeating what he had read in Major Arthur Griffith's, 'Mysteries of Police and Crime'.

James Monro was Metropolitan Police Commissioner during the vital eighteen months following the murders. By rights he should have been a mine of information on the subject. If he was then he divulged very little of it. In 1890 he told 'Cassells Magazine' that he had formed a decided view on the case but added that the Police had "nothing positive" to go on. Irritatingly this was his only public reference to the atrocities which had propelled him into the Commissioner's chair. His unpublished memoirs are barren on the ripper but his grandson, Christopher Monro told Howells and Skinner in the eighties that Monro's theory was, quote, 'a very hot potato'. Unfortunately, Christopher Monro's recollections were third hand and he was recounting them at a distance of many years. All in all, James Monro left crime historians with virtually nothing to work on.

The same is true of Sir Edward Bradford, who succeeded Monro, and Sir James Fraeser who was City Commissioner during the crimes. Neither left any views on the ripper whatsoever. The fifth Commissioner was Major Smith, Fraeser's deputy in 1888 and his successor two years later. Smith appears to have been a vain man and an egotist much given to boasting and exaggeration. Although he was keenly interested in the ripper his memoirs give no clue to his identity.

Of the Assistant Commissioners, Sir Melville Macnaghten's views are already known. This leaves us with Sir Robert Anderson and the three Senior Officers who worked under him on the case, Chief Inspector (later Superintendent) Swanson, Henry Moore, also a Chief Inspector, and Abberline. Moore's precise contribution to the investigation is unclear but he probably acted as a conduit between Swanson and Abberline. He left nothing of importance. Abberline, who coincidentally is buried in the same cemetery as Montague Druitt, endorsed only one candidate for certain and that was Severin Klosowski. Which brings us to two men who did have something interesting to say about the ripper, Anderson and the man he entrusted with the day to day running of the case, Donald Swanson.

Sir Robert Anderson is a puzzle and an enigma. Maybe that is the way he wanted others to see him; the way he wanted to be remembered. He was the sort of man who winks, taps his nose and says "I've got a secret", which would be highly appropriate because for many years he was employed on secret service work at the Home Office. Conversely he was devoutly religious and the author of some 22 books on christian theology.

Anderson was born in Dublin in 1841 and educated at Trinity College. He graduated Bachelor of Arts in 1862 and the following year was called to the Irish Bar. Seven years later he was also called to the English Bar. His secret service work, which was directed against Fenians, began in 1867. He seems to have been a natural survivor on one occasion thwarting a move to sack him because his most successful agent refused to deal with anyone else. Shades of John Le Carre's fictional Karla! How warmly Warren greeted his appointment to succeed Monro in 1888 is unclear. The Commissioner was in no position to object anyway. Their working relationship never had a chance to flower but Anderson seems to have gotten on well with Monro and Bradford. Evidence suggests that he was not overly impressed with Macnaghten, the No 2 foisted on him by Monro.

Donald Swanson was a career policeman who in today's force might well have risen all the way to Commissioner. He appears to have been a quiet, self effacing man. That he was very able no one can doubt. By 1888 he had a long record of successful arrests to his credit. Not being a professional policeman himself, Anderson perhaps singled Swanson out as someone he could lean on. The two men certainly developed a mutual respect and liking for each other. It is therefore no surprise to learn that they both opted for the same suspect, the second man mentioned by Macnaghten, Aaron Kosminski.

Aside from the fact that he was Polish, nothing is known about Kosminski's ancestry or early life. He makes his first appearance in ripper legerdemain in 1882 when at the age of either seventeen or eighteen he arrived in Britain. Whether he came directly from Poland or via some other country is unknown. Nor is it clear if he came by himself or with his family. However, he made his home with his brother, Wolf, in Sion Square, Whitechapel, and worked as a hairdresser.

Three years after his arrival things started to go seriously wrong for Aaron Kosminski. He began to suffer from delusions and ceased to work. On July 12th, 1890 he was admitted to the infirmary at Mile End Old Town Workhouse where it was noted in the records that he had been insane for two years. Three days later he was discharged into the care of a brother (or possibly brother-in-law) and apparently went to live in Greenfield Street, Whitechapel. Who looked after him there is unclear but it may have been a sister. His freedom lasted less than seven months. On February 4th, 1891 he was back again at the Mile End infirmary. This time no member of his family was willing to take responsibility for him and on the 7th he was taken to Colney Hatch Lunatic Asylum and certified as insane. The statements of the lay and medical witnesses in support of his certification ran as follows:

Jacob Cohen (Lay Witness):

'he goes about the streets and picks up bits of bread out of the gutter and eats them, he drinks water from the tap and he refuses food at the hands of others. He took up a knife and threatened the life of his sister. He is very dirty and will not be washed. He has not attempted any kind of work for years'.

Dr Edmund Houchin (Medical Witness)

'he declares that he is guided and his movements altogether controlled by an instinct that informs his mind, he says that he knows the movements of all mankind, he refuses food from others because he is told to do so, and he eats out of the gutter for the same reason'.

The Doctors at Colney Hatch added that Kosminski suffered from extreme delusions and aural hallucinations. These are the hallmarks of paranoid schizophrenia, a condition often attributed to Jack the ripper.

The cause of Kosminski's illness was given as indulging in self abuse. Although this now seems laughable, masturbation was thought in Victorian times to lead to insanity.

Kosminski remained at Colney Hatch for the next three years, during which time his mental condition deteriorated further. He became 'demented and incoherent', was unable to communicate properly and developed visual as well as aural hallucinations. The latter would seem to have been a natural progression of his illness but it is possible that the rest of his decline was also caused by environmental factors; the abysmal surroundings and the constant company of other lunatics. He exhibited no signs of violence except for one instance when he threatened an attendant with a chair. However, given the brutal treatment often meted out to patients in Victorian Asylums it may be that he raised it to defend himself.

In April 1894 he was transferred to the Leavesden Asylum for imbeciles. He was to spend the rest of his life in this wretched place dying there of gangrene in 1919. He was fifty four years old and had spent over half his life in the twilight world of the insane.

Thus Aaron Kosminski. A lunatic, yes. But was he Jack the ripper?

Without wishing to sound like a stuck gramophone needle it has to be said that there is virtually no evidence against Kosminski. Indeed, what we do know points decisively away from him. More of that later. For the moment let us concentrate on what the police, or rather Anderson and Swanson, had to say about Kosminski.

In 1910 Anderson published his autobiography 'The Lighter Side of my Official Life'. What he said about the ripper was highly controversial although strangely it seems to have elicited little comment at the time. Anderson wrote:

> *'During my absence abroad the police made a house to house search for him... And the conclusion we came to was that he and his people were certain low class Polish Jews, for it is a remarkable fact that people of that class, will not give up one of their number to gentile justice.*

> *'And the result proved that our diagnosis was right on every point. For I may say at once that 'undiscovered murders' are rare in London, and the Jack the ripper crimes are not in that category...*

> *'I should almost be tempted to disclose the identity of the murderer... But no public benefit would result from such a course... I will merely add that the only person who had ever had a good view of the murderer unhesitatingly identified the suspect the instant he was confronted with him, but he refused to give evidence against him'*

Now this is astonishing. The man in overall control of the hunt for Jack the ripper was saying that they knew who he was but let him go because the main witness was unco-operative! Yet Anderson's revelations were greeted with an almost universal shrug of the shoulders. Nobody took them seriously. In fact for nearly eighty years crime historians and ripperphiles dismissed them out of hand believing that Anderson had such a poor grip on his facts that he was referring to John Pizer and Emmanuel Violenia. In fact he wasn't. His suspect was Aaron Kosminski.

In 1980 Donald Swanson's grandson inherited Swanson's copy of Anderson's memoirs and made a startling discovery. Slotted in and around the text were some handwritten comments which his grandfather had made in pencil. Seven years later they were reproduced in the 'Daily Telegraph'. These jottings are now known as 'The Swanson Marginalia' and their effect has been to start a bandwagon rolling in favour of Kosminski as the ripper. Ignored for almost a century he has now become a vogue suspect for these horrendous crimes. As I shall show the accusations against him are false. But first the marginalia.

Under the text of the passage from Anderson's book which I quoted earlier Swanson added:

> *'because the suspect was also a jew and also because his evidence would convict the suspect and witness would be the means of murderer being hanged which he did not wish to be left on his mind. D.S.S.'*

Splaying out into the margin Swanson continued:

> *'And after this identification which suspect knew, no other murder of this kind took place in London.'*

At this point he ran out of space so he began again on the endpaper of the book.

'After the suspect had been identified at the Seaside home where he had been sent by us with difficulty in order to subject him to identification and he knew he was identified.

'On suspect's return to his brother's house in Whitechapel he was watched by police (City C.I.D.) by day and night. In a very short time the suspect with his hands tied behind his back he was sent to Stepney workhouse and then to Colney Hatch and died shortly afterwards — Kosminski was the suspect — D.S.S.'

Overall, what Anderson and Swanson were saying is quite straight forward. Kosminski had been identified as the ripper by a witness who had subsequently refused to give evidence against him so the police then kept him under surveillance until he could be safely locked away in an asylum. It appears neat and simple. Unhappily it is not. When we look at it in detail we find a whole labyrinth of complexity, a rubik's cube of riddle and mystery.

First, is the Marginalia genuine? Here the answer is a definite yes. Swanson's handwriting has been verified by experts and although graphology is not an exact science I see no reason to quarrel with it on this occasion. Were the Marginalia faked then it would be more detailed and would not contain the minor grammatical errors that it does.

The next question concerns Anderson's and Swanson's faculties. Had they been diminished by 1910? Once again the answer is in their favour. Anderson was 69 and Swanson 62. Their minds were still sharp and active without signs of decay. Which means that we can take their claims seriously and see where they lead us.

We begin by asking when Kosminski became a suspect. This is important in assessing both the case against him and the viability of Anderson and Swanson's assertions. According to Swanson he was identified at a place called the Seaside Home. This is presumed to be the Police Convalescent Home at Brighton which was known colloquially as 'The Seaside Home'. It was opened in March, 1890 which means that the identification could not have taken place before that date. That being the case it is extremely unlikely that Kosminski had come to the attention of the police prior to March, 1890. Some degree of corroboration for this is provided by Sir James Monro. In July and September of 1889 Monro wrote reports to the Home Office on the murders of Alice MacKenzie and the Pinchin Street torso, pondering whether they could be the work of the ripper. In neither report does he mention that the police were watching somebody or had a suspect in mind. In MacKenzie's case he concluded that she might well have been a ripper victim. Anderson was on holiday at the time but it seems inconceivable that Monro would have written his report without consulting Swanson. Swanson obviously did not mention Kosminski and the logical conclusion must therefore be that he was not a suspect at this time.

The Swanson Marginalia goes on to say that after the identification Kosminski was returned to his brother's home in Whitechapel where he was watched day and night by detectives from the City Police and that in a very short time he was taken to the infirmary with his hands tied behind his back. This seems to give us three possible dates for the identification, March-July 11th, 1890, July 12th-15th (during Kosminski's first stay in the infirmary) or July 16th to February 3rd, 1891. Exactly what Swanson meant by 'a very short time' can only be guessed at but it does seem to indicate that the identification took place towards the latter end of the third period, say around January, 1891. If Swanson can be relied upon then the evidence points to Kosminski not becoming a suspect until over two years after the murder of Mary Kelly. As we shall see, this is a crucial point *against* Kosminski being the ripper.

Even more important than the timing of Kosminski's candidacy is why he actually came to be a suspect. In the absence of the Scotland Yard files we can speculate only.

Donald Rumbelow in 'The Complete Jack the Ripper' thought that Anderson's suspect was John Pizer. We now know this to be incorrect but Rumbelow was perhaps on the right lines. Whether 'Leather Apron' actually existed, whether he was a composite of several different men or whether he was just an imaginary bogey man conjured up by fear we do not know. The important thing is that the police believed he was real and for a time they identified him as Pizer. Pizer was a Polish Jew who lived in Mulberry Street. Kosminski was also a Polish Jew and he lived in Sion Square *which is at the top of Mulberry Street*. Moreover, according to the 'Guardian' (September 12th, 1888) Leather Apron did not work which of course fitted Kosminski. Did the police still believe, over two years later, that Leather Apron was the ripper and that Kosminski (and not Pizer) was the real Leather Apron? The answer to this would seem to be yes and it is provided by Anderson himself.

Anderson wrote that during his absence the Police conducted house to house searches in Whitechapel and concluded that the ripper and his people were Polish Jews. He then goes on to state that this diagnosis proved right on every point. What he is saying could not be clearer. The police decided in 1888 that the ripper was a Polish Jew, never changed their minds and afterwards proved it to their own satisfaction when Kosminski arrived on the scene. Which in turn means that Leather Apron, whether he actually existed or not, was the man they were looking for first, last and always. A careful analysis of the Macnaghten papers bears this out. The missing third copy of the Memorandum seen by Philip Loftus must be treated with great caution but Loftus believes that Leather Apron was one of the three suspects in the copy that he saw. If it was yet another preliminary draft, altered to Kosminski and returned to Macnaghten by Anderson, then that would provide additional confirmation of Kosminski's identification with Leather Apron. It may also explain Macnaghten's claims that Kosminski had strong homicidal tendencies and a great hatred of women, claims which not only cannot be substantiated but which are actually contradicted by the medical reports on Kosminski. They do however exactly fit the picture which the police built up of Leather Apron. As an aside, it is also possible that Ostrog became a suspect because he too was a candidate for Leather Apron.

Now this does not by itself demolish the case against Aaron Kosminski although it does very seriously weaken it. We are still left with one piece of evidence against him his identification at the Seaside Home. Here we must look very carefully at what Anderson and Swanson said.

The Marginalia has been criticised for two minor errors. One is that Swanson referred to Kosminski being taken to a workhouse in Stepney and not Mile End. After almost twenty years one could hardly expect his memory to be absolutely precise on a detail as trivial as this. Mile End is next to Stepney and the error is of no consequence whatsoever. His second error is his belief that Kosminski died not long after being incarcerated at Colney Hatch. Once again the mistake is of no importance; it simply means that Swanson lost track of him after he was locked up and the case closed. He may have been confusing him with a fringe suspect named William Grainger who in 1895 was imprisoned for stabbing a prostitute in the stomach. The police went through the motions of investigating Grainger mainly, one suspects, to avoid the sort of embarrassment caused by the Cutbush affair a year earlier. Later, Grainger's solicitor spread a false story that he was the ripper and had died in prison[*]. Whatever the truth of the matter it really is of no consequence in assessing the Marginalia. For the most part Swanson is clear and specific. Kosminski was taken to the Seaside Home where he was identified by a witness who then refused to give evidence against him because he was a fellow jew. But there is in fact something not quite right about this, something which Swanson may have preferred to gloss over in his memory. The fact is that even if the witness had been prepared to give evidence the chances of a conviction were virtually nil.

For a start the police would have had the upmost difficulty in even getting Kosminski to Court. In July, 1890 the Mile End Infirmary noted that he had been insane for two years. Less than seven months later Colney Hatch certified him as a lunatic. In 1891 fitness to plead was governed by the M'Naghten rules. These dated back to 1843 when a man named M'Naghten attempted to assassinate the Prime Minister, Sir Robert Peel. He was found to be a hopeless psychotic, unable to distinguish between right and wrong, and was sent to an asylum. Given Dr Houchin's report and the diagnosis of the Colney Hatch Doctors, it is likely that Kosminski would have been found unfit to plead by virtue of the M'Naghten rules.

[*] Abberline also believed that a suspect had died in an asylum. It is not clear who he was referring to.

If that had not been the case and he had stood his trial, then even by the standards applied in 1891 Kosminski would have been acquitted through lack of evidence. Indeed, it is probable that the Magistrate would not even have allowed the case to go forward to the higher Court. The only evidence against Aaron Kosminski was the identification and this took place under circumstances wholly disadvantageous to him. He was not taken to a Police Station where the normal rules of identification applied. Instead, he was carted off to the Seaside Home. The way in which Anderson describes the identification implies very strongly that Kosminski and the witness were simply brought face to face without a formal identity parade. Even if there was one of sorts then the other members of the parade would have been Police Officers. Kosminski, a Polish Jew amongst Anglo Saxons, would have stood out like a sore thumb. Any identification in conditions such as these was meaningless.

Nor does the matter end here. Who was the Police witness? All we know for sure is that he was Jewish which narrows it down to two men, Israel Schwartz or Joseph Lawende*. In a Court of Law either man's identification would have been severely buffeted. Almost two years had passed since they had glimpsed the face of a briefly seen man in the darkness. Lawende had stated that he would not be able to recognise him again, whilst Schwartz's description, plus the Ripper's anti-semitic remark, pointed overwhelmingly to his being Anglo Saxon.

There was no other evidence against Kosminski. Had the identification been the centrepiece of a solid case against him then it is inconceivable that the Police would have allowed their witness to refuse to testify. Means of coercion were available.

Perhaps the most puzzling aspect of the Marginalia is the fact that it was the City Police who carried out the surveillance on Kosminski. Why was the Met not involved? We do not know, but one answer is that he was actually the City Police's suspect and that it was they who were trying to work up the case against him. Their files on the Ripper were destroyed during the blitz but there is independent corroboration that they were watching somebody. In 1946 'Reynolds News' printed the following article:

> 'Inspector Robert Sagar, who died in 1924, played a leading part in the Ripper investigations. In his memoirs he said: "we had good reason to suspect a man who worked in Butcher's Row, Aldgate. We watched him carefully. There was no doubt that this man was insane, and after a time his friends thought it advisable to have him removed to a private asylum. After he was removed, there were no more ripper atrocities."'

There are of course two points which do not fit Kosminski. First he did not work and secondly Colney Hatch was not a private asylum. But it is possible that

---

*   See Appendix Seven

he spent his days rambling around Aldgate and the error over the Asylum is probably one of memory. Sagar himself was a Detective Inspector with the City Force in 1890/1 and very highly thought of by Smith who wrote: 'a better or more intelligent Officer than Robert Sagar I never had under my command'. Unhappily Sagar's memoirs were never published and now appear to be lost, but it is very plausible that he was in charge of the daytime team that watched Aaron Kosminski.

If the City Police were in charge of the Kosminski investigation then it would seem that the Met, or more specifically Anderson and Swanson, adopted him as their candidate when the parallel with Leather Apron became clear. But the City Police on the other hand appear to have concluded, eventually, that Kosminski was not the ripper. This would explain a rather comical little row which erupted between Anderson and Smith in 1910.

Anderson's autobiography was first serialized in 'Blackwood's Magazine' before the book came out. Shortly after the 'Blackwoods' articles appeared, Smith published his own memoirs, 'From Constable to Commissioner'. In them he launched a vitriolic attack on Anderson and his claim to have identified the ripper, taking particular offence at Sir Robert's remarks about Jews. This in itself is eye opening particularly as Smith's remarks must have been a late addition to his book (finished manuscripts normally take 18 months to get into print). What triggered Smith's anger? Intriguingly, there is no reference whatsoever in 'From Constable to Commissioner' to the City Police watching a ripper suspect. Yet Sir Henry must have known about it. The City Police is a very small force, Smith was its acting Commissioner in September, 1888 and Commissioner from 1890 to 1901. He was deeply interested in the ripper murders and took personal command of the investigation into Cathy Eddowes murder. So why the silence? And why was he so annoyed with Anderson? Was it because the City Police had wasted their time with Aaron Kosminski only to see him now filched by Anderson as his candidate? Here Smith's summing up on the ripper is most illuminating:

> '...he completely beat me and every Police Officer in London'

Sir Henry's comments prompted Anderson to make some additional remarks of his own when 'The Lighter Side of My Official Life' appeared in book form later that year. Clearly responding to Smith's attack, Sir Robert hit back:

> 'In saying that he was a Polish Jew I am merely stating a definitely ascertained fact.'

But that was not Smith's opinion. Although he must have known about Kosminski, the former City Commissioner was totally unmoved by Anderson's claims. It seems clear that he thought Aaron Kosminski a waste of time and effort.

To sum it up, Kosminski was simply an updated version of Leather Apron. There was nothing to indict him as a gruesome serial killer beyond a so called identification which was in the highest degree unsatisfactory. In fact, what evidence there is exonerates him.

Past writers have generally attributed five victims to Jack the ripper, Nichols, Chapman, Stride, Eddowes and Kelly. If the case against Kosminski is to be believed then after killing Mary Kelly in November, 1888 he went for over two years without killing again, hardly the behaviour of a pathological sex murderer. Once the need to kill and mutilate has become firmly established then the killer's blood lust does not normally abate or go into remission. Paul Begg, 'Jack the Ripper: The Uncensored Facts' plays devil's advocate to this belief by pointing out that Peter Sutcliffe twice went for lengthy periods (although only half Kosminski's) without killing. Correct. But when we look at it in greater detail a different picture emerges. During his bouts of homicidal mania Sutcliffe's periods between attacks averaged nine weeks. But the ripper slew Nichols, Chapman, Stride, Eddowes and Kelly in just one nine week time span. We may find these sort of comparisons obnoxious but they suggest that 'Jack's' homicidal urges were far more pronounced than Sutcliffe's. It is difficult to imagine the London ripper being able to stop for any prolonged length of time. The usual tendency of this type of killer is to carry on until caught and the idea that he lapsed into inactivity for two years is really inconceivable.

Equally inconceivable is the idea that Jack the ripper was an obvious lunatic who scavenged food from the gutter. It has been argued that Kosminski may not have been noticeably insane in 1888. His admission records at Colney Hatch state that his present attack had lasted six months and was not the first, but that they had only commenced when he was 25. This however was an error which the Asylum swiftly rectified, appending their records that the duration of the attack was in fact six years. It is probable that the confusion arose from Kosminski's first admission to the Mile End Infirmary the previous July. He would have been 25 at that time and it seems likely that the Asylum mistakenly assumed that the first attack had taken place just before July 12th, followed by a second shortly after his discharge which then lasted for the six months prior to his arrival at Colney Hatch. Whatever the answer, the mistake was put right. The Mile End Infirmary's records noted that Kosminski had been insane for two years i.e., since the summer of 1888. From this, the evidence of the lay witness Jacob Cohen, and the corrected Colney Hatch records it is a logical deduction that Kosminski's illness began in 1885 and that by 1888 he was clearly insane. If that is the case then it is scarcely credible that this sad immigrant, caked in his own dirt and eating mouldy bread from the pavement, was even able to persuade frightened women to go with him let alone successfully carry out their murders and avoid capture. Nor, as far as I am aware, has any serial killer in history ever deteriorated into the gibbering imbecile that Kosminski ultimately became. It is without precedent.

An even stronger point against Kosminski being the ripper is the very nature of his illness. Without doubt he was a paranoid schizophrenic. At first sight this would appear to be a powerful argument the other way: the ripper may well have been a paranoid schizophrenic and here there are certain similarities between Kosminski and Peter Sutcliffe. Sutcliffe suffered from extreme aural delusions and later, after being incarcerated, visual hallucinations as well. He was subsequently certified insane and transferred to Broadmoor. Now this seems to dovetail neatly with Kosminski and it does except in one crucial way: Unlike Sutcliffe, Kosminski's aural hallucinations were not of a violent nature. Here again the medical evidence effectively demolishes the case against him. His voices told him that he was a God like figure who knew the movements of all mankind. He was paranoid and insane but not dangerous and the argument that he was a homicidal maniac suspends belief. We are asked to accept that the violent persona inside Kosminski in 1888 vanished leaving only the non violent persona who scavenged food in the streets and refused to wash; that the hideously perverted sexual desires just went away. It really is untenable.

The more the medical evidence on Aaron Kosminski is examined the less likely he is a candidate for the ripper. He drifts away on a pacific breeze. Perhaps even that is putting it too high. The reality is that in this nightmarish and bloodstained death race he doesn't even make it off the starting blocks.

It would be easy to criticise the police for wasting their time on Kosminski: easy and wrong. Anderson and Swanson were not simpletons: they were highly educated, conscientious men. They genuinely believed that they had the answer. There are two main reasons why they failed. The first is that the Jack the ripper murders were something totally new, something wholly outside their experience. Crime in the nineteenth century was very largely economic. This was something the police knew about, were comfortable with, knew how to solve. The ripper was completely different. Britain had had multiple killers before but never a serial killer, a joy or lust murderer as we have since come to call them. Suddenly all the normal rules, the established criteria, went out of the window. The police had no idea who they were searching for.

The second problem lay with what is both the police's greatest strength and greatest weakness, tunnel vision. Once the police have decided that they have got the right man or the right theory then their minds tend to close to other possibilities. In cases where they are right this refusal to be detracted is a tremendous asset providing the determination and the impetus needed to bring the case to a successful conclusion. But when they are wrong, as they were with the ripper, then it leads them further and further away from the truth. In 1888 and the succeeding years the deadly combination of tunnel vision and an unprecedented situation meshed together to lead to Scotland Yard's greatest failure. Whilst Anderson and Swanson were mulling over Polish Jews the real killer was already dead and buried. Saddest of all, Jack the ripper had actually come to their attention but because of their preoccupation with Leather Apron he was allowed to keep his cloak of anonymity.

Part Three

The Man Who Was Jack The Ripper

PROLOGUE

There is an old saying that nobody knows what is around the next corner. For Detective Lieutenant James Parr of Dundee C.I.D. thin was particularly true of the afternoon of February 10th, 1889.

It had been a routine day until his colleague, Lieutenant David Lamb, appeared in Parr's Office late in the afternoon.   Lamb was not alone. Indicating his companion, he told Parr:

'This man has a wonderful story to tell you'

Into the room behind Lamb stepped Jack the Ripper.

Chapter Eleven: Decoding Serial Killers

'...human beings have become disposable items. They are murdered by the thousand every year in the U.S.A., bodies used to satiate a perverted lust and then thrown away like so much garbage.'
(Brian Marriner 'A Century of Sex Killers')

Between the end of the 1970's and the middle of 1986 there were a reported 17,617 cases of AIDS in the United States. In that year alone almost 7,000 Americans perished at the hands of serial killers.

Pathological murder has now reached epidemic proportions. Jack the ripper was not the first serial killer, but he was the first to gain widespread notoriety. Since then Whitechapel's nightmare has become all our nightmares.

What is a serial killer? To that there is no specific answer, no single prototype. In the words of one of the worst of the Ripper's children, Theodore Bundy* :

'If anybody's looking for pat answers, forget it. If there were, the psychiatrists would have cleared this up years ago'.

We can only make generalisations. Serial killers are overwhelmingly male, overwhelmingly white and overwhelmingly caucasian. They tend to start killing between the ages of 25 and 30 and they do not stop of their own accord. William Bonin, known as the 'Freeway Killer', raped and strangled 41 young men between 1972 and 1980. After his capture Bonin told a reporter:

'I'd still be killing. I couldn't stop killing'.

William Heirens, a Chicago multicide, scrawled on a wall above one of his victims:

'For heaven's sake catch me before I kill more. I cannot control myself.'

Heirens had been raised by a domineering mother who indoctrinated him with the belief that sex was something dirty and depraved. This also is a common factor amongst sexual killers. John Christie, the Rillington Place strangler, suffered at the hands of a repressive Victorian Father and Peter Kurten, known as the 'Dusseldorf Ripper', had his perversions moulded in childhood by a drunken, violent father who raped his sister and frequently forced his mother to have sex in front of the children. Many serial killers have themselves been subjected to sexual or physical abuse during childhood. In short the message seems to be that serial killers are not born but made.

The child fashions the adult. Serial killers feel no remorse, no pity for their victims. Kurten told a psychiatrist: 'I haven't felt any pricks of conscience... I

---

* executed in 1989 for the murders of at least 21 women.

could not act differently' — Theodore Bundy told a Psychologist that he had felt remorse only for his first victim. After that the craving to kill overtook him, like a drug. He became de-sensitised, his victims no longer people but objects to be used to satisfy his depravity. Brian Marriner, 'A Century of Sex Killers' graphically illuminates the depths of such depravity:

> '*Kurten tore out dogs' intestines. Mullins did the same with the girls he killed. Vacher disembowelled his victims, as did Jack the ripper. Fish butchered his; Gein cut them up and hung them up to cure like animal carcasses. Kemper preferred his women headless—that way there was no face to gaze at him: no eyes to observe him*'.[1]

The ultimate effect of such behaviour on the killer is to de-personalise him as well. Marriner again:

> '*They have become Zombies. Not creatures of legend, but all too true cases of the living dead, stalking our cities as death freaks.*'[2]

What Marriner means by 'Zombies' are not the walking corpses of voodoo legend but men dead inside, devoid of love and conscience, morally insane and seeing people not as human beings but as victims to be killed, used, and then discarded like the empty wrapper which contained the meal. Marriner's is a chilling portrait; it is also horribly accurate.

Outwardly all seems normal. The multicide is not a high flyer but holds down a routine job. He is not an engaging personality and finds relationships difficult but on the surface is nothing more sinister than a run of the mill introvert. He is not a facsimile of Quasimodo. Bundy was handsome and articulate. Dieter Beck and John Norman Collins, dubbed the 'Michigan Murderer', were highly attractive to women. Kurten, Christie and Denis Nilsen appeared to be mild mannered clerks. Peter Sutcliffe seemed to the world around him to be completely sane and normal. Another Peter, Manual, the Glasgow Serial Killer[*], convinced his trial judge that he was: 'very bad without being mad'.

Without being mad. There lies a conundrum which has confounded the experts. The Serial Killer's crimes are mad and like the AIDS virus eventually self destructive. But he functions within society, despite feeling alienated from it, appears rational, and in the legal sense, understands the difference between right and wrong. Some multicides are paranoid schizophrenics but their illness has generally been diagnosed after capture, not before it. In short the serial killer

---

1   A Century of Sex Killers p83
2   A Century of Sex Killers p84

[*]   Manual was executed for 7 murders and confessed to another 4

is insane but not within the legal definition of the word.

Hand in hand with the perverted sexual lust appears to lie an equally perverted desire for fame. Rudolph Pleil[*], one of Germany's many sexual killers, boasted to the Court: "I am Germany's greatest killer. I put others, both here and abroad, to shame". Kenneth Erskine, the so called 'Stockwell Strangler', a moronic psychopath who preyed on elderly and infirm people, told the police: "I wanted to be famous... I never thought you would catch me". Bundy asked his biographers to write about him and not his victims. Manual, a two bit crook who was the butt of jokes in the Glasgow underworld, used his trial to seize the limelight, as if to say: 'See, you should have taken me more seriously'. But significantly these delusions of grandeur only come to the fore after capture. Whilst at large the serial killer, with the exception of a few deranged exhibitionists such as Cream, does not court attention. He seeks to distance himself from his crimes. And somebody or something else is always responsible for them. Christie blamed his victims! Bundy blamed pornography; — significantly though, a member of the Board which heard his appeal against execution was a prominent anti-pornography campaigner. The lesson in all this is that serial killers will always manipulate the situation to suit themselves.

What research has established is that many multicides act under the influence of drink or drugs. Joel Norris, Author of 'Serial Killers: The Growing Menace' outlines the problem as follows:

> *'most convicted serial killers are chronically heavy drinkers and narcotics addicts who are either drunk or high at the time they commit their crimes... during a prolonged drunken state, when the entire brain function is inhibited and social controls are lowered in general, there is simply no form of normal control exerted by the predisposed individual to prevent antisocial activity... alcohol only increases the level of the serial killer's disorientation and further separates him from reality. Much the same can be said for narcotics.'*[1]

Bundy, Manual and Henry Lee Lucas — who may have committed over 200 murders — are prime examples of sex killers with chronic alcohol problems. So too was Jack the ripper.

The Ripper was no exceptional case. He was simply a common or garden sex murderer no different from the legions of serial killers who have preyed on Society since. Even the fact that he was never officially caught endows him with no special mystique: many other unknown killers have had their activities terminated without being brought to trial for them. If we look at the case histories

---

1   Serial Killers: The Growing Menace p68

*   Pleil claimed up to 25 victims

of four other sexual serial killers then a general picture of the sort of man the Ripper actually was begins to emerge.

Peter Kurten. Born in Cologne in 1883 Kurten was executed forty eight years later for nine murders. He confessed to an additional five and attacked no fewer than thirteen other people.

Kurten's childhood was horrendous. His alcoholic father frequently forced his mother to have sex in front of the children, actions which can justifiably be described as rape. It is possible that some of his twelve brothers and sisters were actually conceived in this way, perhaps even Kurten himself.

His father also raped one of his sisters. The effect on a young, forming mind cannot have been more brutalizing or warping. Kurten grew up equating sex with violence and sadism and viewing women as simply objects to be used. In a classic demonstration of this he also attempted incest with the sister who had been raped, and at the age of only nine drowned two other boys in the Rhine.

By the time he reached adolescence Kurten was performing sadistic sexual acts with animals. His first actual sex murder was committed when he was sixteen: he strangled a girl whilst having sex with her.

These activities went unpunished but he was frequently imprisoned for lesser crimes, though generally accompanied by violence. Without doubt the prison sentences prevented his death toll from being much higher. Even so, he raped and murdered a thirteen year old girl in 1913 and tried to strangle four more women between 1925 and 1928.

Following his final prison sentence he moved to Dusseldorf in 1929 and began a two year reign of terror which spread alarm throughout Europe. He murdered five more women, four children (all girls) and a drunken man who possibly reminded him of his father. Another nine women were also attacked.

Kurten's luck finally ran out in 1931. He was captured not through detection but because his final victim survived and described her attack in a letter to a friend which ended up in the 'dead letter' file and was opened by the Post Office. It was difficult to associate the monster who had held all Germany under a red terror with the outward Peter Kurten. A church goer, staunch trade unionist, dapper in appearance, softly mannered and looking like everybody's favourite uncle. He had married in 1924 and treated his wife, probably the one person whom he had ever felt affection for, impeccably. Yet the reality was that Kurten had killed or injured at least 27 people, lived a life of mainly crime, was stimulated by blood, violence and arson and was a professed devotee of Jack the ripper. He was guillotined in Cologne on July 3rd 1931, his final wish that he could hear his own blood running into the basket.

Kurten obviously possessed the same sadistic desires as the Ripper. Whether the Ripper's childhood was similar we do not know. On the surface neither appeared to be a monster. There was nothing in either man's features which suggested the madness lurking beneath. Kurten was a fastidious dresser: likewise the Ripper also dressed respectably. Interestingly, Kurten's modus operandi varied from crime to crime. One victim was stabbed, mutilated and set on fire, another was bludgeoned to death with a hammer, some were strangled and stabbed, others simply stabbed or strangled. Some were sexually assaulted, others not.

Kurten clearly believed (as did most people at the time) that the Ripper himself had written the initial 'Jack the ripper' letter and postcard. Aping him Kurten similarly sent a letter and postcard to the police detailing two of his crimes, hitherto undiscovered. He was not however an exhibitionist. Like the Ripper he showed no desire to be caught throughout most of his crimes. Only at the end was there an indication that he was wearying of his cavalcade of horrors. He allowed his final victim to live on the promise that she would not go to the Police. Nor, amazingly, did she. But for the letter Kurten would have remained at large. However, he seems by this time to have reached what Brian Marriner describes elsewhere in his book as 'a point of inner collapse'.[1]

Gordon Frederick Cummins. Cummins career of murder was extremely short and extremely brutish. Known as the 'Blackout Ripper' he killed four women and attempted to murder two more within the space of a week in February, 1942. The attacks all took place in West London and were reminiscent of the Ripper's atrocities over fifty years earlier. Like the Ripper, Cummins bloodlust seemed to grow stronger with each murder. The first victim was manually strangled, the second had her throat and body slit open with a tin opener, the third was strangled with a stocking and her body mutilated with a variety of weapons and the fourth was garrotted with a scarf and had her body savaged by a razor. In his two unsuccessful assaults Cummins attempted to manually strangle his victims. In the first he was interrupted and in the second fled when the woman fought free and began to scream. The last attempt proved his undoing. He left behind a gas mask with his serial number on it and was swiftly traced to a Billet in North West London where he was serving in the R.A.F. Cummins was hanged on June 25th. He left behind no confession and maintained his innocence to the end. However, the evidence against him was conclusive and he may have been responsible for the murders of two other women, one strangled — the other bludgeoned to death, the previous October.

A major feature of Cummins' crimes was that he always robbed his victims. Here there is an absolute parallel with the Ripper; also with Henry Lee Lucas who stole money and rings from his victims. Like the Ripper, neither Cummins or Lucas gained very much from the thefts. The predominant urge was the sexual desire to kill, neatly summed up by writer Norman Lucas (on Cummins) as the sexuality of death, not life.[2]

1   A Century of Sex Killers p260
2   The Sex Killers (pbk Edition) p45

Once again, nobody would have thought of Cummins as a sex killer. He was 28 and considered by the R.A.F. to be potential officer material. Ostensibly he was happily married (his wife refused to accept his guilt) and there can be no doubt that women found him outwardly attractive. But on the other side of the coin his was not a shining personality. He was vain, arrogant and egotistical. Acquaintances found his constant boastings about female conquests irksome. Although he came from a good background (his father was a Headmaster) Cummins frequently claimed to be the son of a Lord and styled himself 'The Hon Gordon Cummins'. Such behaviour is often a benchmark of the pathological personality. Jack the ripper was also a highly unlikeable man, particularly when drunk.

John Reginald Halliday Christie. Known to crime historians as the 'Rillington Place Strangler', Christie claimed eight victims in his West London apartment between 1943 and 1953, nine if one includes Timothy Evans who was wrongly hanged for one of them.

Christie erupted late for a sex murderer. He was 45 when he killed his first victim, a girl with the sadly appropriate name of Ruth Fuerst. Victim number two followed in 1944 but, unusually for a sex murderer, he did not kill again for another five years, Beryl Evans, the wife of Timothy, a van driver who lived upstairs. Expediency forced Christie to also kill their baby daughter, Geraldine. Timothy Evans was convicted of the Child's murder and hanged the following year.* Another three year gap ensued but in December, 1952 Christie strangled his wife, also probably from expediency. The victims then came thick and fast, three during the next twelve weeks, in what appears to have been a last, perverted spree.

Apart from Geraldine Evans and his wife Ethel who were simply garrotted, Christie's modus operandi was always the same. He gassed his victims into unconsciousness, strangled them with a ligature and then had sex with their dead bodies. Afterwards he either buried them in the garden or entombed them in an alcove behind the living room wall (except for the Evanses). His crimes went undiscovered until March, 1953 when he moved out of the apartment. He was arrested on March 31st by an alert policeman who encountered him, forlorn and derelict, on the Embankment. He was executed on July 15th.

In some respects Christie is a puzzle. There is the advanced age at which he began to kill and the lengthy gaps between the second and third and fourth and fifth murders. The first can be partially explained by what was the happiest normal period of his life. From 1939 to 1943 he was a full time special Police Constable, a role which suited the authoritarian side of his nature. During this period he also enjoyed an apparently normal sexual relationship with a young married woman. This ended when he was beaten up by the husband. The curtailment of this affair seems to have tipped him over the edge. Aside from the question marks, he followed the classic path of the sex murderer; an unhappy childhood during which he went in dread of his austere, Victorian father and

---

*   He was posthumously pardoned in 1966

was bossed about by his four sisters, and an equally unhappy adolescence. An unpopular loner, he was frequently teased with the nickname "Reggie no-dick" after failing during intercourse with a girl.

Like Jack the ripper, Christie was, or rather became, a sexual degenerate of the worst kind. Again like the Ripper he did not appear anything out of the ordinary. He was not an attractive man either physically or personally but he seemed just to be the middle aged shipping clerk which he became after leaving the police force. But the outward appearance belied the real Christie. Behind the respectable facade was a man with several past convictions for petty theft and a sentence for maliciously wounding a prostitute with whom he was living. Here there is a very strong parallel with Jack the ripper.

Peter William Sutcliffe. The memory of 'The Yorkshire Ripper's' depredations are so recent that Sutcliffe requires no introduction. A Bradford lorry driver, he murdered thirteen women and attacked another seven between 1969 and 1980. His actual murders commenced in 1975, his modus operandi being to batter his victims with a ball pein hammer and then stab them with a knife and large screwdriver. Significantly however he altered his M.O. for his twelfth fatal victim who was hit with the hammer and then strangled with a ligature. Sutcliffe's explanation for the change was that he did not want the crime attributed to him. Until his arrest it wasn't. Nor was his attack on a Doctor five weeks later. Once again, he used the ligature.

Sutcliffe was captured by chance in January, 1981 by two Police Officers who found him sitting in his car with a prostitute. In May he was found guilty on all twenty charges and sentenced to serve at least thirty years in gaol. He was subsequently diagnosed insane and is now in Broadmoor Mental Hospital.

There are some interesting similarities between Sutcliffe and the Ripper. Sutcliffe drove a lorry, the Ripper a pony and cart. Both distanced themselves from their crimes. Both hated prostitutes, Sutcliffe because he had been bilked and humiliated by one; the Ripper because he had contracted venereal disease from a prostitute. But at the core both were sex murderers and any woman would do. Their victims were mainly, but not exclusively, prostitutes because they were the easiest victims to present themselves. Sutcliffe amended his m.o. and used a ligature, so too did the Ripper. Both were married. Like the Ripper, Sutcliffe stole rings from corpses.

If we look overall at the four murderers examined in this chapter we find some differences but generally similar characteristics with each other and with Jack the ripper. All, except Christie, varied their m.o. All, again except Christie, began to kill whilst young; they appeared normal and did not draw attention to themselves; each was married but had no children; — their sexuality was of death not life. Each, save Cummins, was a loner and an introvert and although Cummins at times courted popularity he was not liked. All of them hated and feared women. Kurten's dislike of women was apparent from his final speech to the Court; they were husband hunters, mercenaries. Cummins' boasts about his sex life were clearly indicative of seeing women just as objects. Christie was dominated by his sisters and was the butt of jibes by the local girls. Sutcliffe's apparent shyness with women was a mask for his fear, his bragging of non-existent sexual conquests not merely a pointer to his own inadequacy but also of a general dislike of women. The Ripper was habitually violent towards his wife and in the end added her to his victims.

According to this unholy quintet they were not to blame for their atrocities — their victims were. Kurten:

> '...*Many of my victims made things very easy for me... Doubtless, many a one thought that I should become her bridegroom... The pursuit of men by women has assumed many forms'.*

Christie, in a whining and utterly nauseating "justification" for his crimes, claimed that his victims had led him on and demanded sex with him. According to him they had asked for what happened to them.

Sutcliffe claimed to be ridding Society of prostitutes, in his own words: 'just cleaning up streets'. Many of his victims were not prostitutes so he claimed that they were behaving like prostitutes!

Cummins and the Ripper never spoke, never confessed. Had they done so then we can be certain that they would have attempted the same obnoxious self-justifications, the same lies, to cover their behaviour. Perhaps it is better that they didn't.

In 1988 the F.B.I.'s behavioural science (serial killers) unit was asked to prepare a psychological profile of the Ripper. Their conclusions were as follows:

Gender:	Male
Age:	Late Twenties
Work:	Employed
Marital Status:	Single
Social Standing:	Working Class
Surgical/	
Anatomical knowledge:	None
Residence:	Local
Antecedents:	Probably had a Police Record
Personality:	Loner
Childhood :	Abused and unhappy

The Ripper's childhood will remain a closed book but significantly he may have been closer to an uncle rather than his parents. I have not been able to ascertain whether he had a Police Record in England. He was married but the F.B.I. were in fact half right because he married not for love or companionship but for financial reasons.

The rest of the F.B.I.'s profile is highly accurate. We can now turn to the Ripper himself and see who and what he was.

Chapter Twelve: The End Of The Myth

William Henry Bury was a squalid, sordid little man; drunk, dissolute and diseased. William Henry Bury was Jack the ripper.

In a sense his story begins where it ends. A cold, blustery Dundee afternoon, February 10th, 1889, in which the thoughts in Bury's mind were as bleak as the weather. He had been in Dundee barely three weeks, arriving from London with his wife, Ellen, on the steamer 'Cambria' on January 19th. They had first taken a room at No 4, Union Street, before moving to a tenement flat in the basement of 113, Princes Street. It was to be their final address. Ellen Bury died there on February 5th; William was executed for her murder eleven weeks later.

Late afternoon on the 10th found Bury at Dundee Police Station where he asked to see somebody in authority. He was shown into the Office of Lieutenant David Lamb. The story which he told Lamb was a simple but startling one.

On February 5th he had woken from a drunken sleep at the Princes Street flat to find Ellen lying dead on the floor with a piece of rope around her neck. He had stabbed the corpse once with a knife and later crammed it into a trunk. Since then he had had no peace of mind.

Lamb seems to have been in two minds as to whether to take the story seriously but obviously it had to be investigated. He took Bury to see his C.I.D. counterpart, Detective Lieutenant James Parr, announcing him with the words: 'This man has a wonderful story to tell you'.

Bury repeated his story to Parr. His wife must have committed suicide; he had been afraid to come forward in case people thought he was Jack the ripper.

The next step was to visit the apartment at 113, Princes Street. Behind a tenement door was a chalked message stating:

'Jack Ripper is at the back of this door'

On the stairway wall leading down to the flat was a second chalked message:

'Jack Ripper is in this sellar' (sic)

Inside the flat the Police found the naked and mutilated body of Ellen Bury. She had been strangled with a ligature and stuffed into a large wooden trunk. Her body had been ripped open with a knife, the worst injury a large wound in the abdomen from which the intestines were protruding. Her clothes, heavily blood stained, were lying nearby.

That evening a post mortem was performed by Dr Charles Templeman and Dr Alexander Stalker, both Police surgeons. They confirmed that Ellen Bury had been dead for several days. Cause of death was strangulation with a rope. There were multiple stab wounds to the body which had been inflicted after death. Both Doctors were emphatic that she had not strangled herself.

At this point it is necessary only to give the bare details of the Doctors' conclusions. A more comprehensive summary of Ellen Bury's injuries will be given later.

William Bury was now charged with his wife's murder and deposited in Dundee Gaol. On the 11th he was examined by the prison doctor, James Miller, who discovered scratches on his right forearm and wrist and a mark on his left hand consistent with a finger nail. The abrasions were several days old, around four Miller thought. Bury claimed they had been made by a cat.

There now follows a rather odd gap in the story. According to the papers in the Scottish Public Records Office Bury made no statement in his own words; if he did then it is missing from the file. What he told the Police emerges only from the precognitions of Lamb and Parr, both dated the 11th, and there are two very puzzling omissions from these. Apparently neither officer was in any way, shape or form curious as to why Bury had mutilated his wife after death. And there is no mention whatsoever of the chalked, 'Jack Ripper' messages found at 113, Princes Street. That they were there and had been made prior to the discovery of the body, was confirmed by the 'Dundee Advertiser'[*] on February 12th and was never denied by the Police. Yet, like the mutilations, they were seemingly of no interest. The clear impression is that any possible connection with the ripper murders was being played down until Scotland Yard was consulted.

If the Dundee Police imagined that they might eventually be credited with the ripper's arrest then they were to be disappointed. The Yard had to be called in anyway to probe Bury's London background. But significantly the Officer charged with that investigation was none other than Inspector Frederick George Abberline then still very much involved in the hunt for the ripper.

William Bury had lived in Bow, East London, from October, 1887 to January 18th, 1889. Initially he had been employed by one James Martin, who somewhat euphemistically described himself as a general dealer, to peddle sawdust. Bury also appears to have lodged with Martin at his premises at Quickett Street, Bow until the end of March, 1888. From there he moved to Swaton Road, Bow, married, and later decamped (with Ellen) first to No 11, Blackthorne Street and then No 3, Spanby Road, still in Bow. From April to December, 1888 Bury was self-employed as a sawdust merchant hawking his merchandise around the East End in a pony and cart which he stabled in Spanby Road.

Such are the basic facts of William Henry Bury's existence in the East End of London. But Abberline's investigations produced much more than this. On February 14th he took statements from five witnesses who were later to travel to Scotland to give evidence against Bury at his trial. The first was from Mrs Margaret Corney of Stanley Road, Bow, Ellen Bury's sister[**].

---

[*]   A copy of its Report is amongst the case papers.
[**]   Abberline may have detailed another Officer to take her statement as it is the only one unsigned by him.

Mrs Corney's evidence was as follows. Her sister, Ellen Elliot aged 32, had married Bury at Bromley Church on Easter Monday, April 2nd, 1888. At the time of the wedding Ellen owned Bank and Railway shares (a legacy) valued at £300, a considerable sum in 1888 and worth probably £20,000 at today's values. According to Corney, Bury had induced Ellen to sell two thirds of the shares and in her (Corney's) words he had kept a "considerable part of this money" for himself. Some of the money was used to buy his pony and cart. A great deal more undoubtedly went on drink.

Corney deposed that in August the Burys had gone to Wolverhampton for a holiday. She gave no dates or length of time.

Martha Tabram's murder took place on August 7th; Polly Nichols' in the early hours of August 31st.

At the beginning of December, 1888, around four weeks after the murder of Mary Kelly and probably about two weeks prior to Rose Mylett's death in Poplar, Bury sold his pony and cart. He had decided to migrate to Scotland. He told Corney that he had a seven year agreement of work at £2 per week plus a job for Ellen at £1 per week if she wanted it. These were lies.

The statement is at its most illuminating when Corney describes the Burys' life together. She begins:

> *'My sister and her husband did not live happily together.'*

Bury was drinking heavily and was very much given to late hours. He had punched Ellen in the mouth and eye and sometimes slept with a penknife under his pillow. A fortnight before Christmas Ellen had visited her sister bringing her jewellery with her. Corney had formed the impression that she was unhappy about going to Dundee. Corney summarised Bury's behaviour towards her sister in the following terms:

> *'(he had) habitually abused her, given himself up to drink and paid no attention to his business.*
>
> *'Accused has a very violent temper but I never heard it even suggested that he had not all his wits about him. My sister told me she could never scarce believe a word he said.'*

By itself Margaret Corney's description of Bury and his behaviour depicts nothing more than a drunken, violent neer-do-well who had married his wife for money. But then serial killers seem no more, — and at times a good deal less — than this. The picture of a man greedy for money is that of the Ripper who robbed his victims and stole their rings; of Cummins, and Henry Lee Lucas whose wife was amongst his many murders and from whose dead body he stole rings and money. Plainly, Ellen Bury feared that having already had most of her money Bury would also steal her jewellery. Sadly, she had far more to fear than that.

The drink and the violence, clearly interwoven, are classic hallmarks of the serial killer. And right at the end of the statement Margaret Corney provides us with a very revealing insight into Bury's character. He was an habitual liar but appeared sane, another pointer to a pathologically retarded personality. If we add all these factors together then we have a very good portrait of the man who was Jack the ripper.

The second witness's statement adds to that portrait. James Martin had employed Bury up to the end of March, 1888 when he sacked him for theft. Bury seems to have lived at Martin's Quickett Street premises up to that time. There he met Ellen Elliot whom, said Martin, was employed by him as a servant.

Abberline had clearly done his homework on Martin with his 'K' Division colleagues because midway through the interview he suddenly got very tough with him. Now Martin admitted that the Quickett Street house was in fact a brothel and Ellen Elliot a prostitute. He went on:—

> *'Elliot told me on one occasion that she had given birth to a child in some workhouse and I know that she was no better than a prostitute and she occasionally fetched men home and they slept with her at my house.'*

Martin painted the same picture as Margaret Corney about the Burys' life together. He had seen Bury assault Ellen once before their marriage and two or three times afterwards. He had seen her twice in the street with a bruised face.

Bury was in the habit of getting drunk three or four times a week and had seldom been sober since getting his hands on his wife's money.

According to Martin, Bury had been aware that Ellen was a prostitute. He, Bury, had contracted venereal disease in May, 1888 and had passed it on to her. Ellen had confirmed this to Martin and his wife, telling them that she had "the bad disorder".

James Martin was succeeded by Elizabeth Haynes, the Bury's Swaton Street Landlady who told Abberline that on the Saturday after their wedding (April 7th) Bury had demanded money from Ellen and assaulted her. Haynes:

> *'She screamed for help and I went into their room and found him kneeling on her in bed. He had a table knife in his right hand and was apparently about to cut her throat.'*

There followed the same depressing story of violence. Bury had "frequently" attacked Ellen who confided to Haynes that she was afraid he would kill her, a cruelly accurate prophecy. In the end Haynes had asked them to leave.

Quite apart from the general picture of drunken violence and degeneracy painted by Martin and Haynes, there are two particularly interesting points. Bury was clearly in need of money around Easter, 1888. Towards the end of March he stole money from Martin and around a week or so later he demanded money from Ellen and had to be stopped from cutting her throat. This coincides with the attack on Ada Wilson a very short distance away in Mile End on March 28th. Wilson's assailant demanded money and stabbed her in the throat. The second point is that Bury contracted venereal disease, obviously from a prostitute, in May. The course of treatment would have been around ten weeks. The ripper murders commenced on August 7th, perhaps the next time he picked up a prostitute.

The final statement about the Burys' life together in Bow came from their Spanby Road Landlord, William Smith, and was more of the same. Bury was drinking heavily (except on Sundays) and often assaulted Ellen. When they left Spanby Road Bury told Smith that they were going to Brisbane, Australia. And he added a somewhat cryptic rider. Asked by Smith which Docks they were sailing from Bury replied:

'Ah that's what you want to know like a lot more.'

Exactly what Bury meant by 'a lot more' we do not know. He could have meant acquaintances in Bow; on the other hand this may have been a carefully veiled reference to the Police.

The fifth statement which Abberline took that day need not detain us very long. It was from Ellen Bury's Stockbroker and confirmed that on April 28th, 1888 she had realised shares to the value of £39.37 followed by the sale of a much larger block of £194.35 on June 7th. Plainly, as 1888 wore on Bury's thirst was assuming titanic proportions.

The conclusion which Abberline obviously reached was that this was simply a sordid little story of an unpleasant and brutal man who had married a rather sad, lonely woman for her savings and then killed her in a drunken rage. Nothing to do with Jack the ripper or Whitechapel, or so he thought.

The statements were passed to the Dundee Police, apparently without comment (there is nothing in the files). They meanwhile had been making some investigations of their own.

Marjory Smith had gotten to know the Burys during their stay at Princes Street. On one occasion Ellen had bought some pillows off her. Talking about their life together in London Ellen told Smith that her husband: "stayed out late at night" and got into bad company.

On another occasion Bury himself borrowed a chopper off Smith. She asked him jokingly:

"Surely you are not Jack the ripper?"

Bury answered:

"I do not know so much about that."

The ripper did not normally make remarks which might draw attention to himself but according to Smith Bury was drunk at the time.

Another Dundee acquaintance of Bury's, a painter named David Walker, also had a tantalising little story to tell. Bury had visited his house only hours before going to the Police on February 10th and had been very interested in a newspaper article about a young couple who had eloped and then committed suicide. The story was of much less interest to Walker who wanted to know if there was anything in the Newspaper about Jack the ripper whereupon Bury: "immediately threw down the paper". To Walker he appeared very restless and had talked about returning to London.

Without doubt Bury concocted his suicide claim about Ellen's death from the Newspaper story. His obvious agitation at the mention of the ripper could of course be explained by guilt over his Wife's murder; on the other hand it bears the stamp of the ripper himself, a man who shrank from his own infamy, had fled England to escape justice and had then mutilated his Wife's body because he was the ripper and needed to.

A third witness to make a statement about Bury was his Union Street Landlady, Margaret Robertson. The Burys had taken a room there on January 21st at 40 pence per week rent. William Bury had not made a very good impression on Robertson. Repeating his Bow behaviour, he appeared the worse for drink and had looked "wickedly" at Robertson's mother, frightening her. Robertson was obviously glad to see the back of them on January 29th, Bury complaining (not without justification) that the rent was too high. They had moved into 113, Princes Street the same day.

The statements from the London and Dundee witnesses were a very satisfactory piece of work from the Police's point of view. And they needed them. The case had run into trouble. Had it relied purely on the medical evidence then Jack the ripper's luck might have held for a 'not proven' verdict.*

On February 14th Bury's solicitor asked Dr David Lennox, a Dundee Surgeon, to undertake a second post mortem on Ellen Bury's body. Lennox was assisted by Dr William Kinnear. Four days later Lennox presented a comprehensive 14 page report. His conclusion was that Ellen Bury had committed suicide by strangling herself. Kinnear, who submitted a much shorter report, doubted Lennox's suicide theory but did not rule it out entirely.

Here then was a blow for the Police. Lennox appears to have been a more experienced Surgeon than Templeman or Stalker. The Police turned to a prominent local Surgeon of their own, Dr Henry Littlejohn, and, shades of Rose Mylett, a third examination took place. It was almost a case of too many cooks spoiling the broth. Littlejohn discounted Lennox's theory and endorsed Templeman and Stalker's conclusion that Ellen Bury had been murdered. But he quarrelled with their assertion that the mutilations had definitely taken place after death. They might equally, he decided, have commenced before death. The upshot was that Templeman was persuaded to make a statement admitting that his autopsy could have been more thorough. One can only wonder what an advocate of Marshall-Hall's calibre would have made of this mish-mash in Bury's favour.

* A verdict peculiar to Scotland

Dr Lennox's findings will be examined in detail later and will show that Ellen Bury was murdered by Jack the ripper. For the moment it is only necessary to say that Lennox's suicide theory was certainly wrong and that he seems to have taken his role as a defence expert rather too literally.

Bury's trial took place on March 28th, a year to the day after the attack on Ada Wilson. Only the bare minutes are in the Public Records Office. They state that the trial Judge was Lord Young and that Dill Kechnie led for the prosecution with William Hay appearing for the defence. Twenty-two witnesses testified for the Crown and five for Bury who under the rules of evidence in 1889 was not permitted to speak in his own defence. The defence case relied mainly on Lennox and Kinnear. Bury's other witnesses were character witnesses, including a Priest whom he had met during his short time in Dundee. The proceedings lasted only a day and the Jury do not appear to have had any difficulty in deciding that Bury was guilty. There was no court of appeal in the nineteenth century which meant that his fate rested exclusively with Home Secretary Matthews. There is no Home Office file amongst the papers on the case so we have no knowledge of Matthews' deliberations. All we know is that he found no grounds on which to reprieve Bury and that he was hanged at Dundee Gaol on April 24th. Justice had overtaken Jack the ripper at last.

*****

We can now assemble the case against Bury in its entirety. It can be split into four broad categories, psychological, medical, identification and circumstantial. We begin with the psychological evidence.

The value of psychological evidence in helping to determine the identity of a sexual killer is amply demonstrated by the case of John Duffy, known as the 'railway murderer'.

In December, 1985 a young secretary named Alison Day was raped and murdered near Hackney Wick station. Four months later fifteen year old Maartje Tamboezer was raped and murdered near West Horsley station. A few weeks after that another secretary, Anne Lock, was similarly murdered near Brookmans Park in Hertfordshire.

The Police compiled a list of 4,900 suspects. This they whittled down to 1,999. No 1,594 on that list was John Duffy. They then called in Professor David Canter, a leading psychologist. After diligent research into the case Canter produced a seventeen point psychological profile of the killer. When this was fed into the computer it threw up just one name, Duffy. He matched the profile on no less than thirteen counts.

In 1988 Duffy was tried on overwhelming circumstantial evidence and convicted of the murders of Day and Tamboezer[*]. Like Bury he had been

---

[*]   He was also convicted on five counts of rape.

habitually violent towards his wife.

The F.B.I. prepared their psychological profile of Jack the ripper for the Television docu-drama 'The Secret Identity of Jack the Ripper' in 1988 and presented it on screen through special agents John Douglas and Roy Hazelwood.

The basic outlines have already been given in the previous chapter. We can now enlarge on it.

The ripper was a white male, middle to late twenties who lived in the locale of the crimes.

He had been abused as a child, particularly by a domineering mother, and had probably grown up committing acts of arson and cruelty to animals.

In manhood he was of no more than average intelligence (lucky rather than clever) and was employed in a menial job. He possessed no medical knowledge or professional qualifications.

He was single, hated and feared women — probably did not socialise with them at all — and found great difficulty in interacting with people, once again women in particular. Classically a loner.

His habits were nocturnal and he was scruffy and dishevelled in appearance. He was likely to have had a Police record and be prone to erratic behaviour causing neighbours to summon the Police.

Here we have a psychological photograph of William Henry Bury. Bury was born on May 25th, 1859 and was 29 at the time of the murders. He lived in Bow, within easy walking distance of Whitechapel and Spitalfields, and also drove a pony and cart which would have put him only minutes away. His job, hawking sawdust around the streets, would have given him a good knowledge of East London. He was of humble origin, his father a Fishmonger from Stourbridge in Worcester.

Of Bury's childhood we have no knowledge, but according to Elizabeth Haynes he had lived with an uncle in Wolverhampton before coming to London which may possibly be indicative of an unhappy relationship with his parents.

Bury had no known knowledge of anatomy or surgery. His job in London was strictly a menial one, peddling sawdust first for Martin and then for himself. He possessed no great intellect. An intelligent man would have realised that the story of his wife's death would not stand up to examination for very long. On the other hand he was lucky. His luck held time and again in Whitechapel and may have convinced him to try brazening it out in Dundee rather than fleeing. Even here, if Dr Lennox had had his way, that luck would have continued to hold.

Bury's hatred of women is very clearly documented in the Statements of Corney, Martin, Haynes, and Smith. He behaved abominably towards his wife and was married only in name. He had not an ounce of affection or respect for Ellen Elliot. He married her for her money and ten months later he killed her. During that time he continued to behave like a single man. He was clearly unable to forge relationships with women, sought only the company of prostitutes where normal socialising was unnecessary, and in Elliot he married a prostitute who worked in the brothel where he lived.

Aside from three people in Dundee whom he had known for less than a month nobody came forward to speak for William Bury. Even the Dundee witnesses could only testify that he appeared respectable.

The portrait which emerged from people who had known him longer was strikingly different. The Bow witnesses put together a montage of a violently anti-social misfit who hated the world and seethed with frustration. It would be hard to imagine a clearer profile of a serial killer.

Whether or not Bury had a criminal record in England is extremely hard to determine. He may have done. According to my inquiries with the Public Records Office at Kew, they do not keep specific files except in notorious cases. Criminal histories can be gleaned by combing prison records and then fleshing out the details from local newspaper reports. In Bury's case the only extant file is in the Scottish Public Records Office and contains no reference to any past crimes. What we do know however is that Bury was both a man of violence and a thief.

The F.B.I. was wrong in categorizing the ripper as being likely to be dishevelled in appearance. The witnesses who saw him contradict this. Nor was he a man who unduly drew attention to himself, certainly not in the way William Pigott, Charles Ludwig or Aaron Kosminski did. However Bury's behaviour was erratic and violent. Mrs Haynes had to stop him from murdering Ellen less than a week after their wedding and was eventually forced to ask them to leave. Normal men do not sleep with knives under their pillow. Here the psychological point is damning. The ripper raped his victims with a knife. Bury shared a bed with both his knife and his wife. The sexual connotation is obvious. Here there is also a direct comparison with Peter Kurten, the ripper's disciple and admirer. Kurten was only able to make love to his wife by fantasising about acts of extreme violence.

The statements of Margaret Corney and Marjory Smith, Ellen Bury's dead testimony through the lips of the living, show that William Bury's habits were indeed nocturnal.

Taking it step by step, point by point, the psychological profiles of William Bury and Jack the ripper are one and the same. We can extend this beyond the F.B.I.'s assessment. Like many serial killers Bury was a heavy drinker, a man constantly walking through an alcoholic haze which threw off his few social restraints and primed him to violence. As that bloody Autumn of 1888 wore on and the ripper's crimes deepened in intensity so Bury's drinking grew worse and worse, his attention to his business less and less and his grip on reality more and more tenuous. These are the classic symptoms of a man in the throes of self destruction through the murder of others, as Brian Marriner puts it: 'marching towards death like mechanical robots or zombies, locked into their own private nightmares.'[1]

Moreover, a small but possibly crucial point arises from Bury's drinking habits. Of the ripper victims both definite and possible, Annie Chapman was slain in the early hours of Saturday morning, Liz Stride and Cathy Eddowes in the early hours of Sunday morning, Martha Tabram and Ellen Bury Tuesday, Ada Wilson was attacked on Wednesday evening, Rose Mylett murdered in the early hours of a Thursday and Polly Nichols and Mary Kelly on a Friday morning. Missing from this list is Monday, or to be more precise the early hours of a Monday morning. We know from William Smith, Bury's Spanby Road Landlord, that Sunday was the only day on which Bury did not drink heavily.

We can turn now to the medical evidence and Dr Lennox's report. First the strangulation:

> *'Round the neck was a band of blue discoloured skin about half an inch in vertical diameter... In front 3½ inches from the top of the breast bone at the sides 2 inches below the lobes of the ears'* *

Dr Lennox found the head and neck deeply congested, the face swollen, the lips livid, the tongue swollen and protruding from between the teeth, the lower jaw retracted, the eyeballs congested, the hands livid and the fingers of both hands semi-flexed.

There were bruises on the nose and the rib cage although Lennox was of the opinion that the facial injury had been inflicted 18 to 24 hours before death.

Lennox found ten knife wounds in the abdomen, pubes and perineum. In chronological order they were as follows:—

1. A Deep wound in the middle of the stomach beginning 1½ inches above the pubis and extending upwards for 4½ inches. This incision had opened up the abdominal cavity and when the body was found 12 inches of intestines had been protruding from it.

2. A wound beginning 2 inches above and 1 inch to the right of the first, one eighth of an inch long.

3. 2 inches across to the right from the first wound, an incision ¾ of an inch long which had cut through the skin fat and external oblique muscle.

4. 2 inches above the middle of the groin, to the right, a wound ¾ of an inch long which had divided the skin fat and fascia.

5. A superficial wound 1¼ inches long beginning 1 inch above the

---

1 'A Century of Sex Killers' p84

* Examination Report 18.2.89

pubis on the left side.

6. a deep cut 6¾ inches above the pubis on the left hand side, 1 inch from the middle and 1½ inches in length which had sliced through the deep fascia and the oblique muscle.

7. Just above the middle of the groin on the left, a wound of 3¼ inches which had extended into the subcutaneous tissue.

8. Also on the left, an incision running directly across the crest of the pubis for 2½ inches which had again penetrated the subcutaneous tissue.

9. A similar wound on the right, once again 2½ inches long, which extended from the lower edge of the pubis into the vulva and had separated the membrane of the labia and the subcutaneous fat.

10. Finally a wound which ran for 1¼ inches from the posterior to the anus and ended between the vulva and the isobrium, which had parted the skin fascia and part of the sphincter ani muscle.

There were numerous scratches around the wounds. Only one of the abdominal wounds (No 1) had penetrated the belly wall. No organs had been removed. All the cuts were in an upwards (vertical) direction.

Lennox provides no insight into the type of knife used beyond stating that he had been shown a knife which would cause such wounds.

There is of course one very marked difference between the East End victims and Ellen Bury: — her throat was not cut. But, as we have seen, sexual killers do alter their modus operandi, especially when they are seeking to avoid capture. Peter Sutcliffe, with the murder of his twelfth victim and his attack on another woman a few weeks later, is an obvious example. Bury had fled to Scotland for exactly that reason. Interestingly, according to Mrs Haynes, he had attempted to cut his Wife's throat during his first potentially fatal attack on her.

That apart, this was a ripper murder, the victim first strangled and then stabbed. Ellen Bury was asphyxiated by a ligature, a point commonly agreed upon by all five Doctors. Whether or not Rose Mylett was Bury's first victim with a ligature we shall never know. It is not necessary to prove that she was anyway. Bury may have altered his method of strangulation — fifty four years later Gordon Cummins, 'the blackout ripper' alternated between manual strangulation and garrotting — but on the other hand he may not have done. Only in recent years has it been determined through the research of expert pathologists such as Camps and Cameron and researchers like Begg, Fido and Skinner that the ripper victims were strangled before being mutilated. Strangulation marks on the throat were obliterated by the cuts which means that we have no definite way of knowing whether the victims were manually strangled or garrotted*. The point of over-

---

* Elizabeth Stride seems to have been at least partially garrotted with her scarf.

riding importance is the strangulation itself which is bound up with sexual murder.

The ripper was clearly the type of sexual killer who works his way up to peaks and that had been reached with Mary Kelly's murder. The mutilations on Ellen Bury were nowhere as extensive and were more reminiscent of those on Polly Nichols (which they surpassed) as though he was now working himself up to a new crescendo. Here again the major point of importance is the sexual nature of the mutilations themselves. That design is clear and unequivocal in the murder of Ellen Bury. Bury ripped open her pubis, vulva, abdomen and perineum. This was how the ripper gained his ultimate release.

We return to the East End of London for the identification evidence. The descriptions of the ripper are very general. We know that he was short, stout or burly and respectably but inexpensively dressed. Three out of nine witnesses thought he had a moustache, one did not see his features, three took no notice of them and two decided that he was clean shaven although here again they took no particular notice of him. The description which we have of William Bury (there is no photograph) is very scanty and comes from the 'Dundee Advertiser'. He was short with sharp features, a beard, side whiskers and a fair moustache. His Dundee character witnesses thought he looked respectable which suggests that he was reasonably dressed.

In the absence of more specific descriptions of both Bury and the ripper we can only make a number of very general points. The first and most obvious is that both men were short. The second is that Bury fits the age of the man seen with Stride and Eddowes. Thereafter the mirror becomes rather misty. The witnesses Best, Schwartz and Lawende said that the man they saw had a moustache although each had it a different colour, Best black, Schwartz brown, and Lawende fair. Such variations are to be expected. William Marshall and P.C. Smith thought the man they saw was clean shaven or at least that he had no whiskers. Once again the discrepancies are unimportant. However, it must be said that no witness noticed a beard or side whiskers which strongly suggests that the ripper had none on September 30th. Between that time and Bury's arrest in Dundee he had four months — ample time — in which to grow them and a very powerful motive for doing so. The Police were not looking for a man with a beard or side whiskers; they were seeking a man who was clean shaven or at most had a moustache. If Bury read the inquest testimony of Marshall and Smith — no whiskers — then that point would have struck him very strongly.

Evidence of identification is always suspect. Many innocent men have been convicted on it. Doubtless, guilty men have also escaped justice because descriptions varied so greatly. By itself the identification evidence could not convict William Bury, or anybody else for that matter. But it does not stand by itself. It is part of a composite picture of Bury's guilt and what we can say is that the identification evidence does, broadly speaking, fit William Bury into that picture.

The final part of the case against Bury is circumstantial. What is circumstantial evidence? Lord Coleridge at the trial of John Dickman* summarised it as:

> '*a network of facts cast around the accused man*'.

Explaining it in relation to guilt, Coleridge went on:

> '*If we find a variety of circumstances all pointing in the same direction, convincing in proportion to the number and variety of those circumstances and their independence one of another, ...the cumulative effect of such evidence may be overwhelming proof of guilt.*'

In the absence of what is called 'smoking gun' evidence, in this instance a confession, any factual case against the ripper has to ultimately rely on circumstantial evidence.

Before examining the circumstantial case against Bury it will be instructive to look at Peter Sutcliffe, who, along with Gordon Cummins, is closest to Jack the ripper in terms of methodology and behaviour.

Sutcliffe was arrested in January, 1981 during a Police trawl of the Sheffield red light district. Until his ball pein hammer and screwdriver were discovered (by a particularly conscientious Officer) the Police were getting ready to let him go. Had they done so and Sutcliffe had died shortly afterwards the identity of the Yorkshire Ripper would be officially unknown. However, investigators could have built up a strong circumstantial case against Sutcliffe from the Police Files.

In 1969 Sutcliffe was arrested for assaulting a prostitute.

Later that year the Police found him hiding behind a hedge with a hammer in his hand. At the site of his sixth murder the Police found a new £5 note from a batch issued in wages to only 5,943 people, one of whom was Sutcliffe. In August, 1978 he was questioned because of the number of times his car had been seen in red light areas. A year later he was questioned again after his car had been spotted in the Bradford red light district 36 times in a month, and three months after this yet again because his car had been repeatedly logged in red light areas. Two months before his arrest his best friend first wrote a letter to the Police and then made a statement suspecting Sutcliffe of being the ripper. Sutcliffe also fitted two of the surviving victims' descriptions.

Sutcliffe eventually confessed under Police interrogation. No such 'smoking gun' evidence is possible with Jack the ripper. He was never questioned about the murders because the Police were looking elsewhere, another parallel with Sutcliffe who was hitherto ignored as a prime suspect because West Yorkshire C.I.D. were led astray by a hoaxer. Jack the ripper would not have left a confession of his own accord, a point which comes over very strongly from his psychological profile.

---

*   Hanged in 1910 for the murder of a wages clerk

F.B.I. Agents Douglas and Hazelwood describe him as a man who would not seek attention, want publicity or try to inject himself into the case. Gordon Cummins followed the same pattern and also had a practical reason for not confessing; he doubtless hoped that the Home Secretary would reprieve him. Bury too must have hoped for a reprieve, particularly in view of Lennox and Kinnear's testimony.

The circumstantial case against Bury must be seen as part of the picture as a whole, linking up with the psychological, medical and identification evidence. To recap, William Bury was exactly the sort of man who was Jack the ripper, he committed a ripper murder and he broadly fitted the description of the killer.

He arrived in London in October 1887. By Easter the following year he was desperate for money. Just before Easter Ada Wilson was attacked in her room a few minutes walk from where he was living.

In April he acquired a pony and cart. The following month he contracted venereal disease. The treatment probably finished around the end of July. On August 7th Martha Tabram was hacked to death with what could have been a pen knife, the sort of knife which Bury slept with under his pillow. That month Bury went to Wolverhampton. We do not know the dates, but it is very arguable that he needed a break and to lie low after killing for the first time.

Tabram was slain in George Yard Buildings. The Yard had two entrances, Wentworth Street from the North and Whitechapel High Street from the South. In 1888 it was also a stables. Bury stabled his pony in Spanby Road but George Yard itself was an ideal place to park a pony and cart whilst he was in Whitechapel and Spitalfields. And, Polly Nichols excepted, George Yard is central to the ripper murders. Tabram was killed there. Hanbury Street (Annie Chapman) lies four minutes walk to the north either along Commercial Street or Brick Lane. Dorset Street (Mary Kelly) was a bare two minutes walk up Commercial Street. Settles Street, where the ripper drank with Liz Stride, is approximately five minutes walk from the Yard's southern entrance. Cathy Eddowes' murderer first fled due east into Goulston Street and then turned North which led to the junction of Goulston and Wentworth Streets. East along Wentworth Street would have brought him directly to George Yard.

Tabram and Nichols were killed at 3.30 a.m., Stride at 12.45 and Eddowes at 1.40. Bury was continually out late at night during 1888.

Annie Chapman and Mary Kelly were murdered somewhat later in the morning. Bury may have been out all night; equally he could have been out in the morning supposedly peddling sawdust.

Being self-employed Bury was answerable to nobody but himself.

Jack the ripper had a working knowledge of the Streets of Whitechapel and Spitalfields but was not a native hence his failure to strike during the fog bound days of October. This fits Bury to a tee. A further point is that according to Walter Dew pedestrians out late at night were being stopped by the police, particularly Officers drafted in from other divisions. Going to and from Bow Bury travelled by pony and cart.

He sold his pony and cart at the beginning of December and Jack the ripper thereafter never struck in Whitechapel, Spitalfields, St Georges or Aldgate again. Whether Rose Mylett was his victim we shall never know but significantly she was slain off Poplar High Street, about five minutes walk from Spanby Road, after Bury had discarded his means of transport and Whitechapel had become much longer to reach and far more dangerous for him. It is significant that the attacks on Wilson and Mylett were only a short distance from Bury's home when he did not have the pony and cart.

Once again there is a parallel with Peter Sutcliffe whose car enabled him to range all over Northern England attacking his victims. Sutcliffe lived in Bradford. Of his 13 homicides, 5 took place in Leeds, 3 in Bradford, 2 in Manchester and 1 each in Huddersfield, Halifax and Farsley.

There were no more Jack the ripper murders in London after Bury fled to Dundee. He lied about his reason for going and, to William Smith, where he was going. Colin Wilson and Donald Seaman in their book 'The Serial Killers' have this to say about multicides changing their locale:

> *'Statistics show that such offenders... have left the area because the publicity generated by their murders has made them increasingly nervous of arrest. When this happens the move will probably have been planned to avoid arousing suspicion'* [1]

But once ensconced in his new locale the sexual killer will being anew. Wilson and Seaman again:

> *'Had the ripper felt constrained to quit England in November 1888 for fear of arrest — because of the hue and cry — he would still have been unlikely to be able to resist killing again: homicide is the serial killer's raison d'etre* [2]

And in Scotland he did kill again, his ex-prostitute Wife, strangled and sexually mutilated.

Even in 1889 news travelled fast. On February 12th The 'New York Times' tentatively advanced Bury as the ripper theorizing that he had killed Ellen because she suspected him. There are good grounds for this belief, the two chalked messages found at 113, Princes Street, 'Jack ripper is at the back of this door' and 'Jack ripper is in this sellar (sic)'. Who wrote them? Not Bury. The logical answer is his Wife. How long she had suspected him we can only guess

1   'The Serial Killers' Paperback Edition pp74/5
2   'The Serial Killers' P/BK Edition p72

at. Women are often unwilling to face the truth about their spouses. Threatened with exposure Bury was compelled to kill her. The mutilations followed as a matter of necessity for him.

For five days Bury pondered what to do. He spoke of fleeing again and had stuffed Ellen's body into the trunk (breaking one of her legs in the process). Doubtless he hoped to board ship with it and dispose of it overboard. But on the 10th he read the article about the suicides and a new plan came to mind. He decided to bluff it out, ride his luck. The reason? Money. The ripper was a thief. He stole from his victims because he was avaricious and it was in his nature. Ellen Bury still owned around £100 in shares (circa £6,500 at today's values). When Bury was arrested the Police found on him a document, Ellen's agreement to transfer the shares to him. According to the Dundee firm of Halesolin & Ajilurie that agreement was a forgery. Jack the ripper's last gamble had failed.

✵✵✵✵✵

That is the case against William Bury. I have presented it factually, theorizing as little as possible. For example, it would be fascinating to dwell on whether Cathy Eddowes did know Bury and suspected him. Both had lived in Wolverhampton. But any such theory would be pure conjecture and there has been far too much of that already about the ripper murders.

For Bury not to have been the ripper means that living in London at the same time were two men twinned in psychology, both broadly fitting the same description and each with the motive, opportunity and means. One who killed and then disappeared off the face of the earth, the other who precipitately fled to Scotland after the last murder and then started to commit ripper style sexual murders beginning with a wife who suspected him of being the other ripper. Now does this make sense?

What we have in William Bury is at long last a gilt edged candidate for the ripper, one who fits the evidence and not the other way round, a suspect whose case could be presented in a Court of Law. No fantastic theorizing is necessary, no lies, no sleights of hand, no elaborate cover ups. It is the story of a serial killer and how he came to be hanged.

At the end of his miserable life we can only hope that as Bury came face to face with his executioner he felt the same terror as his victims knowing that he too would shortly have the life choked from his body. Spare no thoughts for him; only for those who did not deserve to die — his victims.

Appendix

One: Police Ranks

Metropolitan Police ranks in 1888 differed quite considerably from today. The ranks of Chief Constable and Assistant Chief Constable were abolished earlier this century, the former being replaced by Deputy Assistant Commissioner.

In 1888 a Divisional Head was a Superintendent. Today the equivalent rank is Commander, which did not exist then.

Under Superintendent were no less than four ranks of Inspector, Chief Inspector, Inspector first class, Inspector second class and Local Inspector. Today the equivalent ranks are Chief Superintendent, Superintendent, Chief Inspector, and Inspector. Thus Swanson and Abberline were effectively Chief Superintendent and Superintendent.

Two: The Ripper Correspondence

Interestingly, the writer of the postcard states 'Number One squealed a bit'. Liz Stride did squeal but this fact did not become common knowledge until 1976. However, in this writer's opinion, the correspondent was right by accident and was guessing at the reason Stride escaped mutilation. The succeeding words: 'couldn't finish straight off' support this interpretation.

William Bury, in my view, was not responsible for either the Princes or Goulston Street graffiti. But there is one tantalising little point: Both were reported as being in a schoolboyish hand[*].

---

[*]   Testimony at Catharine Eddowes' Inquest and the 'Dundee Advertiser', February 12th 1889.

Three: More About Elizabeth Stride's Murder

Not all writers on the case have accepted Liz Stride as a ripper victim. Edwin
Woodhall (Jack the Ripper or When London Walked in Terror 1935) and
William Stewart (Jack the Ripper: A New Theory 1939) were adamant that she
was not, and Walter Dew (I Caught Crippen 1938) had his doubts. Begg, Fido
and Skinner, whilst going along with the majority view that she was, nevertheless insert a number of caveats, namely, the lack of mutilation, the different knife,
the positioning of the body, no excavation of blood in the neck and head to
indicate asphyxiation and the murderer's unusual behaviour (for a serial killer)
in attacking Stride in front of witnesses. The first and last points are dealt with
in Chapter Five. Had Schwartz or the other man remained then I have no doubt
that Bury would not have gone beyond the type of assault which he regularly
inflicted on his wife. The different knife was undoubtedly the pen knife which
he slept with under his pillow. The body lay on its left side and not the back as
in the other cases, but the legs had been drawn up, matching Annie Chapman
and (partially) Mary Kelly. As for asphyxiation, Liz's fists were clenched which
is an indication of strangulation. The fact is that no two murders are ever
completely identical and modus operandi cannot be treated in a doctrinaire
fashion (See Chapter Eleven).

As noted earlier, the general opinion amongst previous writers is that Liz
was not always with the same man that night. The reasons proffered are that the
man and woman seen by Brown could have been a courting couple, the slight
variations in the descriptions and whether Stride would have spent the entire
period with the same client.

There was a courting couple in the vicinity, an Edward Spooner and his
young lady. But they were standing outside a pub in Fairclough Street from
12:30 to 1:00. The couple seen by Brown were standing outside the school which
dovetails with the negative evidence of West, Eagle and Lave who saw nobody
outside the Yard between 12:30 and 12:40. The time of Brown's sighting
coincided with Schwartz's but that is not a point of any significance. Such
timings cannot be made to the minute; they are always approximate.

Descriptions of the same man often vary enormously. It is worth mention-
ing that in the experiment recorded by Scaduto (See Chapter Five) 29 of the 30
descriptions bore no resemblance to the subject and the one that did was too
vague to have been of any use to the Police. The six descriptions of Stride's
consort are impressive because of how minor the differences actually are.
Basically, they centre around the man's coat and whether or not he had a
moustache. On the former, most of the witnesses were glimpsing a dark coat at
night. On the latter, Best and Schwartz said he had a moustache, Packer and

Brown had no recollection either way, and Marshall and Smith thought he had no whiskers. Here again, such discrepancies in the darkness are to be expected. And it is worth recording what Marshall and Smith actually said.

Marshall:

'From what I saw of his face I do not think he had (any whiskers)'[1]

Smith:

'He had no whiskers but I did not notice him much'[2]

For good measure, many men in Victorian times effected side whiskers and that is what they may have been referring to, not that it matters very much.

Liz Stride was an occasional prostitute who sold herself for drink money and the price of a bed. If the client was willing to provide her with drink then she had no reason to seek another, and no guarantee of one anyway. Martha Tabram and Mary Ann Connolly drank with their soldier clients for two hours and Frances Coles spent twenty four hours with Thomas Sadler, mostly in pubs.

Matthew Packer was accused of contradicting himself in two ways. First, he made no mention of the couple when interviewed by the Police on September 30th, and secondly he changed the times from 12:00 and 12:30 to 11:00 and 11:30. He also later made some rather idiosyncratic statements about the man he had seen. To take the last first, the East End was awash with gossipy fables about the ripper and that is really all Packer's subsequent remarks amount to. He varied his times only once, to Warren, and may have been flustered in the General's presence. The Police account of what Packer said on the 30th runs as follows:

> *'I saw no one standing about, neither did I see anyone go up the Yard. I never saw anything suspicious or heard the slightest noise. And I knew nothing about the murder until I heard of it this morning'*

Viewed objectively, only the opening statement 'I saw no one standing about' is really contentious and even here it must be remembered that when he last saw the couple they were not standing outside the club but on the corner.

A minor mystery is why Stride and Bury stood around for so long in the Street. Dutfield's Yard was an ideal spot for a prostitute to take a client and eventually Liz manoeuvred him towards it. Bury's reluctance is explained by the fact that there was a pub nearby and he was obviously seeking both a more propitious time and safer place[*]. This would not have suited Liz who wanted to

---

1   Inquest Testimony
2   Inquest Testimony

---

*   The grapes were possibly used to waste time.

earn her doss money and have a few more drinks. His behaviour may have helped spark the unease which led her to reject him following P.C. Smith's appearance.

There is no record of Schwartz having testified at the Inquest. The Police seem to have kept him back and not acquainted Phillips or Blackwell with his evidence. It may well be that the bruising on Liz's chest and shoulders came from the assault.

Israel Schwartz was basically a reliable witness but his evidence was later marred by a highly coloured account of it which appeared in 'The Star' on October 10th. In his statement to the Police ten days earlier he apparently gave no indication of the direction Stride's assailant appeared from. But in 'The Star' he has Bury walking some distance in front of him towards Fairclough Street. Overall, Schwartz's two accounts differ quite considerably. Whether this was due to embellishment on his part or concoctions by the newspaper is unknown. Surprisingly, the Police took no notice of the inconsistencies and did not re-interview him. But the saddest part of all about Schwartz is that if either he or the second man had stood his ground then Liz Stride would not have died that night.

Four: Sir Charles Warren's Subsequent Career

Doors are never closed to the so called 'Great and Good' and Warren next found himself in Singapore as Commander In Chief of the British troops in the straights settlements. It was not the most demanding of jobs but he managed to make a mess of things, quarrelling with local big wigs and falling out with the Governor.

1894 saw his return to England and the backwater command of the Thames Garrison, winding down to retirement which came four years later. The shutters appeared to have come down on a once glittering career but amazingly opportunity — the greatest of his life — beckoned yet again.

The third Boer War broke out in October, 1899. Unlike its predecessors it was to prove a long drawn out affair. Warren, who admitted to very pronounced views on fighting the Boers which might not meet with the approval of his superiors, proposed to go out to South Africa as an Ambulance driver with the St John's Ambulance Brigade. Instead he found himself reinstated to active service and sailing with the Fifth Infantry Division as its Commanding Officer.

British Military History is replete with extraordinary appointments, but none more so than this one. Warren was 59 and an Engineer not a Line Officer. He had served with distinction in a small way, leading irregular forces, but had never commanded so much as a platoon of regular soldiers in combat. It would be naive to imagine that his prominence as a Freemason did not play a part. Even more astounding, Warren found himself as Commander designate of the Ladysmith relief column should its existing Commander, Sir Redvers Buller, be sacked, a very real possibility as Buller had already failed to relieve Ladysmith with much loss of life.

Not surprisingly, Buller and Warren were at loggerheads from the start. On January 23rd, 1900 Warren was entrusted with the task of breaking through the Boer defences at Spion Kop. The result was a disaster which sent shock waves throughout the British Empire. He was repulsed with the loss of 1,200 casualties, a huge Butcher's bill for Victorian times. Six weeks later he was officially posted to Griqualand West which, one supposes, may have been marginally preferable to Upper Zambesi but only just.

In retrospect the Spion Kop defeat cannot be laid solely at Warren's door. He had been appointed to a battlefield Command by men who knew that his practical knowledge of warfare was minimal and under a superior who was not overly disappointed to see him fail. His battle plan was not without merit and might have succeeded had he received more vigorous support from his senior subordinate. But success has a thousand fathers and failure is a lonely orphan and Warren had failed to make the most of the greatest opportunity of his career. At a crucial stage of the battle his morale seems to have collapsed. Whether his thoughts went back to Whitechapel and that disastrous Autumn of 1888 can only be guessed at.

Sir Charles returned to England in July, 1900 and for the rest of his life busied himself with his works on weights and measurements and the boy scout movement. He lived a long time, his acerbic temper faded and he became known as a kindly, good natured old man. He died at the age of 87 whilst playing Billiards at his club.

Five: Hutchinson's Statement

'About 2 a.m. th I was coming by Thrawl Street, Commercial Street, and just before I got to Flower and Dean Street, I met the murdered woman Kelly and she said to me, Hutchinson will you lend me sixpence. I said I can't I have spent all my money going down to Romford, she said good morning I must go and find some money. She went away towards Thrawl Street. A man coming in the opposite direction to Kelly tapped her on the shoulder and said something to her, they both burst out laughing. I heard her say alright to him and the man said you will be alright for which I have told you. He then placed his right hand around her shoulders. He also had a kind of small parcel in his left hand with a kind of strap around it. I stood against the lamp of the Queens Head Public House and watched him. They both then came past me and the man hung down his head with his hat over his eyes. I stooped down and looked him in the face. He looked at me stern. They both went into Dorset Street I followed them. They both stood at the corner of the Court for about 3 minutes. He said something to her. She said alright my dear come along you will be comfortable. He then placed his arm on her shoulder and (she) gave him a kiss. She said she had lost her hankerchief. He then pulled his hankerchief a red one out and gave it to her. They both then went up the Court together. I then went to the Court to see if I could see them, but could not. I stood there for about three quarters of an hour to see if they came out. They did not so I went away.

Description, age about 34 or 35, height 5ft 6in, complexion pale. Dark eyes and eye lashes. Slight moustache curled up each end and hair dark. Very surley looking. Dress, long dark coat, collar and cuffs trimmed astrakhan and a dark jacket under, light waistcoat, dark trousers, dark felt hat turned down in the middle, button boots and gaiters with white buttons, wore a very thick gold chain with linen collar, black tie with horse shoe pin, respectable appearance, walked very sharp, jewish appearance. Can be identified.

George Hutchinson

Six: The Police Assessment of Rose Mylett's Death

The Police gave a number of reasons for believing that Mylett's death was due to natural causes.

She had appeared drunk to Alice Graves at 2.30 a.m.

The body was lying naturally without signs of a struggle and her fists were not clenched.

No ligature was found.

The mark on the neck only circumvented one quarter of it.

There were apparently no footprints in the Yard other than Mylett's.

The Autopsy Report declared that she had never given birth.

Set against the evidence of at least four Police Surgeons, including the Surgeon General, these reasons are both individually and collectively very flimsy.

Graves' anecdotal testimony cannot possibly be preferred to that of Brownfield and Harris who found no alcohol in the body.

The abrasion on the face *did* suggest violence and the other bruising on the neck, attributed to thumbs and fingers, suggest an attempt at manual strangulation first.

No other signs of a struggle would necessarily have been present.

The missing ligature, for obvious reasons, cannot be regarded as a point of substance.

The bruising would not have encompassed the entire neck if the ligature was applied cross-handed, thugee style as was suggested at the Inquest.

Goulding, on finding the body, immediately concluded that death was by natural causes. Whether he therefore checked for other footprints is unclear. Given that he did not suspect foul play it could well be that he, and other officers summoned by him, saw no reason to be careful and trampled over other footprints.

The final point was a rather peevish attempt to suggest that Brownfield and Harris had been negligent. The fact is that they were concentrating on how Rose Mylett died, not on whether she had once given birth. By no stretch of the imagination does it cast doubt on their failure to find alcohol in the body. The contents of the stomach were examined and the remains of a recently partaken meal — meat and potatoes — discovered.

Appendix Seven: Anderson's Witness

The name of the witness who 'identified' Aaron Kosminski will never be known for sure. Process of elimination narrows it down to Israel Schwartz or Joseph Lawende, the only two Jewish witnesses. Paul Begg adds a third name to the list, Joseph Levy, Lawende's companion, but Levy by his own admission took no notice of Bury's features or attire.

Lawende told Cathy Eddowes' Inquest that he would not be able to recognise the man again. For good measure, he was a City Police witness whereas Swanson implies that the Met escorted the witness to Brighton.

Which leaves us with Israel Schwartz who was almost certainly Anderson's witness. Here the Macnaghten Memorandum is of interest again. In the Aberconway version Macnaghten says that Kosminski 'strongly resembled the man seen near Mitre Square by the City P.C.'. In fact the City P.C., Edward Watkins, saw nobody in or around Mitre Square. Macnaghten was actually referring to P.C. Smith in Berner's Street. For once, Macnaghten cannot be blamed for the error: it was Swanson's. On October 19th, 1888, Swanson reported to the Home Office:

> *12.35 a.m. 30th*
> **City** *Policeman*
> *452 Smith saw a man and a woman... in Berner's Street'*

and further on:

> *'Schwartz gave the description of the man he had seen ten minutes later than the City Police'*

Swanson carries on referring to Smith as a City Officer throughout the report which is basically a discussion of Schwartz's evidence. He makes no mention of Stride by name but does refer to Backchurch Lane, easily confusable with Church Passage which is where Lawende and Levy saw Eddowes with Bury.

It is a logical deduction that after reading Swanson's report in the files Macnaghten thought (not unreasonably) that he was referring to the Mitre Square murder, hence the confusion. Both men are in fact talking about P.C. Smith and Berner's Street. Smith himself was not the witness. He was not jewish and even had he been would not have refused to give evidence. Obliquely, Macnaghten is referring to Kosminski's identification by Schwartz (although plainly he was not as impressed by it as Anderson and Swanson), and he is also indirectly verifying the Marginalia.

It is interesting that no other witness was taken to the seaside home. Lawende has already been accounted for. Swanson believed that the man seen earlier by Best, Gardner, Marshall, Packer, Brown and Smith was not Liz Stride's killer. But why they did not take Hutchinson and Emily Walters is unexplained. Presumably the men described by them in no way resembled Kosminski.

Select Bibliography

JACK THE RIPPER

Abrahamsen, Dr David. Murder and Madness: The Secret Life of Jack the Ripper. Robson Books. 1992

Begg Paul, Jack the Ripper: The Uncensored Facts. Robson Books. 1988.

Begg Paul, Fido Martin and Skinner Keith: The Jack The Ripper A to Z. Headline Book Publishing. 1992

Cullen Tom, Autumn of Terror. The Bodley Head. 1965

Douglas Arthur, Will the Real Jack the Ripper? Countryside Publications. 1979.

Fairclough Melvyn, The Ripper and the Royals. Duckworth. 1992.

Farson Daniel, Jack the Ripper. Micahel Joseph. 1972.

Fido Martin, The Crimes, Detection and Death of Jack the Ripper. Weidenfeld. 1987.

Harris Melvin, Jack the Ripper: The Bloody Truth. Columbus. 1987.

Harrison Michael, Clarence: The Life of H.R.H. The Duke of Clarence and Avondale 1864-1892. W.H. Allen. 1972.

Howells Martin and Skinner Keith, The Ripper Legacy. Sidgwick & Jackson. 1987.

Jones Elwyn and Lloyd John, The Ripper File. Arthur Barker. 1975.

Kelly Alexander, Jack the Ripper: A Bibliography and Review of the Literature. Association of Assistant Librarians. 1972.

Knight Stephen, Jack the Ripper: The Final Solution. Harrap. 1976.

Matters Leonard, The Mystery of Jack the Ripper. Hutchinson. 1929.

McCormick Donald, The Identity of Jack the Ripper. John Long. 1970.

Odell Robin, Jack the Ripper in Fact and Fiction. Harrap. 1965.

OdellRobin and Wilson Colin, Jack the Ripper: Summing Up and Verdict. Corgi. 1988

Rumbelow Donald, The Complete Jack the Ripper. W.H. Allen. 1975.

Sharkey Terence, Jack the Ripper: One Hundred Years of Investigation. Ward Lock. 1987.

Underwood Peter, Jack the Ripper: One Hundred Years of Mystery. Blandford Press. 1987.

Whittington-Egan Richard, A Casebook on Jack the Ripper. Wildy. 1976.

SERIAL KILLERS

Gregg Wilfred and Lane Brian, The Encyclopedia of Serial Killers. Headline

Book Publishing. 1992.
Jones Barbara, Voices from an Evil God. Blake. 1992.
Kennedy Ludovic, Ten Rillington Place. Gollancz. 1961.
Lucas Norman, The Sex Killers. W.H. Allen. 1974.
Marriner Brian, A Century of Sex Killers. Forum Press. 1992.
Norris Joel, Serial Killers: The Growing Menace. Arrow Books. 1990.
Seaman Donald and Wilson Colin, The Serial Killers. W.H. Allen. 1990.

GENERAL

Boyle Thomas, Black Swine in the Sewers of Hampstead. Hodder &
Stoughton. 1990.
Carey John (Editor) The Faber Book of Reportage. Faber & Faber. 1987.
Davenport-Hines Richard, Sex, Death and Punishment. Collins. 1990.
Fishman William, East End 1888. Duckworth. 1988.
Goodman Jonathan, Masterpieces of Murder. Robinson Publishing. 1992.
London Jack, The People of the Abyss. Journeyman Press. 1977.
Raynsford Oliver, The Battle of Spion Kop. John Murray. 1969.
Scaduto Anthony, Scapegoat. Secker and Warburg. 1977.
Wilson Colin, The Criminal History of Mankind. Granada. 1984.